ABOUT THE AUTHOR

Sarah Pullen is a full-time, often-harassed mother of a bundle of boys. She worked as a features writer for a national newspaper and for a bank in the City of London, then disappeared into the windy North Downs in Kent to raise her family. *A Mighty Boy* is a book she wishes she hadn't had to write but felt compelled to. It is her first book.

Dear Reader,

The book you are holding came about in a rather different way to most others. It was funded directly by readers through a new website: Unbound. Unbound is the creation of three writers. We started the company because we believed there had to be a better deal for both writers and readers. On the Unbound website, authors share the ideas for the books they want to write directly with readers. If enough of you support the book by pledging for it in advance, we produce a beautifully bound special subscribers' edition and distribute a regular edition and e-book wherever books are sold, in shops and online.

This new way of publishing is actually a very old idea (Samuel Johnson funded his dictionary this way). We're just using the internet to build each writer a network of patrons. At the back of this book, you'll find the names of all the people who made it happen.

Publishing in this way means readers are no longer just passive consumers of the books they buy, and authors are free to write the books they really want. They get a much fairer return too – half the profits their books generate, rather than a tiny percentage of the cover price.

If you're not yet a subscriber, we hope that you'll want to join our publishing revolution and have your name listed in one of our books in the future. To get you started, here is a £5 discount on your first pledge. Just visit unbound.com, make your pledge and type **MIGHTY** in the promo code box when you check out.

Thank you for your support,

Dan, Justin and John
Founders, Unbound

A MIGHTY BOY

This edition first published in 2017

Unbound
6th Floor Mutual House, 70 Conduit Street, London W1S 2GF
www.unbound.com

Text Design by Ellipsis, Glasgow

A CIP record for this book is available from the British Library

ISBN 978-1-78352-384-9 (trade hbk)
ISBN 978-1-78352-385-6 (ebook)
ISBN 978-1-78352-383-2 (limited edition)

Printed in Great Britain by Clays Ltd, St Ives Plc

1 3 5 7 9 8 6 4 2

A MIGHTY BOY

SARAH PULLEN

Unbound

To All My Boys –

B.O.R.I.S.

Always just a smidgin

With special thanks to Mark and Emma, Tanya and
John Crone, Jan Pilkington-Miksa, Patrick Spens
and Olivia Gideon Thomson for their generous
support of this book.

'If you knew how great is a mother's love,'
Wendy told them triumphantly,
'you would have no fear.'

J. M. Barrie, *Peter Pan*

Before

There is a moment I wish my son dead. I wish for him to be killed instantly in a car crash. I even speak the words out loud. What sort of mother must I be? Can you imagine wishing your child dead? It's not something I would ever have thought possible, not until a stranger in a crisp Italian suit and polished leather shoes tells me that my 10-year-old son is going to die in a matter of months. That it's inevitable. That he'll die a tortuous and undignified death that will rob him of his personality and the essence of his being long before his heart finally stops beating. Wouldn't you too find yourself wishing for a quick death for the child you love beyond reason, a child that has never been ill a day in his life?

We stand in a small hospital playroom, my husband and I. The wreckage of cheap plastic toys lies strewn across the floor, the room pulsates with garish colour and the surfaces are tacky with the residue of hundreds of sticky little fingers. We are awash with emotions and the floor rocks with invisible waves. I reach out a hand to steady myself on the wall. Across the room from us perches a consultant with an unpronounceable name. He reminds me of a hawk – talons gripping, eyes watchful, all-seeing and powerful – and I realise, with a start, that we are his prey.

The consultant has introduced himself and we have shaken hands. His grip is cool and his palms dry, these small things I register, but neither of us ask him to repeat his name. We are both too focused on the news we know he has come to impart. He has ushered us from our son's hospital room and swept us across the corridor into this playroom.

Over the next few months we learn that this bedside exodus happens everywhere. Good news of any nature will always be delivered by our

1

son's bedside, the consultant's relief palpable in the smile creasing his face, whereas bad news always takes us into dark corridors or starkly lit empty rooms. We come to dread those words and the unspoken meaning behind them – 'Shall we find somewhere quiet to talk?' So much information and heartache imparted with a few harmless words.

On this day, though, we are novices to the game and still have optimism and hope crammed in our back pocket. I notice that the consultant refuses to hold my gaze. His dark eyes dart between us, avoiding making contact for more than a few seconds. My palms grow clammy and my heart starts beating loudly in my ears. The man keeps calling my husband by the wrong name, Sam not Ben, but we don't correct him.

He looks at us with clinical detachment and draws his lips together. A frown furrows his forehead. I catch a glimpse of pity flit across his face, then his professional demeanour takes over and the shutters come down.

He points to a couple of chairs and gestures for us to sit. We squeeze into the tiny, brightly coloured children's chairs. A crayon mark slithers across the lino tiles by my feet and my eyes follow its convoluted course to its abrupt end. I keep my eyes on the floor.

The consultant waits until we are lined up in front of him and then asks, 'Do either of you have a heart condition?'

I look up and catch Ben's eye. We shake our heads. The same thought pushes through the fog in our brains. We are here to talk about our son's health not our own.

'That's good,' says the consultant, ignoring our confusion. He takes a deep breath and gazes out the window for a second at the grey London skyline. Sounds of a busy hospital drift under the closed door: the squeak of a trolley wheel on linoleum, a tap running in the sluice room, the squeal of a child running up the corridor. Ben shifts on his chair and the leg scrapes on the floor. Prompted by the noise, the consultant begins to speak. A stream of words flows from his mouth, each one tumbling over the last, as though a dam has burst.

'We've had the pathology results back. Your son has a high grade glioma in his left parietal lobe. It's suggestive of a glioblastoma multiforme. It has been partially resected but we couldn't fully remove it because of the risk of right side hemiparesis.' He pauses. I try and decipher his words but they slip and slide away from me.

The bile rises in my throat and my fingers tingle as the blood drains from my limbs. I feel what is coming. I know it in my bones as only a mother can.

His voice comes from a distance; it's silky smooth but every word grates in my mind. I want to scream at him to stop. Whatever he has come to say will not be real until it is spoken out loud. I want to stick my fingers in my ears and chant nonsense to prevent the words from getting through, but I can't move. My muscles are deaf to the clamour of my brain.

'He has an aggressive brain tumour. One of the worst. We couldn't take it all out as we didn't want to risk paralysing him on one side of his body.' He pauses and takes a deep breath. 'There's nothing we can do. There's no successful treatment for this type of tumour.' He looks hard at us and his lips start moving long before my brain actually registers his words. 'I'm sorry but your son is going die. He has 12 18 months with treatment and only a few without.' He drops his eyes. Black spots crowd my vision and I dig my nails into the palm of my hand to stop the scream that is working its way up my throat. He continues, each word thudding into my chest. 'Some families choose not to undertake any treatment. We'll support you whatever you choose. There is no cure.'

'There has to be something,' says Ben, his voice cracking. 'Go back in. Take the rest of it out. Can't you do that? Surely it's worth the risk!'

The consultant shakes his head. 'It's not that simple. This type of tumour doesn't have clear edges. It infiltrates healthy brain tissue. No matter what we do we won't be able to get it all out. At this stage it's simply about quality of life, I'm afraid – we don't want to leave him paralysed for the little time he has left.'

Ben blanches. 'Doesn't anyone survive?' he whispers.

The doctor laces his fingers together and sighs as though he has heard the question many times before. 'I'll be honest,' he says. 'It can happen.' I look up, grasping at the slim lifeline he has thrown.

'So . . . so there's a chance,' I stutter. My voice is hoarse and the words sound alien and robotic. Not mine.

He catches my gaze and I see it written there in his eyes. He shakes his head. The vomit rises in my throat.

'Very few ever survive,' he says. 'I don't want to give you false hope but the truth is less than 10 per cent of these children survive for two years.'

Everything unravels.

The colour bleeds out of the room. The walls close in, pulsating rhythmically, and the only thing that I can hear is the frantic pounding of my heart.

Ben's brain veers off at a tangent trying to buy him breathing space. 'Can I ask why you wanted to know if either of us had a heart problem?'

The consultant nods. 'It's just a precaution,' he says. I can see his mind assessing how much information to give us. He straightens his back. 'I've had parents keel over with a heart attack when I've had to give them this news. I like to be prepared.' He gives us a look full of pity. 'I'm sorry. I really am. I have children of my own.'

That's it. Sentence has been pronounced.

Our bright, beautiful boy's future has been stolen from him with a few brief words, and with it our hopes and our future, the one we had mapped out. It's taken only a few heartbeats, mere moments, to destroy a world and unpick the universe, at least as we know it. All those parental expectations and longings are crushed under a moulded leather heel, as easily as one would crush an ant. I look at Ben and together we shatter into thousands of pieces. Pieces that skitter across the stark linoleum floor and get lost amongst the piles of toys, never to be recovered.

I can't breathe. It feels as though my mouth and nostrils are clogged with dirt. I claw at my face and haul the air into my lungs, wheezing and retching. I grab hold of Ben. Thoughts flail and whip through my head; the past, the future, fast-forwarding then rewinding. Time stretches and I peer at the tattered remnants of my life and the horror that is to come.

How will we go about our lives now? How can the world still be turning? Why doesn't everything just stop as my heart explodes?

I picture the small boy in the nearby room, building his Lego model and laughing at YouTube videos, oblivious to the death sentence that has just been pronounced by an invisible judge and jury. The diagnosis is worse than we could have possibly imagined. We dared to hope and now all hope has been ripped away. We are falling, tumbling into an abyss. We've been left with nothing to hold on to – just a small boy lying alone in the next-door room, dreaming of his bright future.

~

It's August 2012. The sun is shining and the UK is in the grip of Olympic fever. Silas is slightly under the weather and over a couple of days has a few headaches.

The first moment we start to feel something is really amiss is Sunday lunchtime. The women's pentathlon is on the TV in the background and we are all looking forward to watching the closing ceremony. We have guests. The house is full of children and noise but Silas sits on the stairs in our hall with his head buried in his hands.

'You don't understand,' he says, as one of his brothers accuses him of making a fuss. 'My headache's so bad.' He looks at us, his eyes big. 'I need to go to hospital. Please take me to hospital. Please, Please,' he begs. 'I feel like I'm dying.'

My eyes meet Ben's over the top of Silas's head and I see my concern mirrored in his. Here's a 10-year-old boy telling us he's dying. We need to take him seriously. I am, though, a mother of four boys and I don't want to panic and spend several needless hours in our local A&E department on a Sunday afternoon.

We agree to give him some paracetamol and lie him down on the sofa to see if things improve. Outside the room, out of his hearing, we also agree that if things don't get better then we will take him straight to hospital. Thoughts of meningitis fill my head. Like most parents, I have pressed a glass against an unknown rash on a wailing baby. I know the symptoms. They are stapled to the wall in every doctor's waiting room.

I make Silas bend his neck to his chest. I make him turn towards the sunlight streaming through the window and I relax when the light doesn't appear to hurt his eyes.

Within half an hour of the paracetamol, Silas feels better. He joins us for a big lunch full of ripe summer berries and sticky meringues. He chats, he fools around and he bickers with his brothers. He makes us and our guests laugh at his silly antics. We brush off the earlier episode, happy that we've not wasted the afternoon in A&E and reassured that there is nothing seriously wrong with him. We play a big game of family cricket in the garden and Silas hurls the ball down the makeshift crease with deadly accuracy. The delicate song of a thrush is punctuated by the rowdy thwack of leather on willow. The air is filled with calls of 'Howzat!' and the cries of small boys arguing against unfair dismissals.

The shadows lengthen in the garden and we come inside. Ben leaves to take my brother to the station.

Silas walks into the kitchen.

'What do you want for supper, darling?' I ask.

I get no reply. Nothing too out of the ordinary here, Silas often has to be asked things several times.

'Silas, what would you like?' I repeat.

He looks at me blankly.

'Well?' I say, raising my hands in exasperation. 'What do you want to eat?' I turn away to empty the dishwasher and Silas mumbles a few unintelligible words.

'What did you say?' I ask, my head buried deep in the clean cutlery.

'I . . . I . . . I . . . I . . . I . . . I . . . I . . .'

I look up, narrowing my eyes.

'Are you OK?' I ask, coming round the side of the kitchen table. My eyes search his face. He is frowning.

'I . . . I . . . I can't think,' he says. 'I . . . I . . . can't think.' He sounds as though he's been at the whisky bottle.

6

I hold his shoulders and lower myself to his level.

'Do you feel all right?'

He nods his head.

'What's the matter then?'

'I . . . I . . . I . . . I . .' he stutters.

I squeeze my fingers into his shoulders and icy claws of fear curl around my guts.

'Don't joke, Silas,' I say. 'It's not funny! Promise me you aren't joking!'

He shakes his head and the cold spreads deep within me.

'What day is it?' I ask.

'Sun . . . Sun . . . Sunday.'

'What's your name?'

'Si . . . Si . . . Si . . . Si.' His eyes widen in surprise and confusion.

'It's OK,' I whisper, although I know that it's far from OK. 'Let's go upstairs and lie down on Mummy's bed.' I want to get him somewhere quiet and away from the prying eyes of his brothers.

Silas collapses on my bed and holds his hand to his head.

'When's your birthday?' I ask him.

He struggles to answer and lies there touching his head. I make him bend his neck, touching his chin to his chest. 'Does your neck hurt?' He shakes his head.

'I need . . . I need some furonen,' he says.

'You need what, darling?' I ask, trying to stop my hands from trembling. My mind is racing. Where's Ben? How long will it take him to get back from the station? What should I do? Something is wrong, very wrong. Fear writhes in my stomach. I try to stamp on it but it keeps growing. A bumblebee bashes against the open window and I register its angry buzz.

'I need some . . . some . . . some furonen,' Silas repeats. He waves his hand wildly in the air.

'I don't understand, my darling. You need what?'

'Furonen,' he says. 'My head. My head. I . . . I need furonen.' He moans and holds his head.

It clicks. 'You want some Nurofen?'

Relief lights his eyes. 'Yes, yes, that's it. I want some Nurofen.'

'All right, my darling,' I say and leave the room to get the Nurofen. I pick up the phone and dial 999. The operator answers. I hang up. How can it be that serious? How can I need an ambulance? He was playing cricket not so long ago. I stand in the doorway and watch my son for a moment. He is lying on the bed with his hand covering his eyes. I take a deep breath and dial the numbers again.

'I need an ambulance,' I say into the phone, my voice strong.

~

The ambulance arrives fast, although it feels like the longest 10 minutes of my life. I have to stay on the phone to the operator but the reception isn't good in the bedroom so I stand at the top of the stairs. They won't let me hand the phone over to one of our guests so that I can be at Silas's side. This frustrates me and I grow increasingly agitated. The operator keeps asking me to calm down and I try to keep my voice steady and block out Silas's frantic cries.

Ben arrives back and bounds up the stairs. He looks at me in disbelief. He had left his son running around and less than 30 minutes later he has arrived home to be told the ambulance is on its way.

'Are you sure we need the ambulance?' he asks.

I nod my head. He grabs my hand and squeezes it. Fear dances across his face. He takes a deep breath and composes himself, then plasters a smile on his face and walks into the bedroom.

The noise of a siren drifts through the open windows.

'They're here,' I say to the operator, hanging up the phone with relief.

Two green-suited paramedics puff up the stairs carrying their equipment. It seems to take them an age and I stifle the desire to push them faster.

The two girls assess the situation and quickly rule out meningitis. The only symptoms Silas displays are a headache and some confusion and slurred speech. They let us give him some Nurofen.

'Has he been outside in the sun?' one of them asks.

'Yes,' I say. 'We've been playing cricket but it hasn't been that hot today.'

'Has he been drinking plenty of fluids?'

I think back through the day. 'Yes, lots.'

'It looks like sunstroke or heat exhaustion.'

'But what about the headaches he's been having the last couple of days?'

They shrug. 'We see this type of reaction in kids sometimes.'

'It's not sunstroke,' I say, my voice sharp.

One girl looks at me quizzically and raises an eyebrow. The other keeps her head bent and stays focused on the task of taking Silas's blood pressure.

'Don't worry, Mum, we'll take good care of him. He's in good hands.'

I want to scream at them that I'm not overreacting or wasting their time. I want to make them realise what I feel in my gut, but I don't know how to communicate my terror.

I take a deep breath. 'It's not sunstroke,' I repeat slowly.

The other girl turns around and puts her hand on my arm, patting me into submission. 'His SATs are fine and he doesn't have a temperature,' she says. 'We'll take him into the hospital but it's just precautionary because of his confusion – nothing to worry about.'

Silas walks down the stairs to the ambulance. He can walk just fine. That has to be good news, I think. The paramedics know what they're talking about and maybe they are right, maybe I am overreacting. His three brothers stand in the hall, silent and still.

'It's OK,' I tell them as I guide Silas into the back of the ambulance. 'He'll be fine. We'll be back later.'

I squeeze into the ambulance, while Ben follows in the car. Silas is still confused and not making much sense. He describes the feeling a few days later to us: he could think of the answers to all the questions but he couldn't get the answer from his brain to his mouth, no matter how hard he tried. One of the paramedics asks him how many brothers he has. He can't answer, his lips move but no words come out. He shakes his head and holds up three fingers. I nod with relief.

Accident and Emergency is quiet. It's a Sunday night and almost everybody is at home watching the Olympics' closing ceremony. There is no rush to treat Silas. The paramedics must have told the nurses that he was just suffering from heatstroke and dehydration. I am left on my own with him. He becomes less responsive. He is drifting and absent; his eyes lose focus. I call over a junior doctor but he appears nonplussed and shrugs his shoulders in a Continental European way.

Ben walks through the doors, just as Silas's heart rate plummets to 40 bpm. He's clammy and barely conscious. We call the doctor back over and he inserts a cannula into a vein and takes some blood then fits an oxygen mask to Silas's face.

'His SATs are not as good as when he came in,' he explains, straightening the elastic behind my son's head. Ben holds my hand and squeezes tight. I lean over and whisper in Silas's ear. I stroke his head and wipe the cold sweat off his brow.

The doctor disappears to speak to his consultant on the phone.

'Has he hit his head in the last couple of days?' he asks on his return.

We think for a moment. 'No,' we say in unison, shaking our heads.

'Are you sure?' he asks, his voice tinged with urgency.

'Not that we know about,' I say, explaining that he'd been camping with friends a couple of nights earlier but they hadn't told us about any incident.

'We need to know if it's a possibility.'

'I don't think so,' I say, racking my brains. Was there something I'd forgotten?

The doctor looks at Silas and his lips tighten. He spins round and disappears again.

Silas suddenly writhes on the bed and vomits into the oxygen mask.

'Help,' I call, pulling the mask from his face. 'Help,' I scream as he is sick again all over the bed. His eyes flutter but they don't open. There are soft footsteps and a nurse thrusts a kidney shaped bowl into my hands.

I lie Silas back on the bed and start to clean him up. Ben touches me on the shoulder and points. A dark patch spreads across Silas's trousers and my nostrils wrinkle at the sharp smell of urine. The panic rises in my chest. Why is nothing happening? Where are all the people who are supposed to be making him better?

The doctor comes back with a big syringe in his hand and injects it into the cannula.

He glances up at us. 'We think your son has a swelling inside his head. This will help reduce any pressure in his brain.'

'But he hasn't hit his head,' I murmur.

'Until we know otherwise,' says the doctor, 'we're going to assume he has some sort of head injury.'

My hand finds Ben's and our fingers curl together.

The doctor continues. 'We need your permission to do a CAT scan.'

I frown.

'Because of the radiation,' he explains.

We nod our assent, although I itch to grab the young man and shake him. I want to scream at him to stop wasting time asking for permission while my son dies before my eyes.

I dig my nails into Ben's hand and say nothing.

They wheel Silas into a different part of the hospital to have the scan. The wing is undergoing refurbishment and clear sheets of thick plastic hang from the ceiling, muffling all noise and enclosing us. There are no chairs so Ben and I perch on a carpenter's wooden trestle surrounded by tools and equipment. He grips my hand in his. The thick smell of dust mixes with the sharp antiseptic smell of the hospital.

'He's going to be OK,' Ben whispers in my ear. 'He has to be OK.'

My eyes fill with tears. I wish I could share his confidence but I have an eerie feeling that we are barrelling at speed towards an unknown destination. Less than a couple of hours ago we were happily playing in the garden. These things only happen in movies.

I pray, prepared to make a deal, any deal, with any deity willing to listen. Don't take him from me, I beg. I'll do anything. Give him a chance. He's just a little boy. Ben hears me muttering and squeezes my hand harder.

Silas is wheeled back into the resuscitation room. He's completely unresponsive and shows no reaction to either of our voices. A sudden commotion at the other end of the department catches our attention. A grey-bearded man, with spectacles pushed high on the bridge of his nose, storms into the room. The double doors swing shut behind him. Junior doctors scurry to his side. People appear from all directions.

'I jumped five red lights to get here. Now, where's the boy?'

He pushes into the cubicle and his eyes skim over us. He turns to a monitor and switches on the screen. A few seconds later, the screen fills with an image of Silas's brain. My heart fills my throat and my fingers search out Ben's hand next to me. There, on the right-hand side of the screen – the left-hand side of Silas's brain – are two large, circular anomalous masses, one in front of the other. The back one is three times the size of the front one and appears to be the size of a tennis ball.

The man turns.

'Are you the parents of this boy?' he barks.

We nod. I don't trust myself to speak. This is worse, much worse, than meningitis. I blink hard, fighting the tears. The doctor flings his next words at us, each word like a punch to the solar plexus.

'This boy is seriously ill. He has a significant mass on his brain, most likely a tumour. This is a life-threatening situation. We may lose him at any moment. You both need to be prepared for the worst. You can remain if you stay calm, otherwise I will have you removed. Stay out of my way and let me work and I will do my best for your son.' He dismisses us and gets to work. In seconds, we are plunged into a scene from ER, although the doctor isn't dishy and somehow I know the ending isn't going to be happily ever after.

I dare not look at Ben. He is tight and coiled beside me. I look at the monitor again. How can something that size be in my son's head without us knowing? How could I, his mother, not have realised? I learn later that the faster a brain tumour grows, the fewer symptoms there are.

Slower-growing tumours tend to cause repeated visits to GPs by desperate parents before diagnosis. Silas's tumour, though, is so aggressive that his brain has no time to react to the intrusion until it reaches crisis point and starts shutting down in shock. Suddenly, I find myself wishing that it had been meningitis. Anything seems better than this.

The doctor assesses Silas's condition. He warns us that it won't be nice to witness and he's right. He pinches the nerves in Silas's shoulder until Silas groans and writhes in pain. He squeezes the nail beds on Silas's fingers until Silas tries half-heartedly to pull his hand away. Once, even in his unresponsive state, Silas moans something vaguely resembling 'Ger off!' All this prodding and poking is to gauge where Silas is on the Glasgow Coma Scale. He scores around 7 of a possible 15. A score below 8 means the patient is classified as comatose.

The next hour or so is spent stabilising Silas's condition so that he can be moved to King's College Hospital in London. Monitors beep, hushed phone calls are made and throughout it all, Silas lies oblivious on a gurney. They talk about intubating him in case he arrests on the journey. I stumble out of the room, my mouth thick with saliva, and call my mother.

She struggles to comprehend what I'm telling her – she had been with us at lunchtime only a few short hours ago. I want to weep and curl up in a ball and let her stroke my hair and tell me everything is going to be all right, but I'm the mother now and I have to be strong and shore up my heart. I can handle facts but not emotion. Raw emotion will lead to panic and I cannot allow the panic in. I need to keep my wits if I am to be of any help to my child, and panic will steal them away from me. I bury the panic deep inside and ignore it when it attempts to claw its way to the surface. I push it deeper and cage it in my belly, where it festers and grumbles and makes a permanent home. I call the friends who have stayed to look after our other boys. These are friends I've barely seen in the preceding few years as they have been living in India. These are friends who have had to witness our family implode on a hot summer's day.

It's hard to take it all in – our gorgeous, sunny, chatty boy, who only a few hours ago had smacked a cricket ball for six in the garden, is lying unconscious and fighting for his life. I pinch myself to make sure I am awake and I leave dark bruises on my thighs.

~

That journey up the M20 to King's College Hospital in the middle of the night is surreal. There's no room in the ambulance for either Ben or me as they need to have a full medical team, including the paediatric consultant and an anaesthetist. We let Silas go with a bunch of strangers not knowing whether we will ever see him alive again. We sit in stunned disbelief on the empty motorway unable to comfort each other, each lost in our own pain.

We stop at home and gather a few items. It's close to midnight but all our other boys are up. They've been watching the closing ceremony of the Olympics. They know things are serious and their little bodies are taut with worry. They say very little, just give us both a hug.

We arrive at King's in the small hours of the morning and spend frantic minutes trying to find someone who might be able to tell us where they have taken Silas. We end up in the A&E department, the only place in the hospital at that time of night that shows any sort of life. There are rows of people waiting, slumped on hard-backed chairs, some with bloody wads held to their heads, others with arms cradled in front of their bodies. Phones ring and an orderly cajoles a drunken man to a seat. It's busier than our local hospital on a Saturday afternoon but it's just another run-of-the-mill night in an inner-city A&E department.

Before Silas got ill, I used to watch my fair share of hospital dramas and reality TV shows: *ER*, *Casualty*, *Grey's Anatomy*, and even *24 Hours in A&E*, which was filmed at King's. I used to find something strangely compelling about other people's tragedies, but I'm not sitting in the comfort of my own chair now. It is my loved one fighting for his life and that changes everything. Since that night, I now switch channels when one of those programmes comes on the TV.

Even in my befuddled state, I recognise the cropped-haired nurse behind the Perspex window at the reception desk as one that appears regularly on the show. I've seen her dressing down impatient relatives. I spin around looking for cameras, terrified my tragedy will be on display for all to see. There is nothing, only the whirr and flicker of a broken halogen bulb behind me.

The nurse tries to brush us off and send us to another department but then she sees the terror behind our eyes and her demeanour softens. She makes a couple of phone calls to establish where Silas is and she sends us up to the paediatric High Dependency Unit. If the Perspex screen had not been between us, I would have jumped over the desk and hugged her with relief. At least now we know that Silas has arrived at the hospital alive. Up until that moment, we really had no idea if we were going to be directed to a ward or the morgue.

We are buzzed into the HDU. Nurses talk quietly and nod their heads to us. Curtains are drawn around the bed closest to the door and we hear the monotonous beep of machines. We are guided past an empty bed and then we see Silas, in the far bed, lying so small and still, his face pale. The sheets are pulled up under his armpits. A battery of monitors is connected to all parts of his body. Several screens track his heart rate, oxygen levels, temperature and blood pressure. A second cannula has been inserted in his other arm. A tall young doctor hovers over him checking the readings. He smiles when he sees us.

'You must be the parents,' he whispers. He nods towards Silas. 'He's asleep. His condition is stable for now. The neurological team will be here first thing in the morning to discuss his treatment. I'll check on him again during the night. I suggest you try and get some rest.'

He turns, speaks to the nurse at the station at the end of Silas's bed, and then leaves. I lean down and kiss Silas's smooth, warm cheek and bury my face in his neck to inhale his sweet scent.

The nurse puts a gentle hand on my arm. 'There's only room for one of you to stay overnight,' she says, her features dark and soft.

I look at Ben and know that neither of us can bear to be separated from our son again this night.

'But we live in Kent . . . we're miles from home and have nowhere to go,' I say. 'Please can we both stay? We'll stay out of your way. You won't know we're here.'

'I'll get into trouble . . .' she starts, her eyes darting between us. 'But . . .' She hesitates. She checks her watch. 'I suppose it's not far off morning.' She straightens her shoulders. 'OK, you can both stay, but just for tonight.'

Ben and I squeeze onto a tiny single bed. We have one thin blanket and no pillow between us but we bunch up some clothes under our heads and lie on the small cot next to our sleeping son. I'm not sure either of us sleep much that night – the lights are too bright, the machines make too much noise, the nurses swap shifts and tap on computer keyboards, a baby wails on the other side of a partition wall – and every time Silas moans or turns I'm by his side stroking his head. But he's alive and for the moment that's all that matters.

~

In the morning, Silas wakes up and smiles at us.

The massive dose of steroids they have administered has reduced the enormous swelling in his brain and he's back to his good-humoured self. His speech is nearly back to normal. He has some difficulty searching for words and several times he has to describe an everyday object to us.

'Where's my . . . you know . . . Oh, what's it called? It's little and has hands that go round and round. You know, you wear it on your wrist.'

'A watch.'

'Yes, that's it. Where's my watch?'

He can't fetch the words from his battered brain. As soon as we find the word for him, he just slips it back into his speech as though he had never forgotten it in the first place. It's as though his memory just needs to be jogged.

He can recall very little about the night before, although he tells us that at one stage he knew he was in an ambulance – he could hear people talking and the sirens blaring.

There's only one thing he wants for breakfast – a pain au chocolate. Ben hunts one down in the hospital canteen.

No one can eat a pain au chocolate like Silas. Every mouthful has to be savoured and appreciated to the full. He peels back the layers of pastry bit by bit, letting them melt slowly on his tongue, eking out the moments until he gets to the roll of chocolate inside. By the time he has finished, his face and fingers are smeared with chocolate and crumbs of pastry are to be found in every nook and cranny of his gown and the bedclothes, but Ben and I don't mind and we drink him in.

Our happiness is tempered by the knowledge of the monster inside his head. After his morning assessment, the surgical team call us into a side room for a meeting. It's August, the sun blazes into the small room, baking the faux leather seats. The sounds of a busy London street drift in through the open window: horns blaring, engines revving, the clatter of bins being emptied. Normal sounds of life being lived.

The surgical registrar is a small, slight, olive-skinned man. He is flanked by two junior doctors.

'We need to operate immediately to remove as much tumour as possible,' he says.

'When?' I ask.

'Today. This afternoon.'

I edge closer to Ben on the small sofa. 'What are the risks?'

A muscle in the registrar's jaw twitches. His eyes watch us. He doesn't beat about the bush.

'Death. There's always a risk with open brain surgery.' He pushes a piece of paper across the table towards us. 'You'll need to sign this consent form. You need to understand there's a risk, but it's small and your son has to have this surgery.'

Ben picks up the pen. 'And if he doesn't?'

'He'll die.'

I flinch. 'What are the other risks?'

'Paralysis of the right-hand side of his body, as the mass is in the left-hand side of his brain and it's close to where we think his motor tracts are. Loss of speech, as the tumour is sitting right on top of his language centre. He could have a stroke during surgery or a haemorrhage.' His eyes drift between us. 'There are many risks. But you have to understand, we really have no choice. The operation is your son's best chance. If we don't operate, he won't survive the week.'

I close my eyes and take a deep breath.

The surgeon touches me on the knee. 'We do more than a hundred of these operations a year,' he says. 'We'll do our best for him.'

I think of Silas waiting for us in the HDU, of the smile that had lit up his face when he woke up that morning and saw us next to him. We have to put our trust in these doctors. I squeeze Ben's arm. He scrawls a signature on the paper.

'Do you know what sort of tumour it is?' asks Ben, pushing the paper back across the coffee table.

'We won't know that until we get the pathology report back. It will take a few days.'

'Is it likely to be malignant?'

The registrar stands up. 'I wouldn't like to speculate at the moment. I know it's hard but you'll have to wait. We'll let you know as soon as we have the information.'

'What about our other children? Are they at risk too?'

The man pauses at the door. 'It's incredibly rare for two members of the same family to be affected. It's not impossible but I've never seen it.' He turns to leave.

'Look after him today, won't you?' I ask, my voice small.

His gaze swings to me and his eyes soften. 'I'll do my best.'

Leaving our son in the operating theatre is one of the hardest things either of us have ever done. We have little choice, but we have only just got him back after nearly losing him. If he comes through the surgery all right we don't know what deficits he might have, whether he'll even be able to walk or talk.

I cradle his head as they put him to sleep.

'You won't be able to count backwards from ten,' I say. 'You'll be asleep before you get to six.'

'No, I won't. Don't be silly, Mummy,' he says, a broad smile on his face.

The anaesthetist smiles. 'I don't even think you'll make it as far as six,' he says.

'Of course I will,' says Silas. The operation hasn't fazed him and he has taken news of it in his stride. He trusts us and he trusts the doctors and he has no knowledge of the risks involved. He has also never been anaesthetised before.

I watch the syringe of milky liquid empty into the cannula in his arm.

'Ten, nine, eight . . .' we begin together.

'Seven, six, five, four, three . . .' His voice grows quieter and his eyelids flutter.

'Two, one, zero . . . One, two, three,' he mumbles. The anaesthetist raises an eyebrow.

'Four . . . fi . . .' His head finally lolls onto my arm. I kiss his forehead, the tears streaming down my cheeks, and leave the room.

~

Ben and I walk from the hospital to the nearest pub and have a stiff drink each. Ben buys a small pouch of rolling tobacco and we both have a cigarette, although neither of us have really smoked for years. We just need something to do with our shaking hands. We sit there in the late afternoon heat unable to talk to each other. Instead, we watch other peoples' children run across the pub garden screaming and playing and envy those families their happiness.

Hours later we get the call to head down to the recovery room. As we exit the lift and enter the corridor, I hear the screaming.

'That's Silas,' I say, breaking into a run.

'Are you sure?' asks Ben.

'Yes.'

I'd know that sound anywhere. The cries of my children are wired into me. It's an instinctual response deep in the gut that twists your insides, forcing you to respond.

'Where is he?' I gasp, skidding round a corner. The maze of corridors distorts the sound so I can't pinpoint the exact location.

To my left I see a pair of double doors, the words 'Recovery Suite' on the sign above. I push through the doors. The screaming echoes round the room, bouncing off the walls.

Silas lies thrashing on a narrow recovery bed. The metal sides are raised to stop him falling out. His screams are raw and his voice hoarse from the tube they put down his throat during the operation. He is surrounded by nurses and doctors, all at a loss as to what to do.

'Silas, you need to calm down,' one of the nurses says. He throws her arm off and continues howling.

Ben and I rush over.

'It's OK, darling. Mummy's here,' I soothe. 'Shh.'

He carries on crying and pulls his knees up towards his chest. His screams tear through me and rip through my thin veneer of control. Dark spots cloud my vision. The lack of food and sleep catches up with me and I realise with horror that I am about to faint. I grab Ben's arm. His face too is drained of colour. I sink to the floor and put my head between my legs, willing my heart to force blood into my head. A nurse appears at my side.

'I'm OK. I'm OK . . .' I brush her away. 'Just need a moment.'

Silas's cries continue unabated. I haul myself back to my feet and cling to the rail round his bed.

'He's in pain,' I say, rubbing a hand across my eyes and turning to the throng of doctors. 'What's wrong?'

They look sheepish.

The registrar speaks up. 'I'm afraid he ripped out his catheter as he was coming round. We weren't quick enough to stop him. It must have hurt. A lot.'

Ben winces and his hand drops to his crotch.

The registrar continues. 'On the bright side, at least his right hand is working well and he doesn't appear to be paralysed.'

Silas carries on moaning but his cries quieten.

'We did well. We managed to get about 70 per cent of the mass out,' says the surgeon, a smile on his face.

I don't know whether to be pleased or not. My brain is foggy with trauma. It is hard to think straight. How can it be good news to leave 30 per cent of the tumour still in his brain? The surgeon sees my look of confusion.

'The rest of it was too close to his motor nerves. It was too risky to touch but we got the big part out.'

'But what happens to the rest of it?'

'That depends on the pathology. If it's malignant then you'll have to go down the route of radiation and chemotherapy.' He puts a hand on my arm. 'Don't think about it now. We'll know more in a few days. Focus on his recovery and get some rest yourselves.'

Looking at Silas lying on that hospital gurney, his head swathed in bandages, tubes hanging out of his neck, his ankle, his wrists, it seems impossible that he'll recover in a few days. But recover he does in that indomitable way that children have. He bounces. Less than 12 hours after the operation, he gets out of bed and walks across the HDU. He has a slight lean to the right but this disappears as the day progresses.

Various groups of doctors assess his cognitive state over the next couple of days, asking him questions, getting him to touch his nose, their moving finger, then touch his thumb with each finger in turn, faster and faster, testing his involuntary reflexes by tapping his ankles, knees, elbows and wrists. He starts cracking jokes and we know he is back.

A teenage girl in one of the other occupied beds intrigues Silas. She fights and swears at every doctor or nurse who comes near her. We learn, simply by dint of being within earshot, that she threw herself off the roof of a multi-storey car park. She has multiple fractures to her legs, pelvis and shoulder. She has suffered severe internal injuries and is still in a lot of pain more than a month later. She's very vocal and keeps screaming at everyone that they shouldn't bother to make her better because as soon as they let her out of the hospital she's just going to try and kill herself again, that they won't be able to stop her. It's tragic and hard to hear.

'Mummy,' Silas asks after one such outburst. 'Why does that girl want to kill herself so much?'

'I don't know, darling,' I reply. 'Some people are just so unhappy that they can't see any other option.'

He thinks for a moment. 'That's really sad, I wish we could cheer her up.' He fiddles with his covers.

'I couldn't kill myself,' he continues. 'I love being alive and I couldn't bear to be without you and Daddy.'

I nod my head, not trusting myself to speak. His eyes find mine.

'You couldn't bear to be without me either, could you, Mummy?'

I lean down to hug him so that he can't see the fear in my eyes. 'No, darling, of course I couldn't. You know, though, one day you will have a family of your own. You won't need us so much then.'

'Oh, yes, I will. Of course I will, I'll always need you.'

The surgery has gone well; Silas has no apparent neurological damage and we'll be going home sooner than anticipated. He recovers so fast, in fact, that within 48 hours they move him out of the HDU into a private room on Lion Ward. Ben and I are buoyed with optimism and we finally have peace and a good night's sleep. And this is where the oncology consultant, the one with the unpronounceable name, finds us at lunchtime the next day and takes away all our hope.

~

How do you disguise such life-changing news from a smart, articulate child? How do you continue to function and go about your business when your body just wants to shut down and your ears are ringing with an endless inner scream? Is that what being a parent truly means? Parenting a child with no future. Loving them without expectation,

22

somehow living solely in the moment despite the horror that you know is round the corner. Above all, protecting them from any hint of the nature of that horror.

All the parenting books I've ever read have told me how to raise happy, well-balanced, empathetic boys. Boys that will make good husbands, have successful careers and nurture a family of their own. Nowhere have I read anything that has prepared me for the death of my child. I only know about building a child up, not about taking them down piece by solitary piece. I know nothing about how to explain to them that their life, their bright future, has been stolen from them by a disease that they didn't choose.

At that moment in the hospital, after the consultant leaves us to digest his earth-shattering news, I realise I don't know a single parent whose school-age child has died. I know mothers who have miscarried or had a stillbirth and one or two who have lost small babies. Just as hard, but in a totally different way, as small babies can't read expressions, ask questions, pick up on strained undercurrents, sense the metallic tang of the guillotine hanging above their soft necks. And above all, they can't tell you how scared they are of dying.

After our frank talk with the neuro-oncologist, Ben and I are catapulted into a new way of parenting. We force joviality to disguise despair and use distraction to avoid detail, and above all we start to live a lie in order to prevent the truth coming out. Like Cassandra, the Trojan princess, the gift of foresight plunges us into our own inescapable hell.

This can't be happening to us, I think. We're just a normal family with bills to pay, a mortgage to worry about, clothes to wash, mouths to feed and the school run to juggle – since when is death part of that equation? All I can think about is that I'm a mother of four boys. I have four boys! How can it be possible to ever have just three? How can I bear to watch my son slowly die? That's the moment I wish Silas dead and wish for him to be hit by a car. If I can't stop the guillotine, if it is inevitable, then I want it to fall swift and fast and not prolong the torture for any of us.

But most of all I don't want to watch my son suffer and I don't want to have to start grieving when he is warm and vital and beside me.

Ben and I plaster smiles on our faces and scoop Silas up out of the ward and take him home. Silas chats away in the back of the car, excited to be going home, oblivious to the tears that drip down my cheeks and make a damp patch on my shirt.

That's the thing, isn't it? Death comes knocking on your door and all you want to do is focus on your child and enjoy every moment you have left, but all you can see is the immeasurable loss you are going to have to endure. Every word, laugh or cuddle is just another turn of the knife. How can you find happiness living in the shadow of death?

We get home and can't talk to anyone about the diagnosis. Not even my mother who's been looking after the other boys all week. She takes one look at my face and I shake my head.

'It's not good news,' I say, watching Silas run into the house.

'How bad?'

'Bad, but don't ask me any questions. I can't talk about it. Not at the moment. I'm sorry, Mum, you've got to go home.'

I know I'm hurting my mum by pushing her away but I have to be strong for my child. I can no longer be someone else's baby because that makes me want to crumble and weep and howl and scream and have someone kiss it better. There is no 'better', not anymore, not this time. I know I have to hold it together long enough to feed the children and get them into bed and only then can I allow myself the luxury of collapsing. To do this I have to banish my mother and pretend that life is carrying on as normal.

That first night, I go through the motions of motherhood but my mind is far away in a deep, dark place. Ben and I can barely communicate. Neither of us is able to articulate our devastation. We are like two pinballs crashing around in random directions as our brains veer in circles. For brief moments we come together and then we spin away again on our separate paths. At one point, I say that I am glad I have him by my side, that I don't have the strength for this journey without him.

Ben's reply cuts me deep, even though I know he doesn't mean to hurt me; he just cannot contemplate the pain to come.

'I wish we had never met,' he states simply, as if erasing our history together and mapping out a different life for both of us could remove his agony.

~

Silas should have been born a girl. Not because he was dainty and effeminate, far from it, but because at our three-month antenatal scan, the sonographer told us so.

'There you go,' she said, all light and breezy. 'See that line there.' We squinted at the screen, trying to work out what line she could be talking about. 'It's too soon to be sure, but the way that line is pointing means it's probably a girl.'

We had two gorgeous boys already and you can imagine our excitement at the thought that here, finally, was the girl we longed for. I spent the next few months thinking of girls' names and wondering how soon I might be able to buy something pink.

Our optimism had dimmed by the time the next scan came round and I persuaded Ben that we'd better find out the actual sex so that I no longer needed to hide the pink-striped baby tights I had bought in the bottom of a drawer.

I lay in the scan room with gel on my tummy and waited for confirmation that we were having a girl. Ben squeezed my hand.

'It's a boy,' the sonographer said, beaming.

'Are you sure?' we chorused.

She checked again. 'Yup, definitely male. Male and growing well. A bouncing baby boy.'

I looked across at Ben.

He grinned and shrugged. 'Oh well, back to the drawing board with names. At least he's healthy.'

And that's the thing, isn't it? You can cope with just about anything as long as your children are healthy.

A few months later, Silas came crashing into the world. He was overdue by more than a week and I was enormous. We have a picture of me sitting in a deck chair in that last week in glorious spring sunshine and you'd be forgiven for thinking that someone had stuffed a duvet, the pillows and even a double bed under my top.

The birth was quick and once Silas had made the decision to come nothing was going to stop him. I had no pain relief, just a bit of gas and air, and I remember the midwife shouting as his head crowned.

'Oh my God, this is a big one. It's huge. Come and look at this, everyone.' She waved troops of students through the room.

I was still pushing, but if I could have reached I might well have strangled her.

She was right, though. Silas was a whopping 5kg, or 11lbs! He came out looking as though he had fought several rounds with Mike Tyson. His ears were still in one piece but they were swollen and bruised. His nose was flattened and his eyes puffed closed. Ben called him Jabba the Hutt for the first week.

To me, he was battered but perfect, and I was now the proud mother of three boys.

~

Those first few days after Silas's diagnosis, Ben and I function on autopilot. We take the children to their cousin's house in Wales, and while they run about on the beach kayaking, skimming stones and eating ice creams, we hold war councils.

'Whatever you do, do not leave this hospital and go searching on the Internet,' the oncologist had told us. 'Go away, enjoy your holiday and we'll meet in six days to discuss the next steps.'

For the first 24 hours we are too shell-shocked to do much, but soon we put out feelers across the world to neurosurgeons and neuro-oncologists in Australia, the USA and elsewhere in Europe. I need to know what I am dealing with before I meet with the oncology team.

Information on the Internet is sobering and terrifying. Glioblastoma multiforme, or GBM as it is more commonly known, is a frightening disease. It's one of the most aggressive cancers in humans and the average survival is one year. Despite advances in surgical techniques and chemotherapy this survival rate has not improved in more than 30 years. Many of those diagnosed only live a few short months. However, one piece of information stands out: long-term survival, which equates to two years with this type of tumour, is closely correlated with tumour removal. Children and adults who have their tumours fully removed prior to radiotherapy have a greater chance of surviving longer. This is difficult for us to read as Silas has a large portion of tumour left inside his head.

The other thing our research turns up is that recent immunotherapy trials in both Europe and the USA have shown promising results with children. Immunotherapy is a form of treatment that stimulates the patient's own immune system to recognise and destroy the cancerous cells.

During the days, we speak with many top scientists and doctors. One conversation in particular sticks with us. Ben speaks with an eminent neurosurgeon in Virginia, USA. As the conversation draws to a close, the surgeon says, 'Don't forget, it's easy to get caught up in chasing around the world for miracle cures. The truth of it is your son has a very aggressive brain tumour and you mustn't lose sight of that. Remember to live and enjoy every day you have with him because at the end of it all you'll never get those days back. Make the most of the time you have, however little that may turn out to be.'

These words are hard to hear but we are grateful for the brutal truth. The likelihood is that whatever treatment we seek, the eventual outcome won't change. We could drag Silas away from his home and friends to the other side of the world for experimental treatment but he'd be miserable and he'd still die. We have to weigh up our desperate desire to keep him alive with his need to live the rest of his life, however short it may be.

We decide to take charge of his future and of our future and the first step is to name Silas's tumour, to take away the fear it engenders in us.

The children are watching TV with their cousins.

'Hey, guys,' I say. 'We need to think of a name for Silas's tumour. Something silly. What shall we call it?'

At that moment, Rowan Atkinson walks on screen in a rerun of *Blackadder II*. His voice echoes out from the TV. 'Well, Bob, welcome on board.'

Almost instantly, Silas pipes up, 'What about BOB?'

It's perfect. Harmless and silly, especially if you picture Rowan Atkinson saying it in that pursed-lip, tight-arsed sort of way. From that moment on we are in a battle with BOB. It gives us a focus and we set about destroying BOB in every way we can. We have video footage of Silas destroying a plasticine BOB, video animations using toy figures, home movies called 'Killing BOB' and 'Killing BOB II', and even a pumpkin BOB being blown up using explosive bangers. It gives us an outlet and the children some fun. It also gives Silas the belief that killing BOB is what we will do. It becomes a game and BOB killing him never enters into the equation.

～

That first week out of the hospital is fraught with barely controlled panic. Ben and I live in a heightened state of fear, hormones pumping, our adrenal glands working overtime. We survive in a permanent state of fight or flight and any loud noise leaves my heart racing and my palms clammy. Sleep is difficult and we achieve it with the help of temazepam or zopiclone. We spend hours lying awake in the small hours of the night, aware of each other's breathing but unable to talk as we each struggle separately to process our new world.

We watch Silas from a distance. Every laugh, giggle and proclamation of love is a turn of the screw. We are overprotective and alert for the epileptic seizures that are possible after his surgery. We ply him with medicines: anti-seizure, anti-emetics and appetite-inducing steroids. At the same time, we don't want to stop him living and we bite our tongues as he cycles down steep hills and climbs rocky headlands only a week after major brain surgery. He looks just like any other 10-year-old boy on the beach in swimming trunks, running through the surf, except for a striped beanie hat protecting his stitches and the enormous S shaped scar that cuts a swathe through the hair above his left ear.

His brothers show him no allowances and grapple with him on the sofa – their pent-up resentment at being stuck with Granny for a week while he enjoyed both of us in hospital coming to the fore. Games of Twister with the cousins descend into writhing bundles of children, their arms and legs splaying across the slippery plastic mat. Silas is a child first and foremost and for him thoughts of cancer are fleeting and ephemeral. Something he doesn't want to think about and, bar the constant rounds of medication, could easily forget in that wonderful, innocent way that only children possess. The way a scraped knee can be instantly erased by a sticky lollipop.

~

I never took our happiness for granted. I was aware how lucky I was to have had four healthy children and a husband I adored. I said it often – to my mother, to my best friend, to Ben even. We had both had bumpy times in our adolescent years, dark skeletons in the family cupboard, that sort of thing. Life had not been plain sailing for either family and both our fathers had died by the time Silas was born. Mine at only 59 and Ben's before he was 70.

Some people sail through life with barely a cloud in the sky, while others batter through horizontal rain the whole way. There's no gauge to say, 'That's your fair share of luck, let's dish out some trouble.' After Silas is diagnosed, I look at people with what I perceive are gilded, perfect lives and I can taste the bitterness. It's not that I begrudge them their happiness, it's more that I wish we could have that same happiness back. I want to be like them and, although I didn't take it for granted, I didn't realise how precious it was until it was too late.

It is difficult not to feel hard done by when you are hit with odds of 250,000 to 1, as we have been. I know that every family that has ever stood in our shoes feels the same, but still it feels like drawing the short straw.

I sense that people look at us and feel pity but also relief; relief that it has happened to us and not to them. Lightning is unlikely to strike twice. The Pullens have taken the hit so everyone else can relax. The same way everyone always feels a little safer flying just after a plane crash. I wonder how many people stowing their luggage away on flight MH17 felt the same? Or how my grandfather, commanding a destroyer sunk by an E-boat at Dunkirk, felt after the rescue boat that plucked him from the cold water was immediately sunk by friendly fire.

I see it flit across their faces, these friends of ours, relief quickly followed by guilt. Guilt for feeling relief and guilt for not quite managing to hide it. I know this as I was one of those people once. Upset by a tragic story of a child drowning in a swimming pool but also relieved that it was not me and my family living that nightmare. Only now, on the other side of the fence, do I get it. Only now do I finally understand. Others' misfortune serves only to remind us of our own mortality and vulnerability and we inevitably shy away from it, like a contagious disease, grateful that we are still intact. I watch our friends and neighbours hold their families a little closer following Silas's diagnosis and I am jealous.

~

Silas is our third son, but it is amazing how the space in your heart just grows bigger with each new addition.

Even though we knew Silas was going to be a boy, we hadn't chosen a name before he was born. Partly because you have to meet your children before you can saddle them with something, and partly because I still held out the vague hope that the baby would turn out to be a girl.

In the end, Silas was named after the much maligned *Silas Marner*, a book I had enjoyed as a teenager. The main character is a deeply misunderstood hermit with an inherent kindness and a gentle soul – traits that shone out of our Silas early on. More literally, from its Greek origins, Silas means simply 'man of the woods'.

His middle names were Patrick and Somerset. The first was my father's name and he had died unexpectedly the preceding year so it felt only right that our newborn son should carry his name, and the second because that's where Silas was conceived.

We had returned from a stint of living in New Zealand. We had two small children and were toying with the idea of moving down to the rolling hills of East Somerset. Ben had always had a yearning for the West Country and we were staying with good friends of my parents for a few days to look at a selection of local properties.

The reason I know Silas was conceived in Somerset is because I wasn't planning on getting pregnant. We had a two-year-old and a nearly eight-month-old, whom I had only recently finished breastfeeding. Our work was cut out already. We definitely didn't need to add another child into the mix quite yet. However, we'd left the children with my mother for a couple of days and it was our first weekend in months without screaming babies in tow, and the result was a little extra blue line appearing on a pregnancy test a few weeks later. The shock was short-lived; we knew we wanted more than two children and we just accepted that fate had stepped in and expedited the situation.

If Ben had had his way, Silas would have been called Hector. With hindsight, maybe being named after a great warrior would have been more appropriate for him than being named after a gentle woodsman, but none of us knew then what was round the corner.

~

Our first meeting with the multidisciplinary team at the Royal Marsden is a little different from the one Silas's oncologist probably envisioned.

We walk into a room lined with strange faces – paediatric oncologists, clinical oncologists, clinical fellows and neuro-oncology nurses. The walls are coloured in bright murals with aliens poking out of strange moonscapes. Silas is unfazed by all the attention and allows the doctors to prod and poke him. He walks in a straight line, balances on his tiptoes, hops across the room on one leg. He performs and then slinks off at the first opportunity back to the waiting room to continue with the film he had been watching.

Dr S, the consultant we had met at King's, the one with the unpronounceable name, is pleased with Silas's progress.

He turns to us, eager to move us through the system quickly and without complication. He has seen the same queue of patients and bewildered parents waiting in reception that we have.

'Right, the plan is to proceed with radical radiotherapy in combination with a chemotherapy drug called temozolomide, which is well tolerated in children. We would also like Silas to join a Phase II paediatric trial for Avastin, a drug which aims to prevent the tumour making blood vessels.'

I hold up my hand. 'Before we go down the radiotherapy route, we need to find a surgeon who will remove the rest of the tumour.'

Dr S raises his eyebrows and tilts his head. 'It's too risky to remove the rest of the tumour. That's why they didn't do it at King's. It wouldn't be a good idea.'

'I know it's a risk but if it can be done, we need to do it.' I fix my eyes on his. 'I've done my research – Silas has no chance otherwise. We need to find someone who is confident about operating.'

'Well, we can try,' says Dr S, puffing out his cheeks. 'But I can't promise we'll find someone. I can send his scans to a few other surgeons and get their opinions. We really have to move ahead, though, with radiation. Any delay will give the tumour time to regrow.'

'We have to try, though.'

He looks thoughtful. I can feel him sizing me up as a boxer sizes up his opponent in the ring.

'If it was your son, what would you do?' I say. 'Put yourself in our shoes.'

He steeples his hands and nods. Silent.

After a few seconds he sighs. 'Yes, I'd probably do the same.' He scribbles a few notes onto his pad.

'Also,' I say, 'we don't want to do the Avastin trial but we would like to get him onto an immunotherapy trial – anywhere in the world but preferably Europe. It has to be best to get his own immune system to work for him. Can you help us with this?'

Dr S purses his lips and exchanges a glance with one of his colleagues.

'That might be difficult. There's no current trial in Europe that's open for children on primary presentation.'

I catch his eye and hold his gaze. 'We must find something; we want to give him the best shot. Please help us.'

He rubs his hand across his chin. 'I'll have to speak with a few people. There's a trial that they're trying to get off the ground at Great Ormond Street Hospital (GOSH). They've not yet received all the regulatory approvals they need so it might not be open in time for Silas. I'll make some calls though.'

I smile. Perhaps we can make this happen. It's a long shot and we'll have to make some tough decisions but Dr S seems willing to help us if he can. This is a start. I leave the room feeling that maybe we have an ally and that, if so, we don't have to fight the system as well as BOB.

~

Early in my pregnancy with Silas we moved into our house: a red-brick Victorian rectory on top of the North Downs that had been lived in by the same family for the last 50 years. It was tired and tattered and desperately in need of some care and attention. It stood tall and proud to the side of the village green with windows that let the light stream into every corner, beautiful wooden gables painted a deep, rich, papal red and too many disused chimneys that were in imminent danger of falling down. We had to spend large sums of money soon after we moved in repointing them and strapping them securely to the roof before winter and gale-force winds hit.

The house was by no means perfect. It was too close to a busy main road, had been extended poorly by vicars who were long on progeny but short of cash, and had a permanent colony of long-eared brown bats in the roof, which complicated any building works. It did, though, have incredible views from the back down towards the sea and Whitstable, and a rambling garden with hidden nooks and crannies, perfect for vegetables, football and hide-and-seek.

When we bought it, we didn't anticipate staying put. Ben had been brought up all over the world and he had visions of continuing his globetrotting existence, family in tow. But plans have a way of coming unravelled as priorities change and the house oozed happiness and comfort. It was the perfect place to raise a handful of boys and, unsurprisingly, we stayed put.

We moved into the house the week of 9/11 and I've memories of unpacking boxes with the television blaring and footage of the twin towers falling in a seemingly endless loop. We, like so many others, struggled to comprehend the senseless killing and I remember being relieved that my father was not alive to witness such destruction and hatred.

I was violently ill that week. I couldn't keep any food down and had to ensure there was a path clear of boxes between me and the bathroom. I put it down to severe morning sickness, although I had never suffered before. After several difficult days, I went to the doctor. She diagnosed a kidney infection and put me on a course of strong antibiotics and the sickness dwindled away. That same week I felt the first flutterings of the baby in my stomach and I hugged my belly afraid for what it might have to witness in its lifetime. How could I keep it safe from unseen future enemies that flew planes at buildings? Turns out the enemy I actually needed to worry about was lurking within his very genes.

Researchers have yet to discover the underlying cause of childhood brain tumours, and it is likely that, more often than not, there are a variety of factors involved; but there has been a Canadian study that has found a possible causal link with the use of antibiotics during gestation.

Was this when it happened, when the wheels were set in motion? Was it my fault?

It is human nature to want to find a cause, to pinpoint the moment in time when the die was cast, to find someone or something to blame for events outside our control, and it took me months after Silas's diagnosis to stop blaming myself and to stop sifting through the past for an explanation. Finally, I realised that no matter how much I tortured myself, I would never get nearer to a definitive answer. The truth is there were any number of factors that might have contributed to his cancer: my antibiotics, bumps to his head, X-ray exposure or just dodgy genes.

I hated not having a black-and-white explanation but in the end I had to accept that he had just drawn the short straw.

Ten days after that first meeting at the Royal Marsden, Silas and I are on our way to Liverpool.

The day before, Ben and I had been at a preliminary meeting with the team at GOSH, discussing the possibility of Silas taking part in their immunotherapy trial. Our hopes were dashed when the lead researcher told us that the tumour sample removed from Silas's brain at King's had not been stored correctly. It had been pickled in alcohol instead of frozen so they wouldn't be able to use it, and without viable tumour tissue, Silas would be ineligible for the trial. Our anger was nipped in the bud as, during the meeting, we learnt that Silas's oncologist had found a surgeon willing to go back in and remove the rest of the tumour. This fresh tissue could then be frozen for the trial.

Things moved quickly and hours later, I sit opposite Silas on the train.

It is the first day of a new term, a new academic year, and we speed past platforms jostling with uniformed children. I tear my eyes away, but it is too late and I can't wipe the image of my eldest son starting at a new school without me to wave him off and bolster his confidence. I ruffle Silas's short hair but the guilt gnaws away at me as the train hurtles our family further apart.

Silas and I play cards and I notice that he isn't really using his right hand, his dominant hand. It isn't obvious, he's just doing more with his left. He picks up his drink left-handed and reaches round with his left hand to scratch his right ear. He struggles to pick up the cards, the fingers on his right hand failing to grasp the coated plastic and slipping repeatedly. He looks like a baby trying to pick up a pea to pop into its mouth, his face tense with concentration and his brow furrowed.

I cast my mind back a few days. We had fought over a thank-you letter that Silas had been writing. He complained that he couldn't hold the pen properly and I accused him of just wanting to return to the TV. He ended up in tears, his writing scrawled illegibly across the page. Now my heart sinks.

'Is your hand all right?' I ask.

He turns it over and rubs his thumb across his fingers.

'It just feels weird,' he says. 'Sort of like it's not my hand.'

'When did this start?'

'Dunno, I guess just the last few days really.' He shrugs his shoulders.

I sink into my seat. His hand had been fine after the first operation. Why is he having problems now? Is it a delayed response to the trauma to his brain? It can't be the tumour, I think. It's only three weeks since the operation, nothing can grow that fast. I stare at his head wishing for X-ray vision.

I trample down my fear and hold out my hand. 'Shall I deal?'

Liverpool welcomes us with open arms and smiling faces. The neuro ward at Alder Hey fans out into spacious corridors and large rooms, and the soft lilt of Liverpudlian accents fills the air. Ben delivers boys to three different schools and follows us north.

The next day, after a prolonged functional MRI scan during which the operators have Silas wiggling fingers and toes to establish where in his left hemisphere his motor tracts lie, Ben and I are called into a meeting with the surgeon. We leave Silas watching TV and traipse down the corridor, fingers curled together. This is the moment we have to decide whether it's worth risking our son's mobility to get the rest of BOB out.

'Come in,' says the surgeon, beckoning us over towards a screen.

'I've good news and bad news,' he says. He looks at our faces, his dark eyes hooded. 'I'll give you the bad news first.' He points to the screen. 'The tumour has grown massively in the last three weeks.' He holds up his right hand and wiggles his fingers. 'That's why your son is losing the feeling in his right hand. The tumour is three times the size it was after the first operation.'

I gasp. Ben squeezes my hand and the world tilts once again.

'The good news is we have no decision to make. We've no choice – not anymore. We have to operate. We have to take the risk of paralysis as the tumour load is once again becoming too great for his brain to cope with.'

I crumple into a chair and take a deep breath.

'Can you do it?' I ask.

The surgeon looks thoughtful, his white shirt crisp against the dark wool of his suit. 'Yes, I believe I can. His motor tracts run in front of the tumour, which is not where they were originally assumed to be.' He points to flashes of orange on the screen. 'I've a good shot of getting it out and not doing more damage to him.'

He instils us with optimism. He speaks with assurance and confidence and in the end the decision to operate is easy.

Hours later, he tells us that he has successfully removed all the visible tumour. It's apparent in the recovery room that there's no further decline on Silas's right-hand side and we are elated. I bury my anger at the London surgeons for not fighting harder to remove everything during the first operation and focus on the fact that now we have plenty of new tumour material to qualify Silas for the GOSH trial. We have given him a fighting chance and we feel vindicated that we have made the right decision.

Silas makes a quick recovery following his second brain surgery, not as quick as the first time, but still equally impressive. He stops all seizure medication and steroids and with them the anti-emetics – it's a relief to be drug-free.

We speak with the team at GOSH. They have their permissions, are testing their equipment and pushing everything ahead in the hope that Silas can be the first patient on the immunotherapy trial. He's a suitable candidate as long as he does not have too heavy a tumour load after radiation, as the immunotherapy can potentially cause catastrophic swelling in the brain.

The next few weeks are full of preparations for radiotherapy: mould rooms, where Silas is fitted with a hard, meshed, plastic mask that will hold his head still during treatment; CAT scans; more MRI scans; and meetings with play specialists to talk him through the process.

We have to sign consent forms that you would baulk at for yourself let alone your 10-year-old child. Forms which state we are putting him at risk of hearing loss, strokes, growth problems, hormone problems, cognitive problems and, believe it or not, future brain tumours. Radiation to the brain can wipe nearly 10 points off an individual's IQ level, but we have no choice and put pen to paper.

The radiotherapy means daily three- to four-hour round trips up to the Royal Marsden in Sutton on the outskirts of London. We will have to negotiate unreliable stretches of the M25 and long queues of traffic caused by roadworks. It'll be a struggle but, for the first time since Silas's diagnosis, Ben and I feel buoyed with optimism. We allow a little hope back into our lives. Maybe, just maybe, we can beat BOB.

Silas goes back to school and life returns to some semblance of normality.

~

Silas roared. He roared from the day he was born. Not screaming and wailing like many newborn babies, but shrieks of enjoyment and yells of exuberance. He was never quiet and was always shouting. This might have been because he lived in a raucous house full of boys and had to shout just to make himself heard, but I believe that living his life at top volume was just the way he was made. He loved being alive and just wanted to shout about it. This continued as he got older. In fact, to the whole family's great amusement, he couldn't whisper. It was impossible for him. He would try and his voice would get lower and lower and deeper and deeper but his vocal chords were simply not designed to vibrate in such a minimal way.

Chinese whispers round the table at supper would have us all in stitches as his voice carried round the whole room. Sometimes you'd have to jerk your head away as he started whispering – the assault on your eardrum just too painful. Whispering sweet nothings in a girl's ear was going to be nigh on impossible for him, but you can be certain he was going to try.

In one nativity play, when he was about four, Silas played the innkeeper – the main part in this production. He shifted his weight from foot to foot with excitement, unable to stand still. Dressed up in a moth-eaten brown blanket with a rope belt, his voice boomed across the school hall. The more the parents laughed, the louder he got. He played up to the audience until, instead of talking and singing, he was pretty much yelling at full volume. He stole the show.

Almost every photo shows him grinning, laughing, shouting and hollering. Open-mouthed and open-faced. Life was here to be lived and you can be sure that he was not going to miss a single moment of it. He resounded with noise. It bounced off him in ever widening waves, scooping up all in its path and taking them along for the ride whether they were strapped in safely or not.

~

The bubble of hope we have encased ourselves in bursts with a bang. Two days before Silas's radiation is due to start, he complains of a sudden headache on the way to school and vomits into a bag in the car.

The oncologist tells us to take him to the local hospital. We sit in that hospital room in horror. Both Ben and I know the symptoms are signs of increased intracranial pressure, but it's only three weeks after the second operation. Silas recovers, the headache goes, and he thinks we are making a fuss about nothing.

An emergency scan is done and our hearts lift when the paediatric consultant, knowing how worried we are, says that the scan looks all right to him. He admits we'll have to wait for the radiographer's report to be certain. It's a false alarm and we scarcely dare to believe our luck and hug each other with delight.

Half an hour later the consultant returns and says those dreaded words, 'Let's go somewhere more private to have a chat.'

In a quiet side room, he reads out the radiographer's report and apologises profusely for being wrong and jumping the gun. The tumour has regrown. BOB is back.

'But he's meant to be starting radiotherapy in a couple of days,' I say. 'What will happen now?'

'I don't know,' says the consultant. 'He'll have to go back on steroids and the radiotherapy will probably just be palliative now, but you'll have to have that discussion with the oncologist.'

Tears fill my eyes. All of a sudden we are back at death's door. The two and a half months to Christmas alone seem like an insurmountable hurdle. I bury my head in my hands. How are we ever going to tackle a monster as aggressive as BOB – a cancer that can double in size in just days? I realise we have been kidding ourselves.

The consultant puts his hand on my arm.

'I'm sorry,' he says. 'I really am.'

I shrug him off. I'm fed up with people saying they are sorry.

~

Silas had extraordinary hair. When he was a baby we nicknamed him Fu Manchu – a mainstay of comic strips and television series over the last century. He was an archetypal evil genius who favoured bizarre methods of disposing of his victims, using poison or venomous animals.

Silas didn't earn his nickname for similar character traits – after all he was only six months old – but for Fu Manchu's one outstanding characteristic: a long, dark moustache that twirled to sharp points far below his chin. He would rub the tips between his thumb and forefingers as he plotted his next dastardly crime. Silas's baby hair stuck straight up from the top of his head in long, gorgeous wisps – he looked as if he'd stuck his finger in an electric socket – and Ben took great delight in curling these strands into two long horns of hair that drooped much like Fu Manchu's moustache. Thankfully the nickname didn't stick.

Silas had red hair. Not fiery ginger but a rich, dark, molten auburn. He wasn't a true redhead with skin that needed to hide from the sun and freckles littering his face. His eldest brother, Oscar, drew that card. Silas could tan easily. In fact, he would turn nut brown quicker than all his siblings.

Red hair made him a target and he was seven years old when he first came home from school and begged me to let him dye his hair another colour. A year later, a boy told him that the only good redhead was a dead redhead.

'They are just jealous,' I said as I wiped his tears. 'Secretly everyone wants red hair, that's why it is the most popular hair-dye colour sold.'

He narrowed his eyes. 'You're just saying that to make me feel better.'

I shook my head. 'One day you'll be glad that you are not the same as everyone else.'

He sniffed.

I kissed his head. 'Bet you didn't know King Arthur had red hair?'

'Did he?'

'Supposedly.'

'He was cool.'

I nodded. 'And he got to wield Excalibur.'

He grinned and thrust at me with an imaginary sword before rounding on his brothers with a holler.

~

At the beginning of October, Silas starts six weeks of daily radiation and chemotherapy. For Ben and me, this feels like fighting just one small corner of a huge bush fire with a single hose and a solitary fire extinguisher. It is not enough but it is all we have.

Silas's oncologist, Dr S, can't hide his disappointment that BOB has made such a rapid reappearance, but he's not as pessimistic as the consultant in our local hospital.

'I know it's not what we hoped for,' he says on the first day of radiation. 'But he might still have a good response. Let's not make any decisions until his post-radiation scan. Some children respond really well.'

The daily journeys up to the Royal Marsden are an enormous chore, but they give us each precious time alone with Silas – a lot of time is spent singing Silas's favourite pop songs, belting out the words at the top of our lungs, the bass reverberating through the car's speakers.

We've been told we can take a CD for Silas to listen to during his treatment, but the first day, in our anxiety, we forget. The technician fumbles around in a drawer and pulls out a few battered CD cases.

'I'm not sure any of the music will be up his street,' she apologises. 'But it's all we have.'

I flip through the cases. Mostly it's classical music or crooners like Tom Jones and Barbra Streisand – music for an older clientele. Nothing Silas would recognise. The last disc, though, is the Beatles. It's perfect. As a family, we've wasted many a rainy Sunday afternoon singing to 'Beatles Rockband' on the Wii. That first day Silas is bolted to a plastic gurney by a moulded turquoise face mask, embraced by the radiotherapy machine. We leave him immobile and alone, about to have his brain fried, humming along to 'Here Comes the Sun'.

On our return to the room, I put my arm around Silas and ask him how it had been.

'Fine, but I could smell my brain burning.' says Silas matter-of-factly.

I turn to the radiologist beside us.

She nods. 'It's quite common, I'm afraid.'

'Lucky you've got plenty of brains to spare then,' I announce and kiss the top of his head.

We never do get around to bringing in another CD over the next six weeks. It turns out that 'Here Comes the Sun' is exactly three minutes and and four seconds long – the precise length of time Silas requires for his radiation. Somehow the refrain 'It's all right' makes us feel just a little cheerful. Ben and I aren't allowed to be in the room with him because of the radiation, but listening to the same notes echoing down the corridor keeps us connected – a bit like lovers in different countries looking at the same moon.

The days drag on and the rush of cars becomes the endless backdrop to each journey. Every day, we have to pass a family-run supercar show-room called Romans International. Silas ogles the Ferraris, Bugattis and Lamborghinis out of the passenger window.

Halfway through his radiotherapy, Ben stops at Romans on the way home. Unknown to Silas, Ben has already spoken to the manager. The two of them are shown around and Silas is allowed to sit in several cars – an Enzo Ferrari, a Bugatti Veyron and finally a Ferrari 599 GTO. Silas is encouraged to start the engine in the 599 and give it a few beefed-up revs. Ben films the whole thing: the wide-eyed look and enormous smile on Silas's face as the engine roars to life is priceless.

Silas is shown how to adjust the driver's seat so that he can be nearer the steering wheel. He moves himself closer.

'That's amazing,' he grins. 'They even make them for kids to drive!'

～

Ben and I met in a crowded bar. The bar was rented out for a private Valentine's Day party. Ben gatecrashed the party late on with a friend. I spotted him as soon as he walked in. He held himself with confidence and ease and looked out of place amongst all the blue jeans and collared shirts of the other men. He wore leather trousers, a bright yellow gilet and a fluffy, green mohair jumper. He was more than comfortable in his own skin. I begged a girlfriend, Bella, for an introduction. She had known him in Florence some years before and duly obliged, although she spent the next few months complaining that we were too wrapped up in each other to notice her or anyone else anymore.

Ben and I spent the rest of that first evening talking and the next morning, I rang up my best friend and said, 'I've met the man I am going to spend the rest of my life with!'

I had never been so sure of anything before. I can't explain how I knew. I just knew that we were meant to be together. It was as though his angles and bends just slotted into my chinks and gaps and knobbly knees in a perfect fit.

Eight years later we had a mortgage, four sons, two dogs, two cats and a motley flock of chickens.

~

Silas sails through the radiation. The hair across the left-hand side of his head falls out; he is left with just enough of a tuft by his ear so that if he wears a beanie pulled down low, no one would ever know the rest is missing.

He returns to district cricket training at weekends, despite the weakness in his right hand. His dark beanie stands out in striking contrast to his cricket whites. He hesitates outside the door at his first session. He knows that the other boys will whisper about him and laugh at his inconsistent bowling. I see the doubt cloud his face. His hand hovers over the door handle and the seconds tick by. Then he straightens his shoulders, takes a deep breath and pushes the door open.

Cricket has seen him through some difficult moments in his treatment already and his passion for the game is undiminished. Ben and Silas spent the last hour or so before his surgery in Liverpool playing cricket in Silas's room. I lay on the bed as Silas stood by the door, his hospital gown flapping round his legs, holding a novelty cricket bat used for collecting autographs. Ben bowled tricky googlies at him using an old tennis ball. The ball was driven all around the room to hushed shouts of 'Howzat'. The neuro-nurses at the ward station tolerated all the bangs and crashes with good humour and Silas went in for his general anaesthetic with a big smile on his face and talking about 'doing a Dilshan'.

Right at the end of radiation, we get the news we have been waiting for from the team at GOSH; they have done all their testing and got their permissions and Silas will be the first patient on their trial for a dendritic cell vaccine. It's great news. It will mean his treatment can continue in the UK, that we can all stay at home and be a family. We now just have to hope that the radiation has stopped BOB in his tracks, at least for the time being.

~

Having cancer is not all bad. We try to focus on the good things as much as possible. Every day, after our trips to the radiotherapy suites, we list three good things that have happened to us. These are usually simple, like: we've not got stuck in traffic on the M25; we found a parking space outside the children's centre – these parking spaces are free and as rare as gold dust; the M&S petrol station had Silas's favourite Santini tomatoes or strawberries from the Kelsey farm in Kent, whose kids are at school with him. Occasionally, they will be better things like: we've met Silas's godmother for lunch; stopped at the supercar showroom; or Silas has been taken round the set of his godfather's latest film, *Thor II*, at Shepperton Studios. Focusing on the good definitely reduces the power of the bad. We are thankful for small things and try to block out the shadow looming over us.

We write a private blog to keep friends and family updated about Silas's treatment. We keep things light-hearted and never touch upon the truth of his diagnosis. The blog becomes a positive outlet for our journey and a way of keeping the wool pulled over the eyes of everyone else. We always play the bad things down and encourage people to come up with inventive ways of destroying BOB.

There are other things that come out of Silas having cancer. We start reading bedtime stories again. Something that has slipped as the children got older. We snuggle up in our big double bed and read the whole series of *Young Samurai* books to Silas and his younger brother. These eight books by Chris Bradford are full of non-stop action and life lessons but, most importantly for us, they are full of little proverbs that we can relate to Silas's own struggle:

There is no failure except in no longer trying.

Seven times down, eight times up.

Some are particularly pertinent for Ben and me:

The impossible becomes possible if only your mind believes it.

Anyone can give up; it is the easiest thing in the world to do. But to hold it together when everyone would expect you to fall apart, now that is true strength.

And my favourite:

When it is dark enough, you can see the stars.

These are special moments and a chance to regain a small slice of their childhood. They are quiet moments when I get to hold Silas in my arms, breathe in his sweet smell and kiss the top of his head; moments to stop the fight and just be; precious moments that I cling on to.

~

Silas's first MRI scan after his radiation is inconclusive. Inconclusive because the enormous post-radiation swelling in his brain disguises the size of the tumour. Dr S takes us aside, though, and tells us that the general consensus is that the tumour has progressed and we need to prepare ourselves for the worst.

'Things can move very fast if the tumour has failed to respond.' He takes a deep breath. 'It's not the news we wanted, I know.'

'What about Christmas?' Ben asks. 'Will he make Christmas?'

Dr S raises both palms. 'We would be talking anything between two to four months. There's no way of knowing.'

Christmas is only a month away.

'Does this mean they won't accept him on the GOSH trial?' I ask, trying to keep my breaths even and hold his gaze. I study his face. Can I read anything else from his eyes? Is he withholding things from us, the way we are from Silas?

He thinks for a moment. 'It's possible he'll no longer be suitable as the immunotherapy can cause further swelling, but that's their call. We'll have to wait and see.'

The GOSH team review the scans and agree to continue with Silas on the trial, much to our relief. They hope that the scan shows pseudo-progression, which is when radiation-induced changes to the brain can mimic tumour growth.

~

Not long before Christmas, Silas has his dendritic cells harvested via a procedure called a leukapheresis. He has a vascath, a tube the size of a biro, inserted into a vein in his groin under a general anaesthetic and then his blood is centrifuged for the best part of a day and the white blood cells are siphoned off.

The anaesthetic team at GOSH give Silas a choice of being put to sleep by gas or by injection. He chooses gas as it is a novelty. He lies in the operating room, both Ben and me at his side, with a gas mask over his nose and mouth.

'It smells of pears.' He grins and licks his lips.

'It's the same gas as laughing gas. They can get the giggles,' says the anaesthetist. She leans over Silas. 'Silas, why don't you tell us your favourite joke?'

Silas furrows his brow.

'OK,' he says, smiling. 'There were two cats. An English cat called OneTwoThree and a French cat called UnDeuxTrois. They both swam the channel. Which one won?'

The anaesthetist scratches her head. 'I don't know. Which one won?'

Silas is already giggling. His body shakes as he tries to control his laughter. His eyes sparkle. 'OneTwoThree, of course, as UnDeuxTrois cat sank!'

Silas's eyes roll up in his head and he reaches out in a half-hearted attempt to remove his mask. His hand drops to his side and his eyelids flutter closed.

An hour or so later we are brought to the recovery room. As we enter, Silas's voice booms across the other beds.

'That was amazing,' he slurs. 'I feel so great. This is what it must feel like to take drugs. Can I do it again?'

He spots us. 'Mummy and Daddy, I had such a great time.' He looks around him, his eyes big. 'Wow, everything looks so colourful. I feel like I've been taking happy drugs. You're really missing out!'

The nearest nurse stifles a giggle and Ben and I shake our heads and grin. For a moment the hospital recedes and it's just the three of us laughing and it feels good.

The immunotherapy trial involves sensitising Silas's immune cells to his tumour and then injecting these cells back into his body to help his own immune system recognise and destroy the tumour cells. This means a monthly trip to GOSH, large test tubes of blood being removed via a cannula and six agonising injections just under the skin of each thigh.

Silas bears each trip with fortitude – the journey no doubt made a little easier by bribery with a large pain au chocolate. The nurses raise their eyebrows and smile as Silas starts to unpick the pastry, strewing mess all over the hospital table.

The treatment rooms in the research facility are all named after types of trees – Oak, Chestnut and Holly, to name a few – which Ben and I find ironic. All these trees live for hundreds of years, whereas this facility deals only with life-limiting diseases like Muscular Dystrophy, Cystic Fibrosis and various cancers. Is this subliminal focus on longevity somehow meant to reassure those who don't have the luxury of time?

The same is true of the radiotherapy suites at the Royal Marsden; they too are all named after native English trees and the innocuous sounding Rowan was the site of our first foray against BOB.

~

Three boys in the space of three years is hard work. Wonderful, chaotic, rewarding, but exhausting. We spent so much time running after them all it's no surprise that we waited a bit longer for the last one. We always wanted four children. In my mind, two wasn't enough. If one wasn't there the other would be lonely; with three, someone is always left out; so four it had to be.

Silas was a few months past his second birthday when his younger brother, Inigo, was born. Ben and I had agreed to have a fourth child several months before I actually got pregnant. With a house full of boys, we desperately wanted a girl, but we'd decided that we would only go ahead if it didn't matter if the baby was another boy. Short of flying to the USA and having Ben's sperm centrifuged there was little we could do anyway. However, I devoured as many books as I could on the subject of natural sex selection and became an expert on dietary requirements – lots of dairy, wholegrains and leafy greens and a limited intake of salt and red meat – timings within the menstrual cycle and positions. I seem to remember I even made Ben wear tight pants for a while!

After a couple of months, I had still not conceived, so we decided to relax over Christmas and by New Year, typically, I was pregnant. When our fourth boy tipped up nine months later we could only laugh. 'We may not have a girl, but at least we have a boy band,' Ben pointed out.

There should be a word for a group of boys. A collective noun that sums up the energy contained in a raucous band of brothers. The only official term I can turn up is 'a blush of boys' – a fifteenth-century pun on the shyness of male adolescents. How inappropriate for a family full of boys. How much better does 'a bash of boys' or a 'bundle of boys' sound, or even 'a blast of boys'.

Small boys are like puppies, constantly rolling around on top of each other. As a mother of just boys, it's all about damage limitation, both to each other and to the immediate environment. Parents of daughters would invite us over for lunch and then visibly quake with relief when we left. They nicknamed our horde 'the locusts'.

To us, these visits were a minefield. No cupboard locks, ornaments sitting decoratively on tables, loo brushes at floor level, razors within grasping reach. They would frown in disgust when Silas's grubby fingers snaked out to touch something he had been told not to four times already, and tut under their breath about our bad parenting. They had no idea that 'No' to a small boy is simply a challenge, another of life's hurdles to be negotiated like a bull in a china shop. 'No' on its own just doesn't cut it. Not for boys. They need to know what will happen if they put this finger here and nudge that thing there. Will the world fall apart or sweets tumble from the sky? Life is exciting and it's all about dis-covery. Do first and think later.

Silas was the most adept doer of the lot. His eldest brother, Oscar, exercised a fair amount of caution in a simple self-preservation sort of way. Rufus was hampered by shyness, but Silas had no such qualms and lived life with an in-built immediacy, which meant that his inherent curiosity was never curtailed by ifs and buts. Consequences always came later.

We took the eldest three skiing in Austria when Silas was just four. We didn't go with friends. It was just us in a small, family-run hotel in Gargellen, nestled in a picturesque valley. The eldest two boys were put in the same ski group so they could lean on each other for support. Silas, however, was placed in a different group. At first we worried as there was no other English speaking child with him, but he took this all in his stride, despite being barely old enough to take down his salopettes on his own to go to the loo. Within a day or two, he had made friends with every child in his group and communicated using gestures, grunts and hilarious facial expressions. Words were superfluous.

Austrian ski school runs from the morning to mid-afternoon, with the children being given lunch in the hotel, so we didn't see any of them for most of the first five days. Ben and I had long, lazy lunches at remote mountain hideaways and made the most of our time together. The last day we took all of them out of ski school and up the mountain so that we could ski as a family.

It was nearly a disaster: we had completely overestimated Silas's skiing ability after only five days on the lower slopes.

'Look at me,' Silas called over his shoulder as we got off the chairlift. He ducked between stationary skiers and reached the slopes well ahead of us.

'Hold on, darling,' I shouted, helping one of the other boys with their gloves. 'We need to go this way.'

His voice carried in snatches on the wind. 'Look at how fast I can go.'

'Wait for us,' I yelled. But it was too late; he was gone, his blue helmet disappearing down the nearest red run.

Trying to catch a small child with a head start on a ski slope is nearly impossible, even if you are a good skier, especially if you discover they have yet to master the snow plough or turn properly. A small child's low centre of gravity means they don't have to turn much and it is incredible how fast they can go with a couple of waxed boards on their feet.

I left the other boys with Ben and powered my way past unwary skiers, keeping my eyes focused on the little, blue, bobbing helmet that was heading straight down the mountain at high speed, oblivious to the sharp left-hand turn further down the slope.

'Silas, you need to snow plough,' I yelled, making as few turns as possible to keep my own speed just under control. 'Do a pizza. You're going too fast.'

His chuckles floated back on the breeze.

'Silas!' I yelled, my voice shrill, as the turn drew closer. I could see the dark points of fir trees sticking up above the lip of the bend. 'You need to stop!'

The laughter ceased but he carried on and I realised he wasn't going to stop on his own. He had built up too much speed and his little legs weren't strong enough to hold a snow plough at that pace. I could also see that he was too scared to turn. Up ahead I saw the corner, the edge of the piste marked by crossed red poles. The trees loomed beyond.

I did the only thing possible in the short space of time I had left. I skied into my young son and pushed him into the deep snow at the edge of the piste. We crashed in a heap of legs and tangled skis. I pushed up on my elbows. Silas wasn't moving. His face and helmet were covered in snow.

'Silas,' I shook his shoulder. 'Are you OK?'

He spat the snow from his mouth and lifted his mittened hand. He pushed his goggles up. His eyes were wet with tears but they were also sparkling with excitement.

'That was fun,' he said, throwing his arms around my neck and covering me with snow. 'Did you see how fast I went? Can we do it again?'

~

Silas's immunotherapy runs concurrently with his chemo regime. He spends five days each month taking oral chemo and then a couple of days later has his immunotherapy jabs. The rest of the month is spent recovering from the effects of the chemo and monitoring his white blood cell levels and platelets.

Silas tolerates the chemo well. He's sick on a few occasions but we learn how to avoid the triggers and the anti-emetics he has to take generally do the job. His first month's dose causes a bout of shingles, which we are lucky to catch early, but still results in a week in hospital on IV antivirals.

He has several platelet transfusions over the following months. These usually entail evening trips to our local hospital while the platelets are couriered down from London. On a few occasions he becomes neutropenic and his level of white blood cells falls too low to fight infections, but generally he copes well. His hair starts growing back and he has enough energy to do small boy things.

My sister-in-law asks a pertinent question at this time. She wants to know why he looks so well. Why doesn't he look at death's door like many children undergoing chemo? She has a good point. The truth, unfortunately, is simple. Those children who have a fair chance of surviving their cancer will be bombarded with drugs. Their immune systems will, in some cases, be obliterated and then rebuilt. The chemo will ulcerate the linings of their stomachs and throats so that even swallowing is agony. Silas doesn't have this treatment: the medical establishment don't want to ruin what little life he has left.

Such intensive treatments involving stem cell rescue and the like haven't shown any beneficial effect in the treatment of glioblastomas. They aren't a life-prolonging miracle cure, so they're not used in patients who are written off from the start as terminal. Instead, the doctors use the best-tolerated, least life-limiting chemotherapy drugs available. The drug Silas is using, temozolomide, the recommended treatment, adds on average a paltry two months to the life of a child diagnosed with a glioblastoma. The one advantage is that it hopefully doesn't stop them living this short life. This is hard to accept; inevitably you want the medical establishment to throw everything in their arsenal at the monster that's devouring your flesh and blood. But a scorched earth policy is only pursued in cases where there is some hope.

So the healthier a child looks during treatment for cancer, perhaps the more likely they are to die.

The flip side of his gentler treatment is that Silas never feels as though he is at death's door. He always feels that BOB is a mere inconvenience and he never delves too deeply into the truth.

~

We tell very few people about the true diagnosis. Our priority is always Silas. We don't want him to find out that he's going to die. Not yet. Not until he has to. It's an enormous burden for us to carry, but what would it be like for him? We will carry it for as long as we can to spare him.

We tell only our immediate family and a few of our close friends, including Silas's godparents. The circle remains small. We know that the larger it gets the less control we'll have and people will start to gossip and speculate. We keep the news restricted to adults – children are unreliable at keeping secrets, although to my fury my 12-year-old nephew stumbles on the truth not long after Silas is diagnosed – the result of careless chatter by his parents. To his credit, he carries the burden with maturity and sensitivity and never lets his guard slip.

We also tell Silas's headmaster and the deputy head. There are many different types of brain tumour and we're careful not to let it become common knowledge exactly what sort Silas has. We keep things vague or skirt round the question.

In some strange way, cancer is a bit like pregnancy. I remember with each of my pregnancies, people, even strangers, were quick to offer advice. Everybody had stories to tell, good and bad. Cancer is the same. You become a member of an exclusive club and everyone feels in a position to offer you advice or tell you about the friend of a friend they knew who had a brain tumour and is still fighting fit 20 years later.

There are times when I have to bite my tongue and, I'm afraid, times when I find myself saying through gritted teeth, 'There are many different types of brain tumours and not all have good outcomes.' The worst offenders are sometimes those who think they have all the answers: the cancer survivors themselves. They want to give us tips on how to get through the worst bits, despite the fact that they had very different types of cancer.

There's no doubt that these people mean well and have gone through their own struggles. It's just really difficult to keep nodding your head when all you want to do is shout, 'Your experience isn't the same – you weren't told you were going to die and that doctors could do nothing to help you.' The voice storms in my head drowning out their kind words until I feel the mask slipping, and suddenly I have to find a way to end the conversation abruptly before I blurt out the truth. People probably think me rude and abrasive but in the midst of deep grief, it becomes hard to worry about other people's feelings.

It's the same with small talk; listening to other people's problems becomes increasingly difficult. We find it hard to go out and socialise. It all seems so banal and unimportant. The invitations fall by the wayside as Ben and I aren't exactly the life and soul of a dinner party anymore. A few good friends insist on still inviting us but it becomes harder to face the outside world.

A few years previously, my older brother had a German girlfriend. She was charming and engaging, if a little confrontational. At family gatherings she struggled to understand our self-deprecating, sarcastic and very English sense of humour. One such evening, she took affront at some comment or other and burst into a tirade.

'Ze problem wiz you Engleesh,' she growled, 'iz zat you never talks about ze elephant in ze room. It iz ze vun zing you need to do but not vun of you ever ever does! It iz maddening!'

At the time, I remember we found this remark hilarious as, for all intents and purposes, *she* was the elephant in the room that night. I guess, though, she had a point after all. After Silas is diagnosed, *we* become the elephant in the room and, a little like the hikers walking into the Slaughtered Lamb at the beginning of *American Werewolf in London,* a wave of silence descends upon any gathering we enter. This is quickly followed by a stream of forced joviality and raised voices that leave us feeling awkward and isolated. It becomes easier to batten down the hatches and hide away than subject ourselves to the ordeal of plastering yet more false smiles onto our faces.

Other things fall away and our focus shrinks. I stop playing club tennis because it now seems pointless to waste precious time simply enjoying myself when I could be at home with Silas.

For Ben and me, there's no doubt our journey would be easier if the truth was out there. We'd have more friends to lean on and wouldn't struggle to keep up the pretence that Silas is doing well.

'Silas is looking so well; you both must be so pleased.'

'He's doing OK at the moment, yes.'

'Look at him running around – you wouldn't know that there was anything wrong with him. It's amazing what doctors can do these days.'

Grr. 'he's coping OK, I suppose.' My head spins with what I don't say – he's coping OK if you discount the trip to hospital late last night for a platelet transfusion, and the vomiting on the way to school this morning, and the shingles outbreak that required five days on intravenous antivirals . . . and the fact that he's unlikely to see his twelfth birthday!

'You must be pleased because it could be much worse. I had a friend who . . .'

I make my excuses and end the conversation. That's how it goes. We choose to bear the burden on our own to keep Silas safe. It's our choice and I don't regret it, not for a moment, but it's not easy.

Ben and I agree early on that we won't lie to Silas. If he asks us outright if he's going to die, we owe it to him to be truthful. I can't bear the thought of him turning to us down the line and accusing us of lying to him; such betrayal by his parents is unthinkable and unforgivable. We want to keep him innocent for as long as possible, but we are prepared when the time comes, if it comes, to tell the truth. Deep down we both know that there's a chance he need never know. Dementia is common in children with brain tumours as the cancer cells invade their white matter. It's not going to be his body that fails him in the end, but his brain – that sentient part of his being. Perhaps if we are lucky, his brain will fail him before the truth needs to come out.

We don't lie because he never asks. This doesn't mean that we open the door to the discussion. We often head it off at the pass or just refuse to be drawn.

Once, early in his treatment, Silas is walking down the stairs with Ben. Silas is still getting dressed and is pulling his shirt over his ears.

'Daddy, I'm so lucky that I have been born now.'

'Why's that?' Ben asks.

'Because it's really lucky that they have found a cure for cancer.'

Ben stays quiet and straightens Silas's T-shirt.

Another time, Silas is sitting in the bath.

'Mummy, what do you think is the worst cancer to have?' he asks.

I rack my brains for an appropriate response, unwilling to tell him a lie but not wanting to tell him the truth either.

He picks up a flannel and sticks it on his half-bald head. 'Don't worry, I think I remember you told us once that it's pancreatic cancer. You said your friend's father had died from it and that it's really difficult to treat because you can't remove the pancreas.'

I stare at him. Some months prior to his diagnosis, I had told him and his younger brother my friend's story by chance. Now it's a lifeline.

'What an amazing memory, you have,' I say. 'You obviously get that from my side of the family!'

He laughs and the moment passes.

We're also helped by the fact that Silas knows of several cancer survivors: his grandmother had throat cancer; his great-uncle prostate cancer; and several of our friends had breast cancer.

There's only one time that Silas asks outright if he's going to die. We are sitting in the waiting room at the Royal Marsden a few months into his chemotherapy treatment and I have picked up a book with lots of drawings in it. All the pictures have been drawn by children with cancer and depict how they see their cancer. As we turn the pages, Silas becomes quieter. At the back of the book is an epilogue. It reads: 'These pictures were all drawn by children receiving treatment for cancer. At the time of going to print 17 of these children were still alive.'

Silas draws in a sharp breath next to me.

'What happened to the other children?' he asks. The realisation dawns and his eyes widen. 'They didn't die, did they?'

'I guess they must have,' I say, realising it is important for him to understand that children still die from cancer. If we're going to have to tell him sometime in the future, then it will be better if the journey is a gradual one.

His mouth drops open and his face pales. 'That's not going to happen to me, is it? I'm not going to die.' He shakes his head vigorously. 'I don't want to die!'

I look at my 10-year-old son and see the panic building behind his eyes. I decide the time isn't right. Nowhere near right.

'That's why we are here,' I say, gesturing to the room. 'That's why we are doing all this treatment.'

His shoulders relax and his hand finds its way to my hair, his fingers curl the strands. The tears prick my eyes. I blink them away and clench my jaw. I stare at the clock ticking on the wall. I haven't lied, not exactly, but I didn't answer his question.

We become adept at talking about the future, even though we can't imagine a future without him. I constantly talk about what Silas will be doing in a few years' time. Who he will marry. How many children he wants. Whether he wants to go to university. We project his life forward in all manner of ways, every chance that we get, so that he'll have no reason to doubt that his future is assured.

~

Silas held one of the best positions in a large family such as ours. He wasn't the eldest, so he didn't have to live up to unrealistic parental expectations. He was also not the youngest, so he didn't get spoilt and babied by the rest of the family. He got a fair amount of abuse from his older brothers, but he could also dish it out to the one beneath. He sat happily in the middle and got away with much on the back of it. He was quick to disappear when toys needed tidying up or the dishes needed clearing, which drove his older brothers nuts.

'I just need a pee,' he would say as supper finished and that would be the last you would see of him.

He also had the great skill of making it appear as though he was helping while keeping you distracted with singing and jokes, and it was only when you had actually finished whatever needed to be done that you realised that he had, in fact, not lifted even a finger.

Silas was inherently lazy. Not in a sly or devious way, but in a 'there are far better things I'd rather be doing' sort of way. Why waste my time doing this when life needs to be lived?

When the children were small we had a Trail-Gator that attached to the back of Ben's bike. It essentially turned two bikes into an elongated tandem by lifting the front wheel of the child's bike so they could be pulled along. The older two would continue to pedal when they were hitched up like this; Silas, however, just sat back and enjoyed the ride. He didn't make any pretence at pedalling, even if Ben turned round and berated him as they went up a hill. If there was someone else to do the work, then that was fine as far as Silas was concerned.

This desire to make things easy on himself spanned across all walks of Silas's life and led to inventive shortcuts. Once I arrived at school to pick him up and was pulled aside by his reception teacher.

'Mrs Pullen,' she whispered, her cheeks flushing slightly. 'Silas wasn't wearing any pants to class today.'

'Silly boy. How did you discover this?' I didn't manage to stifle my chuckle and she frowned at me.

'The children had to get changed for PE. It caused a bit of a commotion as I am sure you can imagine, especially amongst the girls.'

'Well, I'll talk to him but I doubt he'll forget again!'

In the car I asked Silas if he had forgotten to put his pants on that morning.

'No,' he said, looking at me as though I'd asked if the sky was green.

'Then why weren't you wearing any today?'

He laughed. 'Because it meant I could get dressed quicker, silly!'

Over the years, Silas perfected the art of saving himself time and energy. He was known to wear his pyjama bottoms under his trousers all day so he was already dressed when it came to bedtime. During games lessons at school, he would wear his grey school socks under his white PE socks to save the energy of having to take them off and put them on again.

His energy-saving spread to other areas of his life. He rarely finished reading a proper book. He read a lot but often he would get halfway through and then skip to the end to save himself having to read every word. I was constantly amazed at how many books he claimed to have read when I barely ever saw a novel in his hand. It's just that his idea of reading and my idea were two distinct and separate things, and he was much happier dipping in and out than reading every word.

~

The weeks stretch into months; Christmas comes and goes without incident. In March, Silas has an MRI scan. Waiting for each scan to come round is torture. I wake up in cold sweats for nights beforehand, my heart pounding with terror. I peer at Silas, alert to any changes. Have I missed something? Anything? Something that will give me some warning that the scan will bring bad news. I sell my soul several times over – 'Please give us good news. I will do anything. I'll try and be a better person . . . Take me instead. Let him live and have me!'

Ben and I try to prepare ourselves for the worst. The few days between the scan and the resultant phone call from the oncologist drag endlessly. We try to put it out of our mind but it lurks round every corner. I bite my nails to the quick and snap at all the children. I go for walks with the dogs and scream across empty valleys, releasing my terror. I hit the gnarled trunk of a beech tree until my hand sings with pain. When I speak with one of the other boy's teachers at a parents' meeting, I think, 'Can't they see that I am about to explode? That I will erupt all over them? Isn't it written all over my face? Can't they see I care nothing for equations or chromatography? Are they blind?'

The moment we get good results, we can breathe again. Our taut muscles relax and for a few days we are euphoric. It is like holding a winning lottery ticket. Silas is allowed ice cream or a fizzy drink – healthy eating is discarded with the joy of living.

These are the moments when I want to stop the earth turning. To freeze time and its inexorable march towards the future I haven't chosen. These few days after a positive scan are the closest we come to regaining our past happiness. That's not to say that we are never happy in the months after Silas's diagnosis. We have moments of laughter and joy –

rip-roaring, belly-bursting moments – but always just below the surface lies the truth of our situation, which adds a dash of desperation to the mix.

Silas's scan in March is good. BOB has shrunk against all the odds. It's too early to attribute this to the GOSH trial so the radiation must have been successful after all. We celebrate. We pack our bags and get a travel letter from the Marsden and go on a short holiday between blood tests to Silas's godfather in Ibiza. We celebrate Silas's eleventh birthday by climbing a rocky promontory on the Ibizan coast and carving our initials in the trunk of a tree. As we sing 'Happy Birthday' and Silas blows out the candles on his chocolate cake, my heart clenches. Is it really possible he won't see another birthday?

~

Before I had children, I worked in the City for an investment bank in corporate broking and then in specialist equity sales. There were rumours that my nickname was 'the Corporate Rottweiler'. I'm not sure if this is really true and I suspect it is not something of which to be proud. I think it suggests a certain impatience as well as an inherent stubbornness. I was efficient and got things done, but I was just not very good at waiting for other people, especially if my work was dependent on theirs, and I snapped and snarled at their heels.

As a mother of four boys, my patience was tested to the limit. Boys work on a different timeframe to everyone else. Their yell of 'I'm coming' roughly translates as, 'I'm going to come but first I have to finish climbing this tree then on my way back I might get distracted by an insect on the ground or a friend will tag me and then I will have to play It for at least five minutes.'

I built myself a bit of a reputation in the school playground. When it was time to go, I would take a deep breath and yell for my children. Other mothers learnt to cover their ears. Silas got his booming voice from me, there's no doubt about that. He got the voice and the little ears with tiny earlobes.

When the first yell didn't succeed, I would try again, and then I would hare around the playground dragging my children away from their games, using either gentle force or out and out bribery. The real problem was that I only had two hands and four rambunctious boys. I would get a hold of two, but by the time I collared the third or fourth, one would invariably have disappeared again. It became an endless cycle of round-up or catch me if you can.

Silas tested my patience more than the others. He didn't listen. I would ask him to do something several times. He would nod so I knew he'd heard me, but as soon as I stopped speaking he discarded the request as extraneous to his general existence and forgot about it. This drove me nuts. I took all sorts of measures to counter it. I would crouch down so our eyes were level and ask him. I would then make him repeat the request to me ensuring he had heard it correctly.

'Silas you need to put your shoes on, please.'

He nodded.

'What have I just asked you to do?'

'Put my shoes on.'

'Good.'

A few minutes later I would come back and he would be worrying a scab on his knee, his shoes still sitting under the chest by the front door.

I often sat him down and told him how much more time I would have to play with him if I didn't have to spend 30 minutes each day repeating instructions to him.

When he was eight, it turned out he needed grommets. I felt a bit guilty. He really couldn't hear me. However, with grommets duly in, things didn't noticeably improve. Silas heard but mostly chose not to listen.

I would often whisper 'I have chocolate' behind his head and he would spin round immediately, a big grin on his face and his hand outstretched.

∼

Reading for pleasure is impossible after Silas becomes ill. I have always been an avid reader and devour books within a matter of days. My husband knows that the way to my heart is to buy me a pile of books every Christmas. Our shelves are piled high with poetry, plays, biographies, non-fiction and fiction. Often I threaten to take boxes of books to the second-hand shop just to clear some shelf space for new purchases. Ben digs his heels in. His itinerant childhood has made him a compulsive hoarder. Everything is kept in case it might one day be put to use – pieces of wood, old nails, misshapen bits of glass, cans of paint, rugby shirts he has not worn since his schooldays. Books are no exception, despite the advent of the Internet and tablets, and I have to sneak bags of them onto the stall for the village fete.

Reading now, though, is another country. Words offer no escape. Fiction becomes unbearable. I can't get any solace and enjoyment from someone else's imagination anymore. My own reality is so agonising that there is no room for other's fictional worlds and emotional rollercoasters.

Instead, I bury my head in research papers. BOB appears to be on the run but we have to keep him that way and the only way to do that is to study. Hard facts and statistics become the language I gravitate to. If the doctors can't save my son, then I have to do something. I'm not able to sit back and let him die without a fight. That would be tantamount to putting my own signature on his execution warrant.

I know that my chances of discovering a miracle cure are non-existent but that's not what I am aiming for. Everything I read tells me that cancer survival follows a bell curve and those that make it to the tail end of this curve are nearly always those that are proactive in their treatment. If I can just push Silas further out on the curve, then who knows how long we could have.

I trawl paediatric brain tumour chat forums and speak with other parents or survivors about drug combinations. I read books about surviving terminal cancer. I read articles about the latest drug breakthroughs. I bury my head in research papers about drug synergies, cellular pathways, molecular targets and genetic mutations, grateful that I had taken science A levels. I learn a new language and terminology. I inhabit a world of peroxisome proliferator-activated receptors, histone deacetylase inhibitors, translation and proliferation pathways, apoptosis and autophagy.

One thing becomes clear: to beat BOB we have to attack the cancerous cells from all sides simultaneously. Targeting just one pathway with the chemotherapy drug is never going to achieve this. The cancer cells that survive the initial onslaught will quickly mutate and become resistant. I know it's only a matter of time before BOB takes the upper hand again.

Targeting several pathways isn't possible while Silas is on the immunotherapy trial, as many of the pathways I want to hit might also have a knock-on effect on his immune system.

However, as soon as the trial finishes at the end of May, I have more scope. I set about trying to find prescription drugs and more easily obtainable nutraceuticals that will work in synergy to affect different pathways.

The major flaw in this plan is that Silas is a child and therefore a minor. I have to be careful, as if I cause a detrimental reaction by mixing drugs and do him some harm then I could potentially be treated as a criminal. It's one thing to obtain certain prescription medicines illegally for your own use, but another thing entirely to give them to a child.

I'm not afraid to break the law. If I knew for certain something would work, I would have jumped at it, but I don't have that luxury and I don't want to jeopardise our relationship with his oncology team. I realise how important it is to keep them on side.

I write a paper, which I present in June to Dr S.

'We need to come at the tumour from different sides,' I say. 'These are my suggestions.'

He fingers through my research paper, many pages long, his eyes wide and his forehead furrowed in disbelief. 'You wrote this?' he asks.

'Yes,' I say, impatient to proceed. 'Everything is referenced.' There are nearly 70 references to other research papers attached at the end.

He scratches his head.

'I've tried to find drugs that are synergistic and have a proven track record of being used in children with minimal side effects,' I continue. 'They can also be added to Silas's existing temozolomide regime,' I say, referring to his chemo, 'without overlapping toxicities and each has been shown to have an effect on different growth pathways of GBMs. Some are prescription drugs used to treat things like diabetes and acne, others are nutraceuticals like Vitamin D3 and sulforaphane.'

He blows out his cheeks and shakes his head.

'Both you know and I know that if Silas just stays on the chemo, he doesn't have a chance!' I persevere. 'You told me right from the beginning that you couldn't save him. We have to do something. I know that you're unlikely to agree to them all, or even any of them, but please just take a look and let's see what we can do.'

'OK,' he says finally. 'I'll read it and run it by the pharmaceutical department but I can't promise anything.'

'That's a start,' I say.

He taps the paper on his desk and shakes his head, 'I can't believe you wrote this!'

After I leave the room, I picture him calling in his colleagues to show them what one nutty parent has done, but it doesn't bother me. I am beyond caring what others think and anyway, I heard the grudging respect in his tone

~

Silas had a massive head. This was probably one of the reasons BOB got so large before he started showing any symptoms. His head circumference at four weeks old was off the chart. The health visitor mentioned initiating monitoring for hydrocephalus and other causes of macrocephaly before eventually deciding that he simply had a big head.

When Silas was about four, Ben took him to our local Halfords to find him a bicycle helmet, as the cast-offs from the other boys didn't fit him. The sales assistant passed him a large child's helmet. It perched on the top of Silas's head like an ungainly chicken trying to incubate an ostrich egg. The assistant moved up the sizes – a small adult, a medium adult – eventually, with a look of disbelief on his face, he handed Ben a large adult helmet. It was a perfect fit.

His big head caused other problems. Jumpers were a squeeze and often Silas would hop about in agony with a jumper trapped over his ears, unable to pull it off. Ben ripped many items of clothing trying to haul them on or off Silas's head.

Silas always claimed that the advantage of having a big head was that it was full of brains. He may have had a point. He found work ridiculously easy and never had to apply himself in any meaningful way to get good marks. His mind made startling jumps and he was full of questions and original thoughts. He must have been a nightmare to teach.

At his Year 3 parent's meeting, his teacher confided in me that she was at a loss as to what to do with him.

'You see, Mrs Pullen, I show the children a method in mathematics and then I set them questions.'

I nodded, wondering where this was leading.

'Silas is always the first up to my desk with his questions all finished.'

Excellent, that's my boy, I thought and stood a little taller.

She continued. 'The thing is that he hasn't listened to anything I've told him.'

'What do you mean?' I asked.

'Well, often he doesn't show his workings out and when he does it's not what I have shown them at all.'

'So you're trying to tell me that he gets the sums all wrong?' I said, deflating.

'No,' she replied. 'To the contrary. He gets them all right – all the time!' She noted my confusion. 'It's just that he's not doing them the way he's supposed to. The way I've shown him.'

'And have you asked him why?' I questioned.

'Yes.'

'And . . . ?' I prompted.

'He just says that his way is much quicker and what's the point of

66

doing the sums my way when it takes longer. He says that I am wasting his time.'

I bit my lip to stifle a laugh.

~

Silas's next scan towards the end of June is pre-empted by a seizure.

I am driving Silas to school. He has exams that day, something we aren't too worried about, but we think it good to keep his brain engaged. Anyway, the exams are a welcome distraction from the scan due at the end of the week. Close to school, Silas starts complaining about a headache. Alarm bells ringing, I drive a bit slower. He struggles to find words and keeps repeating himself. I turn the car round and head for home, my palms slick on the steering wheel. Silas moans. I look across at him. One eye is twitching rapidly. I pull in at a nearby petrol station and phone for an ambulance. Twenty minutes later we are in the A&E department of the nearest hospital and Silas is vomiting into a bowl.

Fear grips my stomach. BOB must be growing. I panic and phone Ben. Glioblastoma is *always* fatal on relapse. This is it. We are now in free fall – the safety net gone.

By the time Ben arrives, Silas is in the MRI scanner. A short time later a consultant enters our room.

'The tumour looks stable,' she says. 'At least we can't see any growth since the last scan we have.'

'When was that?' we chorus.

'October last year.'

Before his radiotherapy.

'But it has shrunk since then,' I say. 'If there's no change that still might mean it has grown since March.'

She looks at me with understanding. 'I can't tell you that for sure, but it doesn't look like it is exerting massive pressure. We've sent the scans off to the Marsden.'

I point to Silas, who is fully recovered and alert and playing on his iPod. 'What happened to him then?'

'It looks as if he had an epileptic seizure. Sometimes we don't know what the trigger is, but it doesn't look as though it was caused by tumour growth.'

A reprieve. A small smile creeps across my face. At least I can now stop worrying about his scan in a few days' time.

I turn to Silas. 'Next time you don't feel like taking an exam just let me know instead of going to all this trouble!'

He laughs.

~

Our children have led an idyllic childhood. We live on a dead-end track running alongside the village green. Outside our back gate is 10 acres of open land, a lea containing copses full of succulent blackberry bushes and pockets of wild garlic. At the end of the lea is a small hawthorn wood with hollows for bicycle jumps and lots of loose and rotting branches for making camps.

Down the lane from us are our friends Adrian and Kate. They have lived here longer than us and have three children of their own – two boys and a girl – the same ages as three of ours.

This has provided our children with an extended family and a place to go when they need to escape the wrath of their parents or the irritations of their brothers. Not a day goes by during the holidays without a mixture of children in both houses. These friendships will be deep and long-lasting and Silas often commented that Kate 'was his other mother'.

Their family is so much a part of ours that our youngest, Inigo, saw little difference between the two houses. They were both home to him. One Sunday morning, aged two and unknown to us, he climbed over our back gate and toddled down the lane. When I discovered he was missing a short time later, I ran round the house searching all his usual hiding places. I started to panic when there was no sign of him. His brothers hadn't seen him and no one had any idea where he was. Everyone joined the search. I ran out of the back gate calling his name.

I ran towards the busy main road, my heart in my mouth, but to my relief there was no little bundle of clothes heaped on the tarmac.

I picked up the telephone and called Kate. She was having breakfast. She thought for a moment.

'I haven't seen him but I just heard a noise from upstairs. I wondered what it was. Let me go and check.' She took the phone with her and pounded up the stairs.

I heard the squeak of a bedroom door. 'He's here, don't panic,' she said.

'Thank God,' I sobbed.

She found Inigo sitting on the floor of her youngest son's bedroom with the toy chest open and toys strewn across the carpet. He had unlatched the back door to their house and snuck up the stairs without anyone seeing him.

Despite getting into trouble for this escapade, he used to rock up at their house unannounced so often that they nicknamed him Dobby, after the house elf in the Harry Potter books who appears out of thin air.

Our two families have gone on holiday together and celebrated New Year together more times than I can remember. Adrian and I even held a joint party for our fortieth birthdays.

Silas loved heading off to their house, despite being the only one of our children not to have a direct contemporary in their household. He would play with whoever was there and had as easy a friendship with their oldest child as their youngest, and with their daughter as well as their sons. He could often be found sitting at their kitchen table playing board games.

After his surgeries, he was left with two massive fluid-filled cysts in his brain. This meant he wasn't supposed to bounce on their trampoline – a big draw for our children as Ben had forbidden one at home – because the resultant sloshing inside his head could make him feel quite peculiar.

This didn't stop him. As soon as Kate was distracted, he would join the others playing human pinball, until an adult noticed and he was dragged off and berated. To him, having fun was worth it even if it meant being sick!

~

A week after Silas's seizure we are back with the oncologist. He beams.

'Silas is doing well. The new scans show very little tumour remains. It still appears to be shrinking.'

'Because of the immunotherapy?' Ben asks.

'Perhaps,' says Dr S. 'But it's too early to be sure.'

'That's great,' I interrupt. 'What about the seizure?'

He raises his eyebrows. 'Yup, that's strange. Have you put him on any new supplements?'

'Only GLA.'

He looks at me blankly.

'Gamma-linolenic acid,' I explain. 'An Omega-6 fatty acid – borage oil essentially. I mentioned it in the paper.'

'Is that all?'

'Yes, but I put him on a large dose.'

'How large?'

'About 8g a day,' I say. Most supplement capsules contain around 700mg a day, so I sourced a bottle of organic borage oil and have been giving Silas a tablespoon a day in some drinking yoghurt. It is a large amount but I have been in touch with an 18-year survivor of GBM to discuss the dosage. Silas took the first dose five days before the seizure.

The conversation with Dr S gets me thinking and I switch on the computer as soon as I get home. I type in gamma-linolenic acid and seizures. The results are conflicting, with some reports claiming that it could lower the seizure threshold in patients with epilepsy, making a seizure more likely, and other sources stating the evidence it caused seizures was spurious.

It's enough.

Silas stops the borage oil supplement and I feel guilty that my inter-ference in his treatment may have been what triggered his seizure. It might simply be a coincidence, and a big part of me wishes I have the strength to carry on with the borage oil, but it's a wake-up call. Here I am devising protocols for my son and at the end of the day, no matter how much research I do, he's still going to be a guinea pig – the real danger is I could make things worse.

The rest of my plan unravels a few weeks later. Dr S finally agrees to prescribe one of the other drugs I want – cis-Retinoic Acid. One out of four was a start, and it was synergistic with the supplements I still had Silas on. It's an anti-acne drug that has been used in different types of cancers, most notably neuroblastomas. The only problem is that Dr S wants to put Silas on what he calls a 'therapeutic dose', which is a lot higher than the dose I feel would work for my synergistic purposes. Dr S is adamant that there is no point giving him anything less. I'm unsure about the side effects likely to be triggered by such a massive dose, but I capitulate and Silas starts the tablets.

Within four days, Silas is in hospital on IV antihistamines. He has had an adverse allergic reaction to the new drug that has resulted in a rash all over his body and his arms and legs swelling. The drug is stopped. It is the final nail in the coffin of my plan to attack BOB from many different directions. I have to admit defeat. We have no choice now but to rely on the doctors to make the right decisions, and they have not exactly instilled us with any confidence in his survival since the very beginning.

~

When Silas was five years old, his godmother, Tash, got married. Silas was asked to be a pageboy. This delighted him, not because he had to walk down the aisle and be impeccably behaved, but because he got to spend a whole weekend away with both his parents all to himself, and he got to go to a grown-up party without any of his brothers to spoil the fun.

Dressed in cream Ralph Lauren trousers, a linen shirt and a tartan cummerbund, he thought he looked like a ninja warrior. He spent most of the service, legs spread and hands poised in a fighting stance. In his mind he battled arch enemies and traitorous friends, protecting the unsuspecting bride from an otherwise untimely and grisly end.

At the reception afterwards, he kept going long after all the other children had faded and been carted off to their beds. He danced with the bride, her mother, her father, other guests, anyone bold enough to have a go.

As the evening progressed, he started to fade. I held him in my arms, his hand curled in my hair, his eyes began to lose focus. He drifted.

The band picked up and the opening bars of a Proclaimers song blasted across the dance floor. Silas's eyes shot open at the rhythmic beat and he sat up in my arms.

'You'll like this song,' I said. 'It's good to dance to.'

'Can we dance, Mummy?'

'Sure.'

I stepped out onto the dance floor, my son warm in my arms. I stomped my feet with the rest of the wedding guests and sung at the top of my voice, dredging up a Scottish accent and yelling out the words.

The music finished and, breathless, I tumbled off the dance floor, Silas still in my arms. His cheeks were flushed and his eyes bright.

'That's a good song, Mummy.'

'I told you you'd like it.'

'Did Daddy walk 500 miles for you?'

I grinned and twirled him round. 'Nope, but he drove from one end of the country to the other to see me for half a night once . . . I woke up to find him throwing pebbles at my window. Does that count?'

Silas wrinkled his nose and nodded.

That was the first time Silas and I danced to '500 Miles' but not the last, although more often than not the dance floor was the flagstones in the kitchen and our only audience the dog.

~

It's summer, the holidays are in full swing and BOB is quiet. Silas is in great form. Days are spent crabbing at the beach. Long, lazy afternoons with friends at a rented beach hut, the boys still swimming even as the sun goes down. Barbecues on the sand, fish and chips and ice creams; the smell of vinegar and sun cream intermingled. It's too good to be true and I try to shake off the sense of foreboding, despite the good scan. Deep in my bones, I know the clock continues to tick. I give up trying to monitor Silas's eating. He's a small boy and, above all else, he deserves ice creams at the beach.

I drink Silas in. Trying to capture every moment and freeze-frame it in my brain. I start to write down all the little things he says:

'How lucky I am to have the best mummy in the world!'

'This is the best summer ever.'

'You are so pretty!'

'I don't want this holiday to ever end.'

We hang out with his two best friends, Freddie and Harry, his cousins and the girl of his dreams. It's perfect, too perfect, and perfect moments never last.

Early August, back with the oncologist. I try to voice my fears.

'We need to change the chemo,' I plead.

'Why? It's working at the moment.'

'That's just it,' I argue. 'We need to change it before the tumour becomes resistant. We need to stay one step ahead of it.'

Dr S puts a hand up to stop me. 'You would never forgive yourself if we changed it and the tumour started growing.'

'I know,' I snap. 'But I also know we need to do something. I feel like I'm sitting here on a ticking bomb and it'll be too late to do anything by the time it explodes.' I get up and pace the room. 'We have to change things.'

'Look,' he says. 'We'll change the protocol as soon as there is any sign that the tumour is no longer responding.'

'But what if you don't know until it's too late? We both know how quickly this thing can grow.'

He shakes his head. 'It's OK. There'll be a period of stasis, of stability, when it stops shrinking before it starts growing and that's when we do something.'

I spin round. 'How can you be sure?'

I see the doubt in his eyes. 'You can't be, can you?' I accuse. 'Aside from everything, he's only having a scan every three months – everything could change in that time. We know what it can do in three weeks. We need to bring his scans closer together.'

He sighs. 'OK, if it'll make you happy we can organise for him to have scans every other month.'

'Good, that's a start.' My mouth feels dry. I clench my fists to control my panic. My instincts shout that now is the time to change treatments, but I'm at a loss as to how to convey this. I have to trust the doctors; they deal with these patients all the time but they have also told me that he is going to die and I can't help wondering if they don't want to waste time and resources trying to save these terminally ill children. Dr S is fighting for us, I know, but his hands are still tied by the system and the lack of treatments.

The tears prick behind my eyes. I blink them away.

'We can't give up on him,' I whisper. 'Please, don't give up on him.'

'I won't. He's doing so well. I don't know what you've done, what you've been giving him, but I really think he might have a chance.'

'Don't say that. You'll jinx us.'

He smiles.

'What happens if he relapses?' I ask.

'Then I'll find the best trial somewhere in the world. I promise.'

~

Silas had two obsessions in life. One was ice and the other was hair.

Silas ate ice. He didn't just eat ice, he craved it. He could often be found rummaging in the ice compartment of the fridge rustling himself up a glass full of cubes. Once the thought of ice came into his head, he would stop at nothing until he was crunching on its sharp, moist coolness. The mere mention of the word would have him salivating.

I blame myself for his addiction. All my pregnancies were straightforward and for the first two I had no cravings at all. Then early in my pregnancy with Silas, I wanted ice. I ate it at every opportunity. I would fill a glass with ice and just the right amount of water and then wait until the ice reached exactly the right consistency to crunch. It became so bad that I ended up having to buy extra big ice cube trays to ensure I had a steady supply.

After Silas was born, the craving abated, but then, when I was pregnant with Inigo, it came back. By this stage Silas was two and tailed me around the house. He sat on my bulging lap and watched me eat ice day after day. That's where his addiction started. He always associated ice with comfort and love; happiness and security.

Apparently ice isn't such a strange craving during pregnancy. It's possible that it is a sign of low haemoglobin levels or anaemia. This would make sense, as the doctor often put me on iron supplements during my pregnancies. Silas also became increasingly fixated on ice during his treatment and, since his haemoglobin levels were often low due to the damaging effects of the chemo, there may be some truth in this theory.

The other thing on Silas's mind was hair – my hair mostly, and his own as a fallback. He curled hair endlessly. He would wrap my long hair around and around the index finger of his right hand and then slowly pull his finger free. The sensation of the strands running across the sensitive skin of his finger was addictive. It was like a drug that he couldn't live without. He needed it as much as he needed to breathe. He started hair curling when he was less than six months old and he was balanced on my hip, both hands free to play. It then quickly became a comforter. Some children suck their thumbs or have blankets or special toys but Silas had my hair. When he was tired or under the weather or upset, the hair curling would become more pronounced and frantic.

If my hair was not available, he would curl his own. He lay in his bed at night, head tucked down, finger curling and pulling on the hair of his crown as he drifted off to sleep. We had to cut his hair short – a grade 8 or lower – to stop him pulling out great tufts of his hair in his sleep. He often had a small patch of bare scalp showing on the top of his head from too much vigorous pulling.

By the time BOB came along, he had almost grown out of hair curling. I guess it's a bit like thumb sucking. However, it only took that first week in hospital, with me lying next to him on his bed and him feeling sorry for himself, for the habit to be fully reinvigorated. Only now, he had the strength of a pre-pubescent teenager and often caused me to inhale sharply as the hairs parted from my scalp.

'I'm sorry, Mummy,' Silas would say, wrapping the loose hairs around his fingers and rubbing them across his lips. He would toy with the strands, his apology discarded in his delight at his treasure.

~

In September, just over a year after he had first been diagnosed, our bubble bursts for the final time.

Silas's scan is due on Friday 13th – not a good omen – and the day before, he has the first headache he has had for months. I know instantly what it means. I try to convince myself that maybe it's a precursor to another seizure and I mustn't read too much into it, but I feel it deep in my bones.

Silas sits in the bathroom as I give him some paracetamol.

'I don't think I'm going to have a good scan tomorrow,' he says, hanging his head.

'Maybe not,' I agree, keeping my tone light. 'But it won't be the end of the world.' Just the end of our little world, I think to myself.

The day of the scan, I stop at our village's little medieval church on the way back from the school run; the church where Silas himself was christened and where he had stood up in front of packed pews last Christmas Eve and read a lesson, beanie askew on his head and a sprig of holly painted on his cheek.

I stumble through the graveyard under the drooping branches of the gnarled old yew, hoping that the church will be unlocked. To my relief, the latch lifts and the heavy door swings open. I sit on a hassock up by the altar and I wail. The tears run freely down my cheeks. At that moment I am prepared to make any deal, however dark. I hug my knees to my chest to try and hold my heart together. The pain knifes through me, a physical assault that rips me in two. I sit there until I can cry no more. I know what is coming and I don't know whether I have the strength to walk the road laid out before me. I am so alone, small and inconsequential. The warm autumn light streams through the plain windows catching the dust motes dancing in the air; the trill of a black-bird drifts through the open door. Everything is so beautiful and peaceful despite the pounding in my heart and the frozen scream in my head. Eventually, I pick myself up and head home.

Silas runs out of the door to greet me.

'Mummmmmyy!' he sings and throws his arms around me. I hug him tight but can't help wondering how many more times he will get to welcome me home like this.

A few days later, after the scan, I stop by the church again, but this time the door is locked. My heart drops. I'm not a superstitious person by nature, but I know what this means.

Within minutes of arriving home from the locked church the phone rings. It's the consultant paediatric oncologist at GOSH who has been in charge of the immunotherapy trial.

'Hold on. Let me get Ben,' I say, delaying the inevitable. Ben comes into the kitchen. The boys are at school so I put the man on speaker-phone.

'I thought I'd give you a call as we have the scan results . . .' He pauses.

'Go on,' Ben says.

I doodle nervously on a scrap of paper.

'It's not good news, I'm afraid.'

'We thought as much,' says Ben. My pen tears a gaping hole through the paper.

'It looks as though there is a widespread increase in abnormality. There's a slim chance it could be a delayed immune response but it's most likely to be progression.'

I grip the edge of the table.

'Can we operate?' I ask.

'We have sent the scans to the surgeons and that doesn't look possible.'

'Why not?'

'Because the tumour appears to have spread across the midline of his brain into the other hemisphere. There are spots scattered throughout his brain.'

'There must be something we can do?'

'Well, we can see what trials are available.'

'Dr S said that this wouldn't happen. He said we would have time to change things before it grew.' I raise my voice. 'I knew it. I tried to tell him.'

'It is unusual but it can happen.'

'So that's it, isn't it?' I ask. 'It's 100 per cent fatal on relapse. Isn't it?'

There is silence on the other end of the phone.

'Isn't it?' I repeat.

A beat. 'I'm afraid so.'

~

Ben and I hang up the phone and stand in the kitchen unable to speak. The tears run silently down our cheeks. He reaches out and pulls me into a hug, tucking my head under his chin. We cling to each other.

I have failed my boy, that small boy so full of love and trust. I've let him down. I'd kidded myself that I could make a difference to his journey. He never stood a chance and at the end of the day, for all my research, I've not even lengthened his dismal odds.

We spend that morning walking. We leave the house and trudge across fields in the early autumn sunshine. We pass our neighbour, Kate. She steps towards us, a question on her lips. I put my hand up to stop her and shake my head, my eyes brimming. She raises a hand to her mouth and steps back.

'I'm here if you need me,' she calls after us.

We walk in silence, each tormented by our own thoughts. We stride out with purpose as though distance will make the news easier to bear; as though we can somehow escape from the agony. Eventually, I turn to Ben.

'I'm sorry,' I say.

'What for?'

'For not managing to change things.'

He takes me by the shoulders. 'You don't ever have to be sorry. You fought tooth and nail and you don't have to be sorry for doing that.'

'But he's still going to die and maybe I missed something or should have done something different.'

'And maybe he wouldn't have been this well for the last year if you hadn't done all you did, and maybe he would have relapsed sooner.' He looks me in the eye. 'There are too many maybes and we'll never know the answers. Remember last year . . . how we thought we wouldn't even make Christmas.'

I nod.

He continues. 'We've always been living on borrowed time and maybe you just bought us a little more. Remember, even those who do this for a living don't have the answers.' He wraps me in his arms. 'No boy could have a better mother.'

'But I can't watch him die slowly and in pain.'

Ben shakes his head and gazes over my shoulder into the distance. A tear runs down his cheek. 'No, this is going to be the hardest thing we'll ever have to do and somehow we'll get through it, for him and for the others. We'll just surround him with love. We will build a cocoon of love, that's what we'll do.' He pauses. 'We have no other choice.'

A crow caws above our heads and its black shape wheels over the valley where we stand.

That afternoon, we pick Silas and his younger brother up from school and drive out to the sea marshes near where we live. We tell Silas that BOB is growing again.

'Does that mean I'll have to have another operation?' he asks.

A Mighty Boy

'No, not brain surgery. Not this time,' I say. 'They'll want to change your chemo, though, and you might need a port put in.'

'OK,' he says, shrugging his shoulders. He taps Inigo on the shoulder. 'Race you to the hut. Last one there is a loser.' They streak off, their laughter floating back on the wind.

Ben and I follow in their wake filming them. Clips from this day are added to a video we make over the next week based upon the Ministry of Silly Walks and set to the Monty Python song 'Always Look on the Bright Side of Life'.

The blog entry for the day focuses on the fact that Silas is due to play in his first football match for nearly two years, although we have banned him from heading the ball. Something so important to Silas provides the perfect smokescreen for the truth.

~

Silas had nine lives. At least until BOB came along and, as Ben says, 'ruined the party'.

He had a narrow escape at age three. We had builders working on a new kitchen and an outhouse and there were large power leads running from the house across the garden. One of the men was using a power saw when the machine died on him. He cursed and tried to start it up again but quickly realised the power was off and went to investigate. He found Silas, naked apart from a pair of duck-faced wellington boots, with a huge grin on his face. In his hands he held a pair of green garden secateurs and by his feet lay the mains lead, neatly snipped in two. He had suffered no electrical shock and was unharmed. Either the plastic handle on the secateurs or the welly boots had insulated his little frame enough.

A few years later, Silas decided that his physics experiments needed updating. I was in the kitchen talking with Ben when we were startled by a loud bang. We stopped and strained our ears. I heard the beeping of the alarm control panel and realised the power had tripped. We opened the door to the scullery. A metallic tang hung in the air and the acidic smell of burnt rubber stung my nostrils but I couldn't place it. Ben turned the power back on. We stood in the corridor confused. I heard a tap running in the kitchen.

Silas stood by the sink, his back to me. His hand held out under the water. 'What are you doing?' I asked.

'Nothing,' he said, his voice strained.

'Do you know what that noise was?'

'No. What noise?' He kept his head turned away from me.

Something didn't add up. I went back to the scullery and scanned the floor. I saw a piece of metal glinting by the dogs' water bowl. I bent down and picked it up. It was part of the curved reflective bell of a torch. I straightened and saw the rest of the torch, what was left of it anyway, thrown onto the countertop next to the microwave. I yanked open the door of the microwave, the stench of burnt rubber hit the back of my throat. The inside of the microwave was black with soot and several tell-tale bits of glass glinted on the turning plate.

'Silas,' I yelled. 'What have you done?'

'I didn't mean to,' he sobbed from the kitchen.

'You didn't mean to what?' I said, coming up behind him. 'You put the torch in the microwave, didn't you?'

He nodded, his face tear-streaked. He hid his hand behind his back.

'And then what happened?' I prompted, my voice sharp.

'It exploded,' he said. 'I didn't know that was going to happen though. I really didn't.'

'You silly boy. When will you learn?'

He sniffed and I softened.

'You hurt yourself, didn't you?'

He hung his head, the tears flowing again. 'I burnt my hand trying to get the torch out of the microwave. I didn't want you to see what I'd done.'

I checked his hand and wrapped him in my arms. 'You know you were really lucky, don't you?' He lifted his head in surprise. 'You were lucky that the whole machine didn't explode in your face.' He snuggled into me. I rested my chin on the top of his head.

'What were you thinking?' I sighed, raising my eyebrows to Ben.

'You told me that your father once put a lightbulb in a glass of milk in a microwave and it lit up. I just wanted to see if the torch would light up too!' he said, his voice muffled against my chest.

I shook my head.

Then there was the time Silas came off his bike careering down a steep hill. He had built up too much speed and couldn't make the corner at the bottom. He hit the verge, buckled the wheel on a rock and flew over the handlebars through a hedge into a field. By some miracle he walked away with only a bruised ego and a bust lip – a small price to pay for emulating Superman.

The time Silas gave us the worst scare brought medics and the air ambulance rushing to his school.

Silas was by now a robust seven, loud and fearless and always looking for a bit of fun. I had gone to the school to watch him and his elder brother Rufus play in the same rugby match. They were only a year apart at school and often in the same team. Galling for Rufus as he always had his little brother to annoy him and show him up in front of his friends, and difficult for Silas as Rufus was often captain and this meant he was expected to do what his brother told him.

During half-time, Silas popped into the school building to have a pee. They weren't allowed to wear their rugby boots inside the building and he had to remove them – a time consuming process for a small boy whose life was lived looking for shortcuts. He arrived back on the pitch just as the whistle was blown for the start of the second half of the match. He ran to take his place in the line and then his coach noticed he wasn't wearing his mouthguard.

'Silas, off the pitch. You can't play without a mouthguard. Run and get it quickly,' he yelled.

Silas groaned and his shoulders slumped, but he ran back inside the school to fetch the mouthguard he had left in his classroom.

A few minutes passed and I remember thinking that he had better hurry up as his team were a man down without him and were struggling to contain the opposition.

All of a sudden there was a commotion behind me from the direction of the school building. The parents on the sideline turned round. A teacher ran across the tarmac of the playground, waving her arms wildly in the air.

'Mrs Pullen,' she called. 'Mrs Pullen.' It took me a second to register she was talking to me. I took a step towards her, gesturing at myself.

She nodded as she ran. 'Come quickly, Mrs Pullen. There has been an accident. A terrible accident.'

The blood froze in my veins. I started running, the match forgotten.

'It's Silas,' she said as I reached her.

'What's happened?' I panted.

'He's fallen down the stairs.'

Relief coursed through me. Falling down the stairs meant a twisted ankle or at worse a broken arm or leg. 'Thank God, that's all,' I said.

We ran towards the building. 'No,' she said. 'You don't understand. He's fallen down the stairwell from the top of the stairs! He seems to be having a fit. We think he hit his head!'

My heart plummeted and I pounded into the school. The stairs only went up one floor, but from the bannister at the top it was more than a 15-foot fall onto a hard stone floor.

Several people were crouched around Silas when I got to the foot of the stairs. He lay twisted awkwardly in the corridor, his rugby boots dark against the pale stone. His moans turned to sobs when he saw me.

'Mummy, my head,' he cried. 'My head hurts and my leg.'

'Shh, darling. It's OK. I'm here. You're going to be fine.'

I looked up at the crowd around me.

The school secretary caught my eye. 'The ambulance is on its way,' she said.

'What happened?' I asked.

'I don't know,' she said. 'I was sitting at my desk. Then there was a big crash. I looked up and Silas was lying on the ground.'

'I fell,' moaned Silas, his teeth chattering as the shock took hold of his body. Someone brought a blanket and we tucked it round him.

'From the top?' I asked him.

'Yeesss. I didn't mean to.'

'It's OK, darling. It wasn't your fault.'

He gripped my hand.

'I just wanted to see if anyone was coming.'

'What do you mean?' I asked.

'I didn't take my boots off, so I knew I'd get into trouble if anyone saw me. I leant over the bannister to have a look and I slipped. I'm sorry. My head hurts.'

'I know, darling. It's OK.' I looked up at the landing above me. It seemed to stretch away such a distance. I tried to stay calm but my heart pounded inside my chest. It was a long way for a small boy to fall.

The bell for the end of lessons rang and the corridors filled with children. Somebody made a cordon round us on the floor using chairs.

'Did you fall head first?' I asked. 'Can you remember?'

His eyes fluttered open, his body wracked by shivers. 'I tried to stop myself. I grabbed the bannister as I fell.' He waved his hand vaguely. 'I think I hit the other bannister.'

I looked behind me. The wooden bannister of the lower flight of stairs was right next to me. It was possible that it broke his fall. Was this good? It would mean that he didn't hit the stone floor so hard but it depended which part of his body hit the rail. The doorbell rang and a first responder medic arrived, green bag in hand.

'The air ambulance is on its way,' he said. 'It's standard when a child falls from such a height,' he said, noting my surprise.

He bent down and examined Silas. As he progressed, my fear lessened, Silas could move everything. That was a good sign. The medic strapped a neck brace on.

He looked at me. 'It's just a precaution, Mum. I don't think there is any damage to his neck or back. The good news is that there don't appear to be any life-threatening injuries. In fact, I will tell the air ambulance crew to stand down. We'll still take him to hospital for a full assessment but he can go in the ordinary ambulance.'

I breathed a sigh of relief and buried my face in my hands.

'He's had a nasty fall. He'll be lucky to get away with just bruises.' The medic pointed to his leg. 'He obviously hit his leg hard, so that will need to be looked at, and we will need to be cautious with the head injury.'

The deep rumble of a helicopter sounded overhead. The noise growing louder as the pilot brought the machine down onto the playing field where, only a short time ago, Silas had been playing with his team. There were screams of excitement from all the children who had gathered to watch the helicopter land.

'They're here already,' said the paramedic. 'They'll want to assess him for themselves.'

Ten minutes later, the helicopter took off, the doctor having agreed with the paramedic's assessment, and Silas and I were ensconced in an ambulance. The shock had taken its toll on Silas and he slept the whole way to the hospital. This worried the ambulance crew, as they couldn't wake him, and they put the blue lights and siren on, despite my insistence that he was always difficult to wake.

Silas did indeed escape with no more than bruises from that fall, much to the surprise of all the medical staff at the hospital. He had obviously hit his leg and had a nasty bruise on his thigh, but he hadn't damaged the bone. The lower bannister must have broken his fall sufficiently to reduce the subsequent impact to his head and he only suffered a mild concussion. The school fixed a Perspex barrier in place to prevent future accidents. Ben and I had numerous phone calls from school governors to apologise and obviously make sure that we were not intending to sue. This had never crossed our minds, especially as, in the back of my brain, I had a niggling doubt about the circumstances surrounding his fall.

A few days after the event, when Silas was fully recovered, I sat him down.

'What really happened on the stairs, darling?'

He hung his head.

'It's OK,' I said. 'You won't get into trouble. Just tell Mummy the truth.'

He was silent.

'You went in to get your mouthguard . . .' I prompted.

'I couldn't be bothered to take my boots off,' he said.

'I know. You were worried you would get caught.'

He nodded and looked at me sheepishly. 'I didn't want to miss any of the match. I was in a hurry.'

He hesitated.

'Keep going,' I encouraged.

'I did look over the bannister to check no one was coming but I didn't trip. I tried to slide down the bannisters as I thought it would be quicker.'

'Ahh,' I nodded. 'That makes more sense. I thought something like that might have happened.'

He looked relieved that I was not angry. 'I just lost my balance and fell. I'm sorry, Mummy. I didn't mean to cause all that trouble.'

'I know, darling. You were just looking for a short cut, as usual.'

~

Our next meeting with the oncology team at the Royal Marsden crystallises the hopelessness of our situation.

Dr S informs us that the tumour is 'galloping'. He likens it to an octopus that's spread its tentacles into every corner of our son's brain. There is only one trial in the UK running for children with relapsed GBM and Silas doesn't qualify – he doesn't have the correct genetic mutation. The consultant has looked elsewhere but there are currently no trials in the USA or Europe that are showing any tangible benefit for paediatric patients.

The best Dr S can offer us is a chemo combo known as PCV. These drugs have been around for decades and didn't work for GBM patients 40 years ago. To say Ben and I are gobsmacked is an understatement.

'What about Avastin?' I ask, referring to the trial drug we had been offered a year earlier. I know that although it won't save him, it might buy us a few precious extra months.

'It has been shown to have no benefit in paediatric high grade gliomas,' says Dr S.

'I know it's not going to change the outcome, but it often produces a short-term response for a few months.'

Dr S nods. 'I'm no longer able to prescribe it for my patients.'

'Can we get it elsewhere?'

He shakes his head. 'No doctor will prescribe it in this country.'

'Even if we fund it ourselves?'

'Even then.'

I run through a list of other drugs used with paediatric patients across the world. He continues to shake his head. Some of the drugs have been withdrawn while the pharmaceutical companies make newer versions that they can sell for more money, others are just not authorised for use in the UK.

'But you promised us you would find the right trial if he relapsed,' I accuse.

'There is nothing,' says Dr S.

'You're telling me that there is not a single trial anywhere in the world or a drug that has been developed in the last decade that we can use?' I say, my voice shrill with disbelief.

He shakes his head. 'I'm sorry.'

'You're sorry! You're sorry! Our son is going to die and he's not even going to die taking part in a trial that might help other children and families who have to face this disease in the future.'

Dr S lifts his hands in defeat.

I raise my voice. 'You know that's the only thing that would make this whole situation bearable, that would make his death mean something.' I swipe at the tears on my cheeks.

'I know,' says Dr S, his voice quiet. 'I really am sorry.'

I shake my head, the knife twisting in my stomach. 'Do you think there will ever be any hope for these children?'

'In my opinion, in the next decade or so, cancer will become a chronic disease that can be managed like any other serious illness. It will no longer be a death sentence in many cases. But this one . . .' He pauses. 'They are a long way off finding a cure for this one, and I'm not sure they ever will.'

~

When Inigo was two, he suffered a spiral fracture of his femur – a shove from one of his brothers and a leg caught in an awkward position. The result was four weeks in traction, tied to a hospital bed. Not much fun for a two-year-old, and even less for his parents who had to keep him amused. To add insult to injury, the arrival of chicken pox a week later meant relegation to an isolation unit and hours of wall-crawling boredom.

After he came out of hospital, Inigo had to learn to walk again and we thought it might be wise to give him some space from his boisterous brothers. So Ben took the elder three boys off to stay with a friend – a single father with two boys – who had rented a house in St Malo in Normandy.

I was nervous leaving Ben in charge of three small boys aged five, six and eight but had no choice. The first afternoon, all five boys disappeared on the beach in St Malo. The two fathers couldn't find them anywhere. They called and shouted and asked passers-by in broken French. Eventually they hired two bicycles and both went in opposite directions, struggling to keep their panic at bay. One of them finally found the boys – knee-deep in a tidal pool catching unsuspecting crabs and poking their fingers in sticky red anemones.

You'd think they would learn their lesson, but a few days later they took a day trip to Mont St Michel – a rocky tidal island that used to be cut off from the mainland at high tide, although now a permanent causeway stretches across the sands. The island is topped with a medieval abbey surrounded by a fortified town.

The boys ran around the streets acting out imaginary battles, jumping out at each other from behind pillars and launching themselves down stone steps. They were in heaven.

Mont St Michel gets so crowded in the high summer months that a contraflow system is in place for pedestrians. They are directed up to the abbey by one route and back down by another to keep the tide of humanity flowing in roughly the same direction. On the way down from the abbey, the crowds are crushed into narrow, cobbled streets overhung with timber-framed buildings. Gift shops entice and beckon unwary tourists and relieve them of their pockets full of euros.

On the way down, the boys ran on ahead, charging through the unsuspecting crowds as only small boys can. Ben and the other father felt confident they would stop at the exit and ambled along behind. When they reached the gated tower, with its portcullis hanging threateningly above them, there were only four boys.

'Where's Silas?' Ben asked.

The others shrugged their shoulders. 'We thought he was with you.'

Ben took a deep breath and stared back up the street. There was no sign of Silas.

'What was he wearing? Can any of you remember?'

Ben is colour blind. He can see a field of poppies but only if I point it out to him first. Shades of red and green are difficult to distinguish and meld into one murky colour. To make life easier for him, whenever we had to fly as a family, I would dress the boys in similar outfits, always involving blue, so that when one child momentarily disappeared in the airport, he would only have to glance at the others to know what clothes he was looking for.

'I think he had a blue T-shirt on,' said Oscar.

Ben paced beside the gateway, scouring the stream of people. There was still no sign of Silas.

'You wait here,' he instructed the others. 'I'm going to look for him.'

He pushed his way back up the streets, against the flow of bodies. He shouted for Silas but his voice was lost in the constant rumble of pedestrian noise funnelled upwards by the overhanging buildings. He started walking faster, sweat beading his brow, but there was no sign of him. Silas was only five. *What would he say to me? How could he have lost him?*

He checked his watch. It had been more than 10 minutes since he realised Silas was missing. His heart was in his throat.

'Silas!' he yelled. There was no response bar a few tuts and frowns from those people nearest to him. He glanced into doorways and down stone staircases but Silas was nowhere. He ploughed on, up the steep hill, his heart pounding. Suddenly, out of the corner of his eye, he caught a flash of blue. He swung round and there, under the awning of a shop, stood Silas, his face pushed against the window, his breath misting the glass.

'Thank God,' said Ben and knelt down and pulled Silas into his arms.

'Hey, Daddy,' said Silas, nonplussed, lost in his own world of heroes and dragons. 'Can I have one of those swords?' He pointed through the window at a collection of replica medieval swords, their blades glinting in the sun shining through the window.

'Silas, I've been looking for you everywhere.'

'Have you?'

'Didn't you hear me calling?'

Silas shook his head, his hand curling in Ben's hair.

'Oh, never mind,' said Ben. 'Do you want a piggyback down to the others?'

When Ben got back after that holiday he told me that it was the last time he took the boys away without me, and that he needed another holiday to recover. It took him more than a year to confess to what had really happened.

~

After his relapse, Ben and I start to notice changes in Silas's behaviour and personality quite quickly.

He becomes moody and obstreperous and fixates on things. He becomes difficult to reason with. It's a bit like having a truculent toddler back in the house. He has lost the usual constraints that filter his behaviour. According to the nursing team this is consistent with the tumour invading his frontal lobe and therefore affecting his personality, the very essence of the boy we love.

A simple game of Monopoly, a game Silas has always loved, becomes an exercise in perseverance. Silas just takes the cards for the properties he wants at the beginning. When you point out to him that this isn't fair for the other players, he can no longer empathise and just grows stroppy that you are trying to thwart him. BOB makes him selfish and tyrannical. His brothers grow exasperated and no longer want to play with him. They don't know the truth of the situation and lack patience with his unreasonable behaviour. Playing Minecraft on the Xbox results in cries of anger as Silas single-mindedly keeps killing each of them in turn instead of helping to build their imaginary world. This is a boy who had once been so obsessed with Minecraft that he used to spend hours watching YouTube videos of people playing the game so he could garner tips. Now, it's apparent that he can no longer hold complex thoughts and plans in his head, he just needs immediate gratification of one sort or another.

He does things so out of character that they surprise us all. He's unkind and sticks out his leg to deliberately trip up his younger brother. He curls my hair, but instead of being gentle, he starts wrenching his finger loose with huge strands of hair attached. It's as though he can't stop himself and when he realises he has hurt me, he is contrite. But a few moments later he does it again.

His brothers start to shun him or disappear up the lane to our neighbour's house to escape. It's agony for me and Ben to witness.

I can no longer predict his behaviour. On one visit to our local hospital, we are waiting for a scan. The waiting room is full, disapproving pensioners squeezed in uncomfortable seats next to surly teenagers. A fug of body odour hangs in the air. There is a water station. Silas walks over and gets a paper cone full of water. He comes back to the seat and offers it to me.

'Thank you, darling, I'm not thirsty but it was nice of you to think of me.'

He has a few sips then with no warning throws the rest over me. He smiles, a sly smile challenging me to confront him. There are gasps from across the room. I know that to confront him will make things worse. He can no longer be reasoned with, so I try to ignore him. There are mutters of disapproval.

'She shouldn't let him behave like that.'

'Parents these days have no control.'

I keep my head lowered, fearing that I'll say something I'll regret. Silas gets up and returns with more water. He sits next to me and starts flicking the water at me. Flick after flick. His face is expressionless, waiting for a reaction. Where is my Silas, who has always been kind and thoughtful? Where has he gone? I don't know this stranger. The fear wells up inside me. The snide comments from others in the room hurt, but they are nothing to the agony of watching my son change and disappear before my eyes.

I try to distract him, just like I would do when the children were small.

'Let's play "I Spy",' I suggest.

He flicks the water at me one last time. 'OK,' he says.

'You start.'

He looks around the room for a moment, oblivious to a child pointing at him from the corner and whispering to his mother.

'I spy with my little eye something beginning with F.'

'Floor.'

He shakes his head.

'Frame.'

More shakes. I suggest a few other things but to no avail.

'I give up,' I capitulate.

'Actually, it begins with an A,' he says.

'Oh!' I start on a list of things beginning with A. Everything is met with a shake of the head.

'What is it? I give up.'

'Afraid.'

'But I can't see afraid, darling, so that was a bit tricky.'

'Actually it wasn't afraid,' says Silas. 'It was aface.'

'There is no such word as aface, darling. Are you sure?'

He nods. It all falls into place.

'You mean a face, like someone's face?' I ask, my voice gentle.

He frowns, confusion etched across his forehead and then he nods.

'Of course, silly.'

~

Silas knew how to be a child better than most children I have ever met. He excelled at living in the moment and this gave him an incredible freedom – he wasn't constrained by conventions or other people's expectations. The here and now was what was important.

This liberation gave him a unique perspective on life. He was incredibly kind and forgiving to others. He didn't bear a grudge or sulk – no time for that. Most importantly, he was never mean. He could hurt someone's feelings and throw an unkind word in the heat of an argument along with the best of us – he wasn't perfect – but systematic nastiness was beyond him. It required forethought and planning, both of which factored little in his life.

Silas was guileless and without malice. Far from making him popular at school, this trait caused him problems, partly because he would not return unkindness with further unkindness, but also because he couldn't be co-opted into any gang to inflict misery upon another child. So, more often than not, he was one of the children left out of the gangs and made fun of for no other reason than that he had reddish hair or a large head. This confused him.

'Why do people need to be mean?' he once asked me.

I thought about it. 'Sometimes people are mean because it gives them a feeling of power and if there are other things in their life that they can't control then this is one area where they can have some control.'

'But that can't make them happy. People are only their friends because they're scared of them. I wouldn't like that. Surely if they were nice to everyone then they would have more friends and be happier!'

'You and I can see that,' I said. 'But perhaps they don't know that.'

'Then I should tell them.'

'Maybe you should.'

We never tried to fight Silas's playground battles for him. He needed to step out into the big, wide world one day and schoolyard spats would then seem like a walk in the park. So we monitored the situation from a distance and gave him the tools to cope. We strengthened his friend-ships with other kids and told him that he needed to learn to manage difficult, manipulative people and that there was no time like the present to start that process. Mostly, he weathered the storm, although there were times when the daily taunts chipped away at his confidence and he would burst into tears in the car on the way home.

One time, in the first few months after he was diagnosed with cancer, I picked him up from school. He got in the car.

'You know, Mummy, having cancer isn't all bad.'

'What do you mean?' I responded, unable to hide the surprise in my voice.

'Well, there are some good things that have come out of it.'

'Like what?'

'For one thing, I am now the most popular boy in the class. Everyone wants to sit next to me. They all fight over it.'

'Even you-know-who?' I asked, alluding to the ringleaders of the gang.

Silas laughed. 'Yes, they are the worst of the lot. They really want to be my friends now.'

'And how do you feel about that?' I asked, intrigued.

He shrugged. 'I'm OK with it. I know it's not real friendship like with Freddie,' he said. 'But they are not so bad and it's nice to be popular. I'm going to make the most of it.'

'That's great,' I said, gritting my teeth and squeezing the steering wheel.

My heart ached for him and for his generosity. He could forgive so easily and yet, at that moment, I was consumed with jealously. I resented those children that had made his life a misery. I know unkind words in the playground are part and parcel of growing up and friendships swing and sway, but I could not bear that they were to have a future and he was not.

My knuckles whitened and I kept my eyes fixed on the road ahead.

Perhaps in the future that was to be denied Silas, those children might tell stories to their own children about the friend they'd had who had died of cancer. Perhaps the years would blur their memories and they would forget how little true friendship they had ever actually shown. The jealousy rose up in my throat like bile – I could taste its acidity.

Silas looked over at me. 'Are you OK, Mummy?' he asked.

I nodded, afraid my voice would crack if I spoke. I was ashamed. Ashamed at my bitterness and ashamed that my young son could teach me more about forgiveness than I could ever have taught him.

Living in the moment also gave Silas unfettered freedom to make a complete fool of himself. He didn't worry about what people might think. He could always be relied upon to be the one to run up and say something silly in front of a teacher or be egged on by his mates to make a prank phone call. He would dance round the kitchen at home, music blaring out of the speakers, with his T-shirt pulled up over his face, his trousers and boxers round his ankles and everything in between on show, until he tripped over his own feet and ended up in a sprawled heap on the floor, buttocks wobbling with laughter.

Unselfconscious and infectious.

He knew how good it was to be alive.

~

As the weeks march on, Silas's short-term memory undergoes a rapid deterioration. People's names became impossible for him to hold on to. His godmother, Bumble, visits for the day with one of her daughters, Imogen.

'Who's that?' asks Silas.

'Mo,' I reply.

'Oh, yes. Mo.' He nods his head, rolling his tongue around the syllable.

A few moments later, he pokes me and points at Imogen.

'What's her name again?'

'Mo.'

'Mo. That's right.' He repeats the name under his breath like a mantra. 'Mo, Mo, Mo . . .' Seconds later, the scene is played out again, as though it had never happened.

'Remind me what's she called?'

His memory weakens but other aspects of his character become increasingly overwhelming. Always loving, he becomes obsessive and his behaviour borders on inappropriate. He kisses me but is unable to stop. He holds my face and plasters my lips with kisses even in public. He starts to try and kiss me with an open mouth and he grows irate when I try to turn my head. He climbs on top of me and wants to touch my face. It is as though he has lost all of his inhibitions and the sensual aspects of his character are heightened.

This disinhibition rears its head in other, more ugly, ways. One day, I'm digging around in the chest freezer trying to find some fish fingers for his lunch. He starts picking at the ice that has built up around the edges. He finds it hard to separate the ice from the side of the freezer and he kicks the freezer in disgust and disappears. He returns a moment later with a large kitchen knife in his hand.

'Silas, put the knife down,' I say.

He starts to hack at the ice.

'No,' he says, watching me as he stabs at the freezer.

'Come on, darling, put it down. I'll explain why you can't hack at the freezer with a sharp knife.'

'No.' He leans closer to me.

I step back, suddenly uncertain of my 11-year-old son.

'Someone will get hurt. Please put it down,' I cajole.

'You can't make me,' he says, waving the knife in my direction.

'Probably not,' I say. 'But I shouldn't have to make you.' I edge further away. 'Ben,' I call over my shoulder, fearful that I will be unable to disarm him on my own.

'Look, Silas, I'll make you a deal,' I plead. 'You give me the knife and I'll get you a big glass full of ice.'

He weighs up my offer.

'OK,' he shrugs and drops the knife by my feet. It clatters onto the stone floor. 'But it had better be a really big glass!'

We are living with Jekyll and Hyde. There is no warning when he might flip. For Ben and me it is soul destroying; for Silas, who knows? Is he aware of the changes? It's difficult to know what thoughts are running around his head, but the messages in his brain are so confused and disrupted that he knows no different.

∼

Of all my boys, Silas was most like Ben in character. They shared the same zany sense of humour and unquenchable enjoyment of life. If the Ministry of Silly Walks had not been invented by John Cleese and Monty Python, they would have kicked it off. The two of them would make up stupid voices and talk nonsense to each other for hours. They would make up crazy words to songs in the car and sing them at the top of their voices. They would dance around the kitchen, pretending to waltz or foxtrot, until the giggles became too much.

I remember in one anonymous hospital room they played an unknown game on a tablet for hours. Neither of them knew the rules but they made it up as they went along. Their shoulders shook with laughter and their cheeks flushed with pleasure until Silas eventually tossed his head back and roared with hilarious abandon.

The nurse knocked on the door. 'What is going on in here?' She smiled. 'We've never heard so much laughter coming from one of these rooms before! All the nurses want whatever you've had for breakfast, Silas!'

They were both so comfortable in their own skin that they weren't hampered by shyness or embarrassment. Ben has never been curtailed by convention. Once, early in our relationship, he picked me up from a City wine bar after work. Wearing jeans and a white T-shirt, he pushed through the hordes of dark-suited traders. There were murmurs as full wine glasses were jogged and briefcases were knocked over. I turned to introduce Ben to my colleagues and stopped mid-sentence. On his feet, Ben wore sandals and each of his toenails was highlighted in bright scarlet nail varnish. There were mutters from those around me. A flush rose on my cheeks.

'What are you doing?' I hissed.

'Seeing if you really love me,' he grinned. 'Red toenails and all.'

I shook my head. 'You just want to embarrass me.'

He chuckled. 'Mission accomplished, then.'

Silas was the same. He would let his cousin, Selena, plaster his face with make-up and dress him up in a skirt. He would prance around for the rest of the day and be so relaxed in his outfit, that he'd answer the doorbell to a complete stranger and not even notice the double-take.

For both Silas and Ben, the cup has always been half-full. Such enormous positivity cannot help but rub off on others. I have always been the more cautious one in our relationship, the one who wants to save pennies for a rainy day. I learnt my lessons young when my family ran into trouble during my teenage years. However, Ben has taught me that memories are more important than money, and that none of us know what is round the corner. We could scrimp and save, never have any fun, and the nest egg would undoubtedly grow. Before we knew it, though, the kids would have left home and the rainy day would still be a speck on the distant horizon, and we could never get that time back; never get a second chance to blow it all and build those memories that can never be ripped away.

Both Silas and Ben have taught me to live in the moment, in different ways and for different reasons, and for that I am grateful.

~

Desperate people do desperate things. We have no way of saving our son and the doctors can't do anything, so we clutch at straws.

In the course of all my research I come across the use of cannabinoids against gliomas. We pursue this through various nefarious routes: trading bitcoins in dark corners of the web and conducting late night rendezvous at motorway service stations until we finally obtain some cannabis oil with the right concentration of chemicals. The psychoactive component of cannabis is a chemical called THC – tetrahydrocannabinol. We need a plant that has lower levels of this and higher levels of the non-psychoactive CBD – cannabidiol. The final ratio of each chemical needs to be 1:1. We also get cannabis leaves with the right concentration. Ben juices the leaves and freezes them.

We start to give Silas the juice mixed up in a spinach smoothie and the oil spread on toast disguised with Nutella. Ben uses himself as a guinea pig first to no ill effect, so we feel confident that Silas will not get high.

What are we doing? Giving our 11-year-old son a form of cannabis. It makes me nervous, but it pales to nothing in the face of losing him forever. I have read about many success stories with parents in the USA trying something similar. I know that a Phase 1 trial is about to start investigating the synergistic effect of cannabis with the same chemo Silas has been on.

We have nothing to lose by giving it a try and there seem to be no obvious side effects from the cannabis, so we continue with a daily dose.

Here we are, desolate and desperate, and prepared to play with fire.

~

The new chemo regime requires Silas to have an operation to insert a port-a-cath under the skin of his chest. This will provide permanent access to his veins either to infuse a drug into his body, such as the chemo drug vincristine, or to remove blood samples. It will be easier than constantly battling to insert cannulas into his arms – or so we hope.

In the days before the operation, Silas has been having an increasing number of headaches. He wakes at night in terrible pain and we struggle to get any pain relief into him, as he instantly throws it straight up. We have been given different levels of pain relief. Step 1 is paracetamol; Step 2 is codeine; Step 3 is morphine. When all three fail to help him, due to the sickness, we end up phoning the local hospital and being admitted at 5am. Silas grips my hand, his eyes closed tight against the pain.

'Mummy, please . . . Please get someone to help me,' he moans. 'The pain is terrible. Why can't anyone help me? Why is this happening to me?'

So by the day of the port operation, our nerves are frazzled. We're uncertain if we are doing the right thing, giving Silas yet another general anaesthetic.

Dr S runs through his usual battery of tests with Silas. Silas smiles his way through the exercises but I see Dr S frown as he makes Silas scrunch his face up. He looks thoughtful as Silas walks the length of the room and even I can see the slight lean in Silas's gait. It's a bit like the listing of a yacht that has been swamped by a large unexpected wave, the water sloshing below deck tilting the mast just slightly off the vertical. Silas heads back to the teenager's day room where his cousin is waiting to amuse him, and Dr S calls the palliative care team into the examination room.

Ben and I blanch as we see the diminutive Mary, who heads the team. There's no escape. They are there to ensure that Silas's end-of-life care is coordinated and appropriate. There can be no burying heads in the sand now. End of life. Permanent and inevitable. How can we sit here and discuss how best to help our son die? I picture him in a nearby room laughing at cartoons with his cousin. I fold my arms across my chest, creating a barrier between them and me.

Dr S loads Silas's scans onto his screen. 'The tumour is still marching. It has spread throughout his white matter tracts,' he says. 'It is acting more like gliomatosis cerebri now. He is symptomatic.'

'How do you mean?' asks Ben.

'He struggles more with his expressions and has more facial palsy and he's definitely weaker on his right-hand side; you can see it when he walks.'

I turn away and stare out of the small window – a thin strip of glass at ceiling height, just enough to let some natural light into the room, but not providing a view to escape into.

Mary rests her gaze on me. Her soft voice lilts. I register it as if from a distance. 'It's throughout his brain now and is affecting all aspects of his personality. It's very common for patients to lose their inhibitions as he has.'

'How bad is it going to get?' I ask.

She inclines her head. 'I don't know. No one can say for sure. Each child is different and it depends on the part of the brain affected. The dementia is inevitable, I'm afraid.'

'I don't want him to not know who I am,' I whisper. 'To no longer recognise me.' My head is full of stories from other mothers. 'And I don't want him to be in pain.' My voice cracks. 'I can't bear the pain.'

Mary puts her hand on my knee. 'I can't promise he will always know you, but I can make sure that we manage his pain and make him comfortable.'

'Maybe you should think about not putting the port in,' says Dr S. 'We can continue the chemo without the vincristine. There is some evidence that it doesn't add much to the treatment and he will tolerate the other two drugs better.'

Ben and I look at each other. Neither of us want to put Silas through an unnecessary operation, but we still want to fight tooth and nail for him. We aren't prepared to hang him out to dry yet and if there is even the smallest chance that he might have more of a response to the three drugs then the third has to go in the mix too. We know now that we are working with months, maybe even weeks, and we cannot stave off the inevitable, but suddenly every extra day seems vital. We aren't able to face the thought of life without him and the misery that will entail. At least fighting gives us a purpose.

'No, we want to continue with the plan. Let's give him the best chance,' says Ben.

'Do you think we should stop?' I ask, catching a glance between the doctor and Mary.

'I'm not sure about the benefits of the port and the vincristine but . . .' Dr S holds our gaze. 'I guess you could look at it this way: if you could hold on to Silas as he is now, with all the changes in his personality, for a little longer; if we can stabilise him – would that be enough? Do you want to hold on to him like this?'

We hesitate. We know the answer for ourselves; there is no question, but we have to look at it from the view of what is best for Silas. 'He still has a good quality of life,' says Ben. 'He's happy and loving and eating so . . .' He looks at me, I nod. 'Yes, yes we do.'

Dr S claps his hands together. 'So, let's do it.'

The outcome is a traumatic operation for both Silas and ourselves, which ends up with Silas screaming at us and telling us that he hates us and that we are torturers, and the extra drug that is infused through the port a couple of hours after the operation makes no difference at all in the end.

~

Silas slept with his eyes half open. This is something we noticed when he was a small baby, but he never outgrew it. I've recently discovered that this is called nocturnal lagophthalmos and it affects about 10 per cent of the population. It's not so unusual and sufferers tend to sleep with their eyelids only partially closed.

It could be very disturbing, and when he was small, Ben and I would often try and force his eyelids down gently with our fingertips. But as soon as we removed the pressure they would ping open again.

It made it very difficult to tell if Silas was awake or asleep. It also made it very difficult for him to pretend he was sleeping, as he would automatically close his eyes tight shut when he was pretending, something he never did when he was actually asleep.

One Christmas Eve, when Silas was eight, I crept upstairs to the attic room, where all four boys were sleeping together, to put their stockings at the foot of their beds. Inevitably, by this stage of the evening, Ben and I had had too much to drink and so our attempts at being subtle and quiet didn't amount to much. We got the giggles and tripped up the stairs.

Silas was in the top bunk and had hung his stocking on the door of the cupboard next to his bed. I filled his stocking and crept past his sleeping form and tried to hook the rustling stocking on the handle of the cupboard. The room was in shadow with only a strip of light from the corridor falling across the floor. I misjudged it in the half-light and the stocking slipped and fell.

'Shh,' hissed Ben from the stairs in a loud stage whisper.

I picked up the stocking and tried again. Success. I turned to leave. I stopped in my tracks. Silas lay on his side, the light reflecting in his open eyes. I froze, one foot hanging in the air, waiting for him to say something. How was I going to explain this one? I dared not move a muscle. Time passed and he didn't move. I edged closer. His eyes weren't fully open but half closed and I realised that he must actually be asleep. I let out the breath I had been holding and left the room.

A few hours later, the children came bounding into our room, each lugging their stockings to open in our bed. Their eyes glinted in excitement and they rubbed their hands in anticipation. I rolled over hoping to be able to shut my eyes for a few minutes more.

A low voice hissed in my ear.

'I saw you, Mummy.'

'Mmmn,' I murmured, unwilling to surface.

'I know you're Father Christmas. I saw you bring my stocking in last night.'

'What!' I said, sitting bolt upright in bed, rubbing the sleep from my eyes.

Silas sat on the bed next to me. A huge grin stretched across his cheeks.

'I don't know what you are talking about,' I blustered, trying to gather my wits and kick-start my brain.

'You thought I was asleep,' he crowed in glee, delighted to have caught me out. 'But I wasn't.' He danced round the room singing.

'I know Mummy is Father Christmas. I know Mummy is Father Christmas!'

Ben looked at me. 'Totally busted!' he said and we both shook our heads and laughed.

~

Early on in Silas's treatment, during those first few hectic, surreal weeks after BOB makes his presence known, I make Dr S promise me that he will let us know when it is time to stop treatment. That he will make the call when we are blinded by our emotions. I tell him that we are logical, intelligent people and we will be able to listen.

How does a parent choose when to stop trying to save their child from a monstrous death? How do you choose when is the right time to let go? When that child is laughing and joking with you and telling you how much he loves you – is that the time? When his body is failing so gradually that even he is not aware – is that the time? Where do you draw the line in the sand? It's bad enough to know they are going to die but to speed the process up and rush yourself at headlong speed towards the abyss when you know there's no going back, no second chance – how can that be possible? How can you floor the accelerator into a brick wall?

That day at the Marsden when we chose all three drugs haunts me; Dr S tried to tell us it was time to stop, but I was wrong about us being able to listen. All I can think about is not being able to hold my boy in my arms ever again; not being able to wince as he pulls out more hair from my head; never dancing around the kitchen with him; never having him bound into my bedroom with a smile on his lips first thing in the morning; never getting to hear him say one more time, 'I really, really love you, Mummy.' How can I live without those things? How can I even begin to?

~

Not only did Silas sleep with his eyes half open, but he also slept more deeply than all our other children. You could pretty much do what you liked to Silas when he was asleep and he wouldn't wake up. Ben and I used to spend minutes every night kissing his soft cheeks when we went to bed. Often we would go at him in a pincer movement, one of us on each side of the bed and we would kiss him and nuzzle him and get the giggles when he didn't even stir. He wouldn't even raise a hand to brush us away. He just slept on.

It became such an in-joke that when we had guests staying they would often join in. We went on holiday with an old school friend of mine and every night she would join in the kiss fest on Silas's sleeping form; Ben on one side and her on the other. Each consecutive night their kissing would increase in intensity, but Silas never woke and they would end up rolling around in hysterics on the floor.

Once on an earlier holiday, when Silas was no more than two and still sleeping in a cot, some slightly inebriated, childless friends of ours initiated a game of chucking other guests in the pool. One of the guests decided that she really didn't want to be thrown in fully clothed and made a beeline for the boys' bedroom as an inviolable sanctuary. Every self-respecting parent in the world who knows the trials and tribulations of getting small children to sleep would honour this tacit understanding. However, as most of the marauding guests didn't have children of their own, they had no qualms about waking up a room full of small children.

The reluctant swimmer clung to Silas's cot as the marauders dragged her out of the room by her legs. The cot screeched across the tiled floor, rucking up the carpet. The wood groaned and creaked under the strain.

'You'll wake the baby up!' the girl screamed.

Her pursuers grunted in response, tried to stifle their giggles, and tugged harder. Oscar and Rufus sat up, rubbing sleep-clogged eyes, their bewilderment turning to wails of confusion. The cot crashed into the doorway and shuddered to a stop. The girl's fingers were prised free and the victors carried off their bounty towards the pool, whooping with delight. Ben and I raced into the room to calm down the screaming children. We manoeuvred the cot back across the room. Silas lay on his back, his arms thrown above his head, one foot stuck through the bars, his breathing steady and regular, still fast asleep. We shook our heads in disbelief.

Sleeping so heavily has its advantages but it also has some distinct downsides, especially when you sleep in a room full of plotting, scheming brothers. Many times Silas slumbered on oblivious and awoke to find drawing and writing all over his face in felt tips, and even once in permanent marker pens.

~

Within a few days of the port operation, Mary, the head of palliative care, arrives at the house. Her arrival has been timed to coincide with the local community children's nursing team. This is the team that has been responsible for taking weekly blood samples from Silas. Prior to the port being fitted, rather than have to search for an unwilling vein each week, they pricked his finger and patiently squeezed drops of blood into a container. Our assigned nurse has been brilliant at milking Silas for blood. She has a small son of her own so knows how to distract and entertain.

Mary enters the kitchen laden with paraphernalia. She heaves what looks like a large locked toolbox onto the kitchen table and has plastic bags full of recycled cardboard bedpans and containers for pee.

'Will we need all those?' I ask.

'It's likely, and it's better to be prepared for any eventuality,' says Mary. She rests a hand on the toolbox. 'You'll need to find a home for this here.'

'Why, what is it?'

'This is our war chest,' says Mary. 'It's full of restricted medicines, everything we might need to keep Silas comfortable – anti-emetics, analgesics, anti-seizure meds – these have been prescribed by a doctor just in case.' She unlocks a large padlock and lifts the lid.

The chest brims with vials and boxes and syringes. I draw my breath in sharply.

'I know it's a lot to take in,' she says. 'But it's better that it's all here on-site. The aim is to keep Silas out of hospital as much as possible and keep him home with you.'

Silas runs into the kitchen to get a drink. He pauses when he sees Mary, his brow furrows. She snaps the box shut.

'Mary's here to talk to the nursing team,' I say, 'about the new chemo drugs you are taking.'

'Oh, OK,' says Silas. He fills up his glass and disappears.

There is a beat before anyone speaks.

'He's looking well,' says Mary.

'I know.' I smile.

Her voice drops. 'How are you and Ben doing?'

I swallow and the tears spring into my eyes. I shake my head. How can I put into words how I am feeling? To voice my fears will make them real. How can the nurses round the table understand, even though they deal with dying children every day? The difference is these aren't their own children. They're not children whose dreams they have soothed and whose scraped knees they have bathed; children for whom they have high hopes and eyes full of motherly pride.

'I know it's hard,' says Mary, her eyes soft and full of understanding. 'And it's difficult to take it all in, but we will be with you every step of the way.'

I turn away and find a tissue to wipe my eyes.

Mary digs in her briefcase. 'I'm afraid, while I am here, we also need to discuss a Personal Resuscitation Plan for Silas.' She pulls out some sheets of paper.

Ben and I look at her blankly.

'Whether, in the light of his circumstances, it's in his best interests to be resuscitated.'

It clicks. 'What, you mean like a DNR form?' I say, years of watching medical dramas finally paying off.

She nods.

I blow my cheeks out, letting the air escape slowly. Here is a lady I barely know, sitting with a cup of coffee at my kitchen table, asking me to fill in a form that stops my son being resuscitated by emergency services in the event of a sudden deterioration in his condition.

She spreads the forms on the table and starts filling in boxes. She ticks the box allowing comfort and support to be offered to the parents and the child. She ticks the box allowing the medical teams to offer oxygen to support my son's breathing. She ticks the box allowing the use of antibiotics and analgesics but she crosses the box allowing CPR or heart massage, and she crosses the box allowing intubation or assisted ventilation. There will be no intensive care bed for my child. Then she passes the forms across for Ben and me to sign.

I stare at her in disbelief and denial. How can she expect me to sign this form? How can I agree to let my child die?

'It's the best thing,' she encourages.

I know she's right. When the time comes – and each tick of the clock is taking us inexorably closer – I won't want to prolong his agony. Any desire to keep Silas alive will be only for my own selfish reasons. So that I can snuffle in his neck one last time; so that I can kiss his soft lips or run my fingers over the familiar places on his body – the scar on his leg where he kicked a window, the large mole on his left bicep, his short bitten nails; so that I have a few more moments with him and a few more precious memories to cling on to.

The logic is indisputable but the emotional weight of putting pen to paper cripples us.

Silas's laughter floats into the kitchen.

He is so vital and alive, yet here we are, in the next room, preparing for his death.

~

Silas was a mighty boy.

He was big in stature, as hinted at by his 11lb birthweight, and he was physically strong. We have marked the boys' heights on a wall in the kitchen annually, and Silas outstripped all his brothers at the same age. In fact, at seven he was more than 20cm taller than his youngest brother at the same age, and neatly topped out all the childhood growth charts. He was going to be a bear of a man and the tallest of all our boys. I expect he would have even towered over his father's six foot two frame. He was never fat, just square-shouldered and solidly built. He was built for a purpose.

He excelled at schoolboy rugby. He wasn't fast but he was quite simply unstoppable. Once he built up a forward head of motion, he steamrollered anyone in his path. His teammates called him The Tank.

At Under 11 level, players aren't allowed to hand-off, meaning they aren't allowed to put out their hand to stop an incoming tackler. One match, I watched Silas run the length of the pitch, ball tucked firmly under his arm, as the first tackler arrived on the scene he stuck out his free hand and fended him off. The ref blew the whistle.

'No hands,' he called.

The match continued. Silas regained possession and carried on his way. The next tackler launched himself and Silas stuck out his elbow, hand tucked towards his chest, and pushed him away. The whistle blew again.

'That includes elbows . . .' said the ref, raising his eyebrows.

The game continued. Silas charged on. The opposition's try line was in sight. A new tackler came in from the left. Silas tucked his whole arm into his body and twisted so that he led with his shoulder. His shoulder connected with the would-be tackler and sent him flying, in the manner of a charging bull, and Silas neatly placed the ball down over the try line to the cheers of his team. The ref raised his arm in the air to signify the try and shook his head in disbelief.

At a different match, the opposition's coach grew exasperated with his team's performance. His instructions grew louder and his voice carried over the pitch to where the parents were standing. Finally, a penalty was awarded against them and his controlled demeanour snapped.

'Look,' he shouted at his boys. 'Are you all idiots? You all know what they are going to do with the ball. They are going to give it to the big ginger one, as they keep doing every time, and unless you work out a way to stop him, he's going to score yet another try!'

Silas looked up and grinned, his eyes sparkling, he caught the ball that came his way and ploughed through their line. One boy gamely hung on to his leg and was dragged several yards, his shorts slipping down his thighs, until Silas reached the try line.

The opposition coach turned away in fury and kicked the ground.

'That's my boy,' Ben muttered from the sidelines, his chest puffed out with pride. 'My big, mighty, ginger boy.'

~

A couple of days after Mary's visit, the reality of our situation is hammered home. Silas has a massive seizure.

He wakes up that morning and thunders down the stairs. His mood is buoyant and his smile wide. He helps himself to two large bowls of Weetabix. Ben takes Inigo to school and one of the community nurses arrives to check Silas's blood count and remove his port-a-cath dressing. The nurse and I are talking while Silas finishes his breakfast. His spoon suddenly clatters into the bowl. We look up startled.

'I don't feel right,' he says.

'What is it, darling? Have you got a headache?' I move to his side.

'No, I just feel strange.' He hesitates. 'Something's wrong.'

He starts to shake, not massive convulsions, just a continuous sort of shiver and twitch.

'It's all right, Silas,' the nurse says, putting her arm around him. 'You're having a small seizure. It's OK; it'll be over in a minute.'

The shakes tail away. Silas takes a deep breath. 'I feel better,' he says and picks up his spoon to continue eating, but within seconds he buries his head in his hands.

'My head,' he moans. 'I've got a really bad headache now.'

'That's normal after a seizure,' says the nurse. 'Let's lie him down in a dark room and let him sleep it off.'

I make Silas comfortable on the sofa. He sinks into the dark cushions and covers his eyes with his hand. The nurse leaves, mouthing goodbye.

Things don't get better; they get worse. Silas starts being sick and cannot keep any pain medicine down. I call the community nurses back. They access his port for the first time, giving him intravenous anti-sickness drugs and morphine for the pain. He sleeps for a bit, but when he wakes he's totally unresponsive. His eyes are open but they are both vibrating rapidly from side to side. The sickness continues and the nurses return.

'He's having continuous seizures,' says one. They give him a dose of Buccal Midazolam, an anti-seizure medicine that goes in the mouth, and they set up a continuous syringe driver to administer a steady dose of morphine and anti-emetics.

The syringe driver is a basic piece of equipment involving the judicious use of rubber bands. It feeds drugs into the body slowly through a needle that sits just under the skin. One of the nurses sees my frown when I clock it.

'We are getting new ones any day,' she says. 'The beauty of these ones, though, is that they never go wrong. There is nothing electronic to break.'

Famous last words. The alarm on the syringe driver goes off time and time again over the next few hours, leaving Ben and me jumping at every beep and constantly checking the flashing red light to see if it's still working. In the end, the nursing team have to come back out and change the machine twice during the evening, much to their disbelief and our frustration.

'Things are changing quickly,' says Ben as we finally get into bed. His face looks drawn.

I nod. The same thoughts stamp through my head.

He continues. 'We might not have long left.'

I sigh and rub my eyes. 'I know.'

He takes my hand and squeezes it in his. 'We need to start preparing the boys.'

'But how do we stop Silas finding out?'

He shakes his head. 'I don't know. We'll have to find a way. We have to think of them too.'

~

The days after the seizure are difficult for Silas. He remains on a constant stream of morphine through the driver. He drifts in and out of sleep. He knows who we are and he reaches out to curl my hair, but his words are muddled. He sort of makes sense, but then he wanders off on a tangent and drifts into non-sequiturs.

The morphine confuses him and causes him to hallucinate. He sits at breakfast 48 hours after the seizure and starts picking at his hand. He holds his hand up close to his face and plucks at it with the thumb and index finger of his other hand.

'What are you doing, darling?' I ask.

'There it is,' he says.

'There's what?'

'Do you see it?'

I shake my head. 'See what?'

He points to his hand. 'Look there.'

I stare hard at his hand. What am I missing?

'I don't see anything, darling. What is it?'

'Look there. A spider. Can't you see it?'

I look again. Maybe I have missed a money spider. There is nothing. 'There's no spider, darling.'

'Yes, there is! Here, I'll get it.' He pincers his thumb and finger together and lifts them up, his eyes following an invisible spider hanging on an invisible thread of silk. 'Do you see it now?'

'I think you are imagining it. There's nothing there.'

'Yes, there is! It's right here. Look, a spider!' He holds his hand up triumphant.

I reach forward. 'OK, let me take it. I'll get rid of it.'

He passes me the spidery figment of his imagination and tucks back into his cereal.

The morphine dose is gradually reduced and the hallucinations stop. The house is full of people that day. Everyone feels that things are happening fast; that Silas's decline will be quicker than we have all anticipated. The troops are rallied. Mary comes back down from the Marsden, the nursing team are in and out, the paediatric oncologist from the local hospital turns up and our GP arrives.

Ben and I feel like we are in a fish bowl. Everyone is standing on the outside looking in and jostling for the best positions for the final push. I know this is uncharitable and cynical of me, but these tumours are rare and most doctors only get to see one or two patients in their whole careers. Silas is a novelty and needs to be studied.

Mary pulls us to one side. 'From now on, your GP will need to come and see Silas every two weeks.'

'Why?' I ask.

'It's required by law,' she replies. 'Silas has to have been seen by a GP within two weeks of his death so that the coroner doesn't get involved.'

'I don't understand why,' I probe. 'We all know he's going to die from a terminal illness. Why would the coroner need to be involved?'

'It's just much easier and less problematic if the GP has been seeing him regularly. Then there can be no question about the cause of death.'

'Oh.' My thoughts whirr. 'Is that to make sure that we don't do anything to speed the process up?'

She inclines her head slightly.

I have difficulty keeping my voice down. 'So Ben and I have to be watched now to make sure we don't do anything stupid like killing our dying son to put him out of his misery!'

Ben puts his hand on my arm, but the horror in my mind is reflected in his face.

'It's just easier this way,' says Mary in a calm voice. 'No one is suggesting anything. We just want the end to be as smooth as possible.'

~

Things are out of our control.

We are on a conveyor belt and the red emergency stop button has been sabotaged. The more we try to run back the way we've come, the faster the motor turns, its whirring growing in intensity until it drowns out our cries for help. Family members drop in, but neither Ben nor I can cope with their grief. We've pulled up the drawbridge and there's no room for anyone else in our little keep of misery. I can be practical and matter-of-fact and discuss statistics and outcomes. Facts and figures are within my grasp, but I'm not able to deal in my battered emotions. We're moving from fighting for Silas's survival to accepting his imminent death, and we battle every inch of the way, kicking and screaming.

'You're so strong,' friends say.

'No, I'm not,' I reply. 'I just have no choice.' Inside I want to scream that they would do the same in my situation and that I'm no stronger than them. That I don't deserve this any more than the next person does.

'You'll get through this,' they say.

How? How would they know? They have no idea of what this is. How will I ever get through his death? Their words are just meaningless spouted platitudes with no substance. They might help them feel better, but not me.

The most help I get at this time is through conversations with mothers whose children are fighting brain tumours or who have just lost their battle.

One mother in particular gives me support: her beautiful daughter died a month earlier. The girl was the same age as Silas and had been diagnosed a few months before him. Her mother gives me time when she's thick in the goo of her own grief. Her voice steadies me and anchors me to the truth of our situation.

She doesn't offer platitudes or sympathy but she gives me an honest, searing account of the torture of watching your child slip away as their mind fails. She gives me an idea of what to expect. She offers practical advice on how to help when your child can no longer eat or communicate or eventually swallow. She deals in harsh realities and that's what I need. I need to brace myself for the storm that is on the horizon. She calms my fears about uncontrollable pain and gives me hope that we can navigate the journey ahead of us. She reassures me that I don't have to tell Silas that he's dying, but that I should be prepared for him to come to his own conclusions. She didn't tell her daughter, but in the last few weeks before she died, her daughter asked when it would all be over. It was unspoken, but children have a way of comprehending things outside of adult experiences and accepting things on a different level.

I don't want Silas to spend his last weeks living in terror. I know that this is what he would feel if he knew death was waiting round the corner. He'll be unable to bear the thought of no longer being with us, of having to journey somewhere new and unimaginable on his own.

It will consume him just as it's consuming me.

~

Sometimes I catch myself looking at Silas, staring at him, soaking him in but also trying to picture the life he will no longer lead. I visualise a little tow-headed girl running to put her hand on his knee. His hand reaches down to stroke her hair, his fingers absentmindedly twisting through her long ponytail. She reaches out to him and he lifts her into his arms. She buries her head in his neck and he holds her tight.

'I love you, Daddy,' she whispers.

'Not as much as I love you,' he whispers back.

'How do you know?' she asks, leaning back in his arms.

He smiles. 'I just know these things. That's my job.'

Her brother runs into the room, bouncing a ball. He sees his sister and without thinking bounces the ball so that it pings up and hits her on the arm.

'Ow,' she cries, rubbing her arm.

'Don't be such a crybaby,' says her brother.

Silas beckons his son over. He bends down, his daughter still in his arms, until their eyes are level.

'You mustn't hurt your sister,' he says.

'It was an accident,' says the boy, holding his gaze. 'I didn't mean to.'

'That may be so,' says Silas. 'But there are enough people that will end up hurting her during her life. It's your job as her brother to look out for her and always protect her.' He picks them both up. 'If you always look out for each other then you always know someone's got your back. The two of you against the world.' His son nods his head solemnly.

'Now I've got you both,' Silas growls, 'I'm going to have to tickle you!' Both children squeal with delight and terror.

The image fades.

Silas watches me, his head tilted to one side.

'You look sad, Mummy. Why are you so sad?' he asks.

~

Why does Silas never worry about what BOB might mean to his existence? I torture myself about this. Silas is a bright, intelligent boy. He's quick-witted and sharp. Why does he not wonder about BOB?

I think part of the answer to this lies in his ability to live in the present. He deals simply in black and white; yes and no; the here and now. Things that don't fit so easily into these categories are harder to compute, so he chooses not to dwell on the murkier aspects of being diagnosed with cancer. Only twice during his whole treatment does he ever ask, 'Why me? Why did I have to get cancer? It's so unfair.' Both times triggered by a more trivial event that has upset him and his emotions have spilt over to find something bigger to blame.

Right from the beginning we give him the option of remaining in our discussions with the oncologist, but he isn't interested. He doesn't want to waste time on the nitty gritty of his illness when he can be watching a film or playing Angry Birds.

That's our job as his parents.

That's the crux of it, then, the real reason he doesn't ponder over what BOB means to his existence. He's a child and in his mind it's our job as his parents to look after things. He trusts us. He believes so implicitly in our ability to make things better that he doesn't waste time wondering what the outcome will be. In his mind, BOB is never going to kill him because he has us on his side. We're his front-line troops and we'll never be routed. This utter belief in us gives him the freedom to live his life unfettered by doubt.

His eldest brother is very different. Oscar is a worrier and has been since he started to talk. He worries about the planet, fossil fuels, the Hadron Collider, and most of all his health. If he'd been the one in Silas's position, we would have had no choice but to confront the situation head on. Would this have been harder for us as parents? Possibly in the short-term, but all the literature suggests that terminally ill children take the news of their impending death with calm assurance and often even with relief, suggesting that they suspected as much but didn't want to worry their parents.

Should we have told Silas that he was going to die? This is a question I torture myself with on a daily basis. I feel enormous guilt as his mother that perhaps I could have prepared him for his death and helped him come to terms with it, and by not telling him I stole something from him. This is my burden and one I'll always carry. Would I do it differently if I could do it again? The truth is no. As his mother, I did what I thought best for him. I tried to protect him right to the very end. It was the one thing I could still do, and his short-term memory was so poor that it would have been like Groundhog Day: every day we would have needed to break the news afresh – a torture none of us needed, least of all him.

~

Ben tells Oscar that his brother is going to die first.

The seizures Silas has in October precipitate us into action. We have no idea how much longer we have left but we know the nursing team think things are moving fast.

Oscar is 14, on the cusp of adulthood, growing like a weed, wrapped up in his own life like any other self-obsessed teenager. He has a typical older brother relationship with Silas. He'll knock him into place both verbally and sometimes physically when he feels Silas has stepped out of line. He can be a little too rough and he has made few allowances for Silas's treatment, but he'll also stick up for him in times of need. Oscar is away at boarding school during the week and is not at home when Silas has the latest seizure. He's heading off to Spain for a Spanish exchange at half-term and we're worried that things will take a turn for the worse while he's away.

Ben makes some excuse about passing through town and arranges to meet Oscar for a coffee. They stroll through the lower reaches of the town and stop by the river. They lean over the railings watching the ducks dabble in the water. There's still a hint of autumn warmth in the air although the clouds scud across the sky.

'You know BOB has come back,' starts Ben.

Oscar glances at him, narrowing his eyes against the glare of the sun. He nods, uncertain where the conversation is heading.

'Well, Silas has had a series of seizures this week.'

'That's not good,' says Oscar.

'No,' agrees Ben, fiddling with the flaking paint on the railing.

'He'll be all right, though?' asks Oscar.

Ben sighs. 'No. No, he's not going to be all right.'

'What do you mean?'

'The doctors have said that Silas isn't going to get better.'

Oscar looks at him in surprise, his jaw slack.

Ben ploughs on, staring at the dark water. A fish bubbles to the surface. 'He's not going to make it. We are going to lose him.'

'What?'

The tears start down Ben's cheeks. 'There's nothing they can do. They can't stop BOB. Silas is going to die.'

'There must be something they can do,' exclaims Oscar, his cheeks stained with tears too.

Ben shakes his head. They stand in silence for a few minutes, waiting for the cheerful chatter of passing walkers to fade into the distance.

'How long have you known?' asks Oscar finally, wise beyond his years.

'From the beginning,' acknowledges Ben. 'But we needed to have hope. We had to believe that we might get the miracle. We had to protect you all.'

Oscar nods and then takes a deep breath. 'How long? How long has he got?'

'We don't know,' says Ben, shaking his head. 'Two months, maybe. Four if we're lucky, but maybe less.'

Oscar kicks at the ground. Ben puts his arm around him and draws him close.

'How will it happen?'

Ben tightens his lips. 'We don't know. He may have a haemorrhage and die in his sleep, but the most likely thing is that he just slips away bit by bit.' Ben kicks the rail, a muscle in his jaw twitching. 'The only thing that's certain is that it's not going to be easy. It's going to be torture for us all. We're going to have to find the strength, though – all of us – for Silas.'

He looks at his son. 'Silas mustn't find out. It would destroy him. I know it's a terrible secret to burden you with, but I have no choice.'

They stand there a while longer and Ben answers Oscar's questions as best he can. Finally, Oscar wipes the tears off his cheeks with the back of his hand. 'Let's go home,' he says.

He walks into the house that evening and greets Silas with a smile.

Silas bounds up to greet him. 'Oscar, what are you doing home?'

'My half-term has started,' Oscar lies. He cracks a joke about Silas's seizures and his need for all the attention, then he turns to me and wraps me in his arms.

~

Many windows have been broken in our house over the years. Battering boys and intact panes of glass do not go hand in hand.

Silas broke more than his fair share. The first window he broke was in the drawing room on a hot summer's day, not long after his fifth birthday.

'Kick that glass, Silas,' said his oldest brother.

Silas looked at him. 'Why?'

'Because I know you won't do it,' taunted Oscar. 'You're not brave enough!'

Crash. The glass splintered as Silas put his bare foot straight through the pane. Beads of blood dropped from his lacerated leg onto the carpet.

'Silas, you idiot!' shouted Oscar.

'You told me to do it,' accused Silas, his bottom lip wobbling as he saw the blood.

'I know,' replied Oscar. 'But I never thought you would be stupid enough to actually do it.'

I cleaned up the mess and butterflied the nasty cuts on his leg, knowing that they probably warranted a trip to A&E, but not wanting to face the resultant interrogation.

'You don't always have to listen to your brother, you know,' I said as I cleaned his tear-smudged face. 'What did you think would happen when you kicked the window, anyway?'

He shrugged. 'I guess I just don't know my own strength.'

I laughed and ruffled his hair. 'That's one way of looking at it.'

Silas looked at me, his eyes serious. 'At least I showed Oscar that I'm brave.'

I nodded. 'You certainly did. That's one thing your brother won't be able to accuse you of ever again.'

That wasn't the last time he broke a window in our house with his feet. He also broke windows with cricket balls, footballs, tennis balls and once even with his hand, banging to get our attention when he'd been locked in his bedroom by a wayward brother. More often than not, a trail of broken glass would lead you to Silas, a sheepish expression on his face and a ready apology on his lips.

~

A few days after telling Oscar about Silas, Ben repeats the process with Rufus. I remain at home with Silas. Rufus is only 12. He's the closest in age to Silas and their relationship is not straightforward. They have very different personalities. Rufus is self-contained and private. When the house is full of kids, playing games of kick-the-can or sardines, we'll often find him squirrelled away in his room doing something on his own, whereas Silas will be in the thick of things. Rufus likes his own space whereas Silas is happiest in a crowd. Rufus is a home boy whilst Silas loves nothing more than a sleepover. Being only a school year apart, the competition between the two of them is fierce. Silas's disorganised, easy come, easy go attitude drives Rufus nuts. Rufus is a grafter and often believes, sometimes quite rightly, that he has to carry the weight of his younger brother too. There's love in their relationship, but also tension.

Ben takes Rufus to a coffee shop. With hindsight, it was much too public for the discussion they had to have, but at the time Ben thinks the relaxed environment will make things easier.

They sit down at a small table, their chairs scraping against the scrubbed wooden floor. The murmur of voices fills the air. Rufus orders a hot chocolate with all the trimmings, delighted to be treated and to spend rare time alone with his father. The waitress puts the drinks down.

Rufus dips the marshmallow into his drink.

'You know Silas hasn't been doing so well lately?' says Ben.

Rufus nods, his mouth full of sticky sweet.

Ben plunges on. 'Well, it looks as if he's not going to get better.'

Rufus halts mid-chew. He swallows. 'Does that mean he's going to continue to have seizures?'

'Worse than that, I'm afraid,' says Ben. He gazes hard at Rufus knowing the damage his words are going to do. 'The doctors think he'll probably die.'

It takes a moment or two for his words to sink in, then Rufus crumples and starts to cry. People at nearby tables look over, frowning at Ben. Ben pulls his chair closer to Rufus and puts his arm around him.

'I thought he'd be OK,' Rufus sobs.

'You know that children die of cancer,' says Ben. 'Did it never cross your mind?'

'No, I just thought he'd get better.' Rufus looks at Ben, tears streaking his face. 'Why can't the doctors do anything?'

'BOB's too strong. We're trying different drugs but it's unlikely that they'll be able to stop BOB growing. So we have to be prepared that we might lose Silas.'

Rufus pushes his hot chocolate away and covers his face with his hands.

Ben pulls out a hanky and gives it to Rufus. 'We all have to be strong for Silas, darling. We need to make the most of what time we have so that we don't have any regrets. I know Silas has changed and he's not easy to live with anymore, but we have to remember that it's not his fault. We have to be patient and surround him with love. You can do that, can't you?'

Rufus sniffs and nods.

'Does Silas know?' he asks.

'No.' Ben pauses. 'If it was you, would you want to know?'

'I don't know. I don't think so.'

They come home and Rufus is subdued and withdrawn. He disappears up to his room and then a short time later, I discover him playing

FIFA with Silas on the Xbox. For the first time, they are playing on the same team instead of going head to head, and Rufus is gently encouraging Silas and helping him with the controls.

~

Telling Inigo, our youngest son, that his brother is dying is a different matter. We know he's too small at nine to handle such difficult information and we aren't convinced that he'll be able to keep it to himself. We are terrified that it's the sort of thing a young child might blurt out in the heat of an argument – 'I don't care what you are saying. Anyway, you are going to die soon.' Or: 'I wish you'd hurry up and die.'

We know we have to drip feed him the information in the course of ordinary conversations. So that it just becomes something he's gradually aware of, not something special that we sit him down to say.

My opportunity arrives one night in November when Silas and Ben are in London at an Arsenal match with Silas's best friend Freddie. Inigo and I are having supper alone in the kitchen.

'Silas isn't very nice to me anymore,' says Inigo.

'I know, darling,' I reply. 'You know that it's not his fault, though. It's the cancer. It's messing with his brain.'

He nods. 'Cancer sucks.'

'I know.'

'When will he be better?'

This is my chance and I seize it. 'He might not get better, you know.'

Inigo carries on eating. I focus on the rhythmic movement of his jaws. How can I tell him? Small children think their parents can keep them safe from all the world's horrors. Here I am about to destroy all his belief in our capabilities. How can I be sure that he will not blurt out the truth to Silas in an unguarded moment? I blunder clumsily on.

'What do you think will happen if he doesn't get better?'

Inigo shrugs. 'Dunno. He'll keep having to see the doctors.'

'Sometimes the doctors can't help children with cancer. They don't know how to get rid of it and the cancer keeps growing, just like BOB is growing now.'

'What happens then?' asks Inigo

I breathe in and bite my lip. 'Sometimes those children die.'

'Does that mean that Silas might die?'

I nod. 'It's a possibility.'

He freezes with his fork halfway to his lips. 'I don't want Silas to die.'

'Neither do I, my darling, and the doctors are doing everything they can to sort BOB out, but if they can't then there is a chance he might die.'

Inigo's eyes well up.

'So you've got to be really grown-up and brave and be really nice to Silas, even when he's not being nice to you. It's a bit like you are the older brother now and he's your little brother and needs extra special looking after. Can you handle that?'

Inigo nods. A solitary tear runs down his cheek.

I carry on. 'He wouldn't want to know that there's a chance he might die, would he?'

'No,' agrees Inigo. 'He definitely wouldn't.'

'So we have to keep it a secret and I'm only telling you because you're so grown-up these days.'

'OK, Mummy.'

I point at his food. 'Now you'd better hurry up and finish supper before it gets too cold.'

The next morning, I worry that I have made a terrible mistake. He runs into our bedroom when he wakes up and jumps on Ben, who had arrived back late the night before.

'Daddy,' he says, his voice loud in the quiet house. 'Mummy says there's a chance Silas might die!'

'Shh,' I hush, worried about Silas asleep across the corridor. 'Remember what we talked about.'

'Oh, yes,' says Inigo, dropping his voice to a stage whisper. 'I forgot.'

Ben catches my eye and frowns.

'You can't forget,' I say. 'It's really important. I was wrong about how grown-up you are. I shouldn't have told you.'

'I won't forget again,' says Inigo. 'I promise.'

'You mustn't,' I say, my voice sharp. 'You must put it to the back of your mind and try not to think about it.'

Have I done the right thing? In trying to prepare my family for Silas's death and give them time to absorb the enormity of it, I have potentially exposed Silas to the knowledge himself. Can I really rely on a nine-year-old boy to keep the biggest secret of his life?

~

Silas took his job as a big brother very seriously. His job was to protect Inigo and keep him safe. One lazy summer afternoon when Silas was just four and Inigo verging on two, I called them in from the garden where they had been playing with Ben.

'Come on, you two. It's teatime.'

'You'd better head in boys,' said Ben.

Silas looked at me and then he turned to Inigo and held out his hand. 'Come on, Inigo, let's go and get some tea,' he said.

Inigo reached for Silas's hand and they headed down the garden joined together, their shadows long across the grass.

Inigo stopped and turned back to wave at Ben. He slipped his hand out of Silas's so he could wave properly. Silas turned round to gather his little brother again but his attention was caught by something lying on the grass. He bent down and picked up a piece of blue and yellow plastic. I sighed as soon as I saw what he had in his hands. It was a discarded water pistol. This was a recipe for disaster. What small boy could resist turning the pistol on an unsuspecting little brother? I waited for the tears that I knew would be coming.

Silas tested the gun out to see if it still had water in it. He sprayed two long squirts across the garden. A grin split his face as he realised that the pistol was full. He turned back to Ben.

'Look, Daddy,' he called. 'Look what I've found.' He squirted the pistol in Ben's general direction. The spray fell short of his target.

'Here we go,' I thought, resigning myself to the fallout, as Silas turned back to Inigo.

Inigo held out his hand, his eyes fixed on the water pistol. 'For me, Silas,' he pleaded. Silas didn't hesitate. He grinned and raised the water pistol, but then just handed the weapon over to his baby brother and watched Inigo try and spray Ben. He cheered him on. Then they took each other's hands again and toddled inside. I stared at them and all I could do was shake my head in amazement.

Don't get me wrong, Silas wasn't always such a perfect older brother. He meted out swift justice when his younger brother got out of line, but he also took great delight in looking after Inigo and showing him things.

When Inigo was learning to read at school, I would often find Silas sitting with him, a book in hand, helping him sound out the words phonetically one by one. Silas can't have been older than five, but he had immense patience, and instead of jumping in with the word after one or two attempts from Inigo, he would wait and encourage.

'That's right, Inigo, it's a "h". No, it's not "he" – try again. You've nearly got it.'

Encouraged by his enthusiasm, Inigo persevered. 'Her?' he said, looking at Silas questioningly.

'That's brilliant, Inigo,' Silas crowed, patting his little brother on the back. 'You're right. It's "her". Well done.'

Inigo puffed up, his face glowing from the praise, but Silas hadn't finished. He pointed at me. 'Mummy is a "her" but you and me we're both "hes" – that's because we're boys and Mummy is a girl. Do you understand?'

Inigo nodded his head knowingly, his eyes never leaving his brother, staring at him in awe. Silas slipped his arm round Inigo's shoulder and hugged him. He looked at me. 'Inigo's doing really well, isn't he, Mummy? He's going to be reading better than me soon.'

Silas knew how to get the best out of people. He was slow to criticise and swift to reward. A great skill, and one that few adults display, let alone children. Inigo benefited from this more than anyone else.

~

During the following weeks, Silas talks about death a lot. Not his death but ours – mine and Ben's.

One afternoon, Silas and I sit on the bench in our kitchen. He plays with my hair and somehow he gets onto the topic of dying.

'Mummy, I would hate it if you died.'

'I'm not going to die, darling, not for a long time yet.'

'I know, but I couldn't bear it if you did.'

'Yes, you could. You would manage.'

He shakes his head. 'No, I would have to kill myself if you died because I wouldn't be able to live without you. I love you too much. I couldn't be happy without you.'

'You wouldn't kill yourself. You would have your own family by then and they would need you.' I look away knowing this will never happen, and turn back with a smile plastered on my face.

'I'd be an old lady by then and they would need you more than you needed me. What about the two children you want. Your son and daughter. You wouldn't leave them all alone.'

'I suppose not,' he murmurs. His finger gets caught in my hair and he tugs. I wince and he pulls away a few strands and starts playing with them. 'But you'd better not die for a long time because I need you.'

'I'll try not to,' I say, coughing to clear the choke stuck in my throat.

We have long chats about death and what happens after you die. I find myself telling him in great detail that in my imagination dying is like going to Narnia – that time will flow differently in heaven for the person that dies. Time slows down in Narnia so that Edmund and Lucy and the others can spend years pursuing their adventures but not ageing a jot back in the real world. I tell Silas that my thoughts on death are similar but in reverse, so that a few decades on earth will pass in the blink of an eye in heaven. So that the person who goes through that cupboard door first will only be on their own for a few brief moments before their loved ones join them. I tell him the parting will be brief and magical.

I tell him all this with the smile on my face, hiding the silent scream that is tearing my heart in two.

I wonder all the time whether this talk of death is a way of preparing himself. He must know at some level what is happening to him, even if it is only in his subconscious. I give him many opportunities during those last weeks to step towards a discussion of his own death, but he never chooses to go down that route. Some psychologists believe children are relieved to hear their worst fears confirmed, that this gives them some sort of release and that they handle their imminent death in a different way to adults, with a maturity and acceptance way above their years.

As Silas's mother, I know that the thought of being separated from me is unbearable for him. As unbearable as it is for me, and I decide not to put him through the pain of that knowledge on top of everything else he's dealing with. Not unless he chooses to know. Am I right or wrong? Do I really even give him the choice? I'm not sure there is an answer to this question. I act on instinct, a mother's instinct – a leonine and purely animal instinct. It's my job to protect. Deep down, though, I will always wonder if it's my fear, my cowardice, that stops me being honest with him. I can't face destroying his world and the little happiness he has left. To witness the realisation of his imminent death flash across his face would have destroyed me. But perhaps, just perhaps, it would have in some way empowered him. This thought haunts me, stalks me through my waking hours and ambushes me when I sleep.

~

We have a brief stay of execution. The seizures in October do not precede a rapid decline as the nurses have anticipated. We have Silas back for a few, all too brief, weeks. He's not the same – cognitive changes are apparent almost daily. His mind is slipping away from us, eroded and pitted like the chalk cliffs under which we have spent many happy hours fossil hunting.

One evening, I catch him on his iPod, a wild stare in his eyes.

'What are you doing?' I ask, trying to peer at the screen over his shoulder.

'Just buying an app,' he says, turning his back to block my view.

'What app?'

'Just a game.' His fingers flick over the screen in a frenzy.

I frown. 'Silas, can I have a look?'

He looks at me, a strange expression on his face as though he has been caught red-handed in the sweet jar.

'In a moment,' he says, fingers skipping rapidly.

I lean forward and take the iPod out of his hand. I stare at the screen. It's full of the circular discs of loading games. I swipe back. The previous screen is the same. App after app is downloading onto his iPod. Some are games he might play, others are games for toddlers, like Peppa Pig. Then there are a host of random apps: apps for monitoring sleep cycles, apps for TV shows, an app for the Driving Theory Test, a meditation app. The list is endless; page after page of random apps. He has just pressed 'Buy' on every app that appeared on his screen.

'Silas, what have you been doing?' I ask.

He shifts on his feet and hangs his head. 'I was just buying some apps,' he mutters.

'You've bought hundreds!'

'I just wanted them.'

'But you've spent so much money.'

'I didn't mean to.'

I shake my head in disbelief.

'I'm sorry, Mummy,' he says. 'I don't know why I did it.' He sits down heavily on the bench in the kitchen, deflated and confused. I sit down next to him and put my arm round his shoulders. How can I get cross with him? He no longer understands the consequences of his actions. It's not the end of the world; iTunes will refund us if I explain our situation.

I hug my son. He is regressing to an unruly toddler with no inhibitions; flailing around in an adolescent body without control. He is broken. I am broken. We sit together staring at the screen. My throat is tight, damming the tears. His hand works its way into my hair, curling the strands round his fingers.

Silas's balance deteriorates, the slight list to the left increasingly visible, like a ship gradually taking on water. He takes a few tumbles down the stairs. Not good with his platelets low, and so we start accompanying him up and down the steps. In fact, his platelets struggle to recover from the last round of chemo and he has several transfusions to boost his levels. His next round of chemo is delayed, giving BOB ample opportunity to thrive.

I take Silas into school whenever I can to have lunch with his friends and also to squeeze in some cricket coaching. His supportive coach rearranges schedules at short notice and never passes comment on his unsteady gait and mistiming, but just structures the sessions so that Silas always feels he can manage.

Silas becomes ravenous, filled with an insatiable hunger. It becomes a battle to just stop him eating. He delves into the fridge at every opportunity.

'I'm hungry, I can't help it. It's not my fault,' he states.

He gets maddened if we try to restrict his food intake and we have battle after battle. The weight piles on. He gains 8kg in only a few weeks. His face puffs up. He looks as though he is on steroids.

Halloween is a nightmare. We go to a friend's house, an annual event, with the long awaited Cupboard of Doom. The Cupboard of Doom is a darkened cupboard under the stairs in which trays of eyeballs and tongues and hair and other bodily parts have been hidden behind a curtain. You have to finger each one and guess what it really is: cooked spaghetti for hair; olives, cherry tomatoes and button mushrooms for eyeballs. It is always a highlight of the evening for the children. This year, I go into the cupboard with Silas and before I know it he is popping

130

the props into his mouth, munching on the eyeballs and devouring the severed fingers. I have to drag him away with brute strength so there will be some body parts left for the other children to guess.

Policing his eating is exhausting. We have to have eyes in the back of our heads. It makes us miserable, and him even more so.

'Why's he eating all the time?' I ask Mary one day at the Marsden.

'Maybe the tumour has infiltrated his hippocampus – the part of the brain that controls appetite,' she suggests.

My shoulders sink.

'It can happen, I'm afraid,' she says.

That night I get home and I start to research the hippocampus. I discover that the hippocampus has cannabinoid receptors. I trace back the days trying to find out when Silas's appetite became obsessive and I discover, to my horror, that it's only a day or two after Ben started him on the cannabis. It all falls into place: Silas just has the mega-munchies.

'We have to stop the cannabis,' I tell Ben.

'No, we need to keep going. It might be helping.'

'It might,' I agree. 'But I also think it's driving his hunger.'

'How can you be sure?'

'I can't, but let's stop it for a while and see if things get easier.'

Ben finally agrees and we stop the cannabis. Over the next couple of weeks, Silas becomes less ravenous and his appetite returns to normal.

I rip up my research notes. I am furious with myself; furious that I didn't make the connection earlier, furious that I made things harder for a boy already struggling to live, but most of all I rage at my own impotence. Despite all the research I've done, I still know so little. I've broken every parental taboo and yet it has got us nowhere.

∼

A house full of boys is a house full of balls, bats, racquets and nets. Every corner and every container has balls of one shape or another. Silas was a natural sportsman. He had exceptional hand-eye coordination. Ben and I noticed this when he was very small. Silas would pick up a tennis racquet and ball aged two and throw the ball up in the air and hit it, every swing timed to perfection.

Ben and I were so excited by his skill that we even videoed him, just in case we ever had to wheel the footage out when he was a famous tennis star.

Silas was hampered by the fact that he ran with a peculiar gait. He ran with his arms hanging awkwardly down by his sides, his feet turned in slightly and his knees slightly too stiff. Ben used to laugh when he watched him and then say he ran just like his mother!

Luckily, he played all sports with his head first. He approached cricket, tennis, football and even rugby in the same way as he would consider a game of chess. He calculated his opponent's weaknesses and was quick to exploit their errors in judgement.

Playing sports with his brain stood him in good stead after BOB came along and he lost much of the feeling in his right hand. His cricket swing weakened considerably and it became harder for him to reach the boundary. He could still direct the shots with his left hand so he focused on placement rather than power.

Ben and I stood on the boundary during the summer after his diagnosis and watched him steadily bat his way towards a half-century. He had been struggling with his chemo and was tired and sick but he batted on. The opposition bowlers were good, the fielding was tight and boundaries were hard to get. Silas crept closer to his target. Finally, he was two runs away from his half-century and three runs away from a victory for his team but it was the last ball of the final over. He had one shot at it. The spectators held their breath. It was a big ask for an able-bodied batsman, let alone a boy sick with chemo and with little feeling in his right hand. The ball curled down the crease, Silas clipped it with the outside edge of his bat and it ran away past third man and rolled across the boundary for four runs. Silas's team yelled with delight and Silas raised his bat in the air, a big grin splitting his face beneath his helmet.

Ben hugged me, the tears cascading down his cheeks. Most of the spectators were on their feet and cheering.

It was a lesson in perseverance for us all.

~

Both Ben and I want Silas to die at home. It may be impossible to keep him out of hospital, but the nursing team have assured us they will help us if they can.

We never truly consider a hospice, but Ben does go to have a look around our local children's hospice, the wonderful Demelza House. I can't bring myself to go. I know there is only one place Silas will want to be and I won't really consider an alternative. However, Ben wants to assess all our options. He also wants to see what sort of grief support and bereavement counselling Demelza House might have in place for families; perhaps this could be useful for the other boys.

There is a nip in the air on the day he goes. Winter is looming. He turns up the collar of his coat and wraps a scarf round his neck. He arrives back a couple of hours later.

'How did it go?' I ask.

He shakes his head. 'It's an amazing place but not what we're after.'

I relax. The box has been ticked and found wanting. They can't offer more than we can at home. I can breathe more easily.

'What about the counselling?' I say.

He snorts. 'That's no good either.'

'Why?'

'I was introduced to the counsellor. She took one look at me and recognised me.'

'What do you mean?' I ask.

'She knew my name. She said I wouldn't remember her, but that our kids had been at nursery together. Then she asked whether one of my sons was ill.' He pauses. 'She was right; I had no idea who she was, but she's too close to home. There's too many people we know in common. It's no good for us.'

I nod in agreement. We need to keep Silas's death apart from all other aspects of our lives. We need to make this journey on our own and in private. I am relieved to be able to shut the door on the hospice route.

~

As we draw nearer to Christmas, Inigo becomes Silas's nemesis. None of us know why, but Silas fixates on Inigo and says increasingly unkind things. He worries away at his little brother like a dog with a bone, snapping and growling. Silas, who has always been amongst the kindest of our boys and used to sing his youngest brother's praises, can barely tolerate his presence.

A daily torrent of abuse that he seems incapable of stopping flows from Silas's mouth, even when we chide him. We know BOB is invading his frontal lobes and altering the essence of his personality, but it's still hard to stomach. I guess it comes from somewhere deep inside. Inigo is a constant reminder to Silas of all he has lost. Inigo plays lots of sport and Silas now struggles to pick up a ball, let alone run. Inigo is at school every day having fun with his friends. Silas hates being stuck at home. He once said to Ben, 'You know, Daddy, everyone thinks it's really fun to miss school all the time but it's not. It's OK for a day or two and then it's really boring and lonely.'

Inigo has everything that Silas once had and still desperately wants. I suppose every time Silas looks at Inigo it's like a kick in the face.

Silas no longer has control over what comes out of his mouth, not really. He says what he thinks, even if that thought is unkind or inappropriate. For example, we go to the cinema and Silas talks all the way through the film. He just speaks his thoughts as they pop into his head, almost as if he's thinking out loud. He cannot physically stop himself no matter how often he's told to be quiet, and I spend most of the time placating irate cinemagoers.

During these weeks, Silas showers us with kisses. Love oozes out of his every pore. At bedtimes, he constantly calls us back for kiss after kiss, just one more, then another one, then a last one. It's never enough;

he's insatiable for love. He sucks up all that we give him but is never satisfied. I whisper in his ear as he sleeps about how much his mummy and daddy love him.

He rolls over without waking and says clearly, 'Same – I love them so, so much.'

He lies on the bed next to me as Ben reads a book to him and Inigo. He gazes at me, his eyes large with love and wonder. My hair is wrapped around his finger.

'I love you so much, Mummy,' he says. 'I can't begin to tell you how much I love you.'

'I love you too.'

'I love you more.'

'No, that's impossible. I will always love you a smidgen more as I am your mother. That's my job!'

Silas weighs these words. 'OK, but just a smidgen.' He plays with my hair. 'You know I love you more than I love Daddy!'

'No you don't,' I say. 'You just love us both differently.'

'No,' he shakes his head vehemently. 'I love you more.'

'Shh,' I say 'That would make Daddy sad and it's not really true.'

'I don't want to make Daddy sad but I do, I do just love you more. It's just what I feel. I can't help it.'

His voice carries across the room. I hear the pause before Ben continues reading the next sentence and I know he's heard.

The old Silas was always scrupulously fair in his affections but as his mind is taken from him and he becomes more child-like, he loses the ability to moderate his thoughts and all his empathy for others.

We bear witness and it is agony.

~

I gave up a lucrative job in the City to raise my family. It was only a semi-hard decision. I knew that I didn't want anyone else to bring up my children. If mistakes were to be made, then they were to be mine.

I now resent every minute of every day that Silas ever spent at school or on a sleepover. Those are memories that I don't have and can never obtain. Imagine how I would feel if I had juggled my children with ridiculous working hours and only spent time with them at weekends. I don't regret one single minute that I spent with Silas, or with any of my boys. Those memories are more precious than any City bonus – although my kids tease me that they would rather have the chalet in Verbier and fast cars in the driveway.

~

Scans at the end of November show that the first round of PCV chemo has not stopped BOB. The drugs have not even slowed the tumour down. BOB is in a rush to finish his mission. We change the chemo again in desperation, back to the original temozolomide on which Silas had relapsed in the first place. This time we throw in several extras, including some of the drugs I had wanted months before. It is too little too late and we know it, but we can't just stand back and give up the fight.

We've been waiting a couple of months for GOSH to genetically sequence Silas's tumour, in the hope that this might give us more drug options. If we know which genetic mutations are dominant and driving the tumour's growth, then maybe we can find drugs to target them more specifically. The researchers have run his DNA through the machine several times and each time the machine has broken and failed to get a reading. We are told this is unprecedented, and the hospital is increasingly apologetic, but each failure steals precious time from our fractured future.

Ben and I clutch at straws. There's not one single drug trial that Silas can go on in Europe. We talk about travelling to the USA to join a trial, but we know it'll only give us a few extra weeks, and will split us all up for the little time Silas has left. He's happiest at home and we can't trade that for a bit of extra time. We want to; our hearts scream out for time – whatever we can take: a few weeks, a month, days even – but our heads know any time gained is for us, not for him. Our job is simply to wrap him in love and keep him tucked up safe in the house in which he has spent his entire life, surrounded by familiar sights and smells and noises. In truth, our job is to lock away our desperation and make his last weeks as easy as possible.

~

Silas had an enormous heart.

He wore it slap bang on the middle of his sleeve. He was dog-like in his affection and handed it out with innocent ease, with no thought of the heartache that might come his way with such liberal generosity. When friends and family arrived at the house by car, he would be out the door before their engine was cut, flinging his arms around them in delight. He had no tail to wag and stopped short of licking them, but it amounted to the same sort of greeting.

When it came to girls, he was an open book. He loved to discuss his plans for his future love life and, most annoyingly for his brothers, he was just as happy to discuss their girlfriend gossip with us too. If I wanted to know exactly what Oscar was up to at school, I just had to give Silas a gentle nudge and he didn't so much spill the beans as scrape the tin out.

Silas loved pretty girls and was constantly making plans as to how he was going to ask so and so out when her current beau was no longer in the picture. He never hid the fact and most of his school friends were fully aware of which girls he liked most.

One time, before morning assembly, there were just a few boys in the classroom larking around. Silas, being Silas, picked up a red marker pen and wrote on the whiteboard several times, 'Silas loves Flo. Silas loves Flo. Silas loves Flo,' in a large untidy scrawl.

Flo's twin brother, Ed, danced around Silas, laughing and giving encouragement, a willing co-conspirator. The strident ringing of the school bell echoed down the corridor and drowned out their giggles. They froze, Silas with the pen poised incriminatingly in his hand, and their faces fell. They knew that the rest of the class would be coming for the register to be taken. Silas dropped the pen and started to rub the whiteboard with the sleeve of his jumper.

'Hurry, Silas,' called Ed. 'The girls will be here any moment.'

Silas rubbed but the writing stubbornly remained.

'It's permanent marker,' he stated. He licked his finger and rubbed the text but the lines remained in all their solidity. 'I can't get it off!'

'What will you do?' asked Ed, looking over his shoulder at the door. 'Everyone will see it. Flo is going to kill me.'

Silas tapped his fist against his mouth, lost in thought.

'I know,' he said. He ran to the teacher's desk and scrabbled through the drawer. He pulled out a black felt tip pen.

'What are you doing?' asked Ed, his voice sharp with urgency. The sound of girly chatter grew louder in the corridor.

Silas returned to the whiteboard and with his back to the door blocking the view of those coming in, he wrote over the red marker with the black pen.

'Silas loves Flo, Silas loves Flo, Silas loves Flo.'

'Silas, you are making it worse,' said Ed.

Silas shook his head and snapped the lid back on the pen. 'Watch this!'

He rubbed the board with his sleeve and the pen lifted, pulling the red ink with it too and leaving only the pristine white of the board underneath.

Ed's jaw dropped, the classroom filling up behind him. 'How did you do that?' he exclaimed.

A voice bellowed across the room. 'What are you two boys up to?' They turned to see their form teacher standing in the doorway, a scowl narrowing his eyes.

'Nothing, sir,' said Silas, stepping towards his desk. 'We were just making sure your board was clean before the first lesson.'

'Oh, OK. Well done then, boys. You can both have a good mark.'

Silas gave Ed a nudge. They stifled a giggle and took their seats.

∼

December comes. The days rush by. I want to dig my heels into the ground and pull on the sun as it disappears beneath the horizon every evening. It's one of those strange things; the slower you want time to pass, the more it gallops. I want to freeze-frame every hug in my mind and capture everything about my son: his smell, his giggle, the curve of his hip, the way his hair ducktails at the back of his neck, the soft down on his legs. Everything that I know my fickle memory will one day struggle to recall.

Silas's memory continues to worsen. I find him in bed night after night reading the same page of the same children's picture book, the memory leaching from his failing mind. When we read a book, I spend more time reminding him who the main characters are and what they have done so far than reading any new material.

I take pictures of him on my phone as he opens his chocolate advent calendar so that I can show him when he comes back later.

'But I haven't opened my calendar today, I promise,' he argues.

'Yes, you have, darling. Look, today is open already.'

'Someone else must have eaten it then,' he says, fingering the flap.

'No, you had it.'

'I didn't!' he shouts. 'I know I didn't. I'll just have to take another one.' He starts to open another date.

I pull up the picture taken earlier on my phone.

'Look, darling. Here. I took a picture of you.'

Silas looks at the image, a frown etched on his forehead. 'Are you sure that was today?'

I nod my head. 'Look, you're wearing the same clothes.'

He looks down at his blue jumper and his shoulders sag. 'Oh. I'm sorry.'

'It's OK, darling. You just don't remember.'

This same process ends up being repeated several times during the day. Whenever Silas comes into the kitchen and sees his advent calendar, the process starts again.

Christmas looms. A time for celebration and festivities, but we have nothing to celebrate. We're facing Silas's last Christmas and we want to spoil him rotten, but how do you buy Christmas presents for a child you know is dying? Do you buy them clothes that you know they'll never get a chance to wear? Do you buy them toys that they no longer have the dexterity to play with? Do you buy them books that they can no longer read? A football that they can no longer kick? Shopping for Christmas is minutes spent away from my son; minutes I can no longer spare; minutes that can never be recovered. I resent every second away from his side.

Chemo is delayed yet another week as Silas succumbs to an infection. His temperature spikes for a few days and several trips to hospital ensue, leading to IV antibiotics and eventually a decision to remove the port, as the most likely source of the infection.

The port: the tubing under his skin that we had been so sure would make his life easier; that had been so traumatic to put in only a month or so earlier; that the oncologist had tried to talk us out of, sort of. The removal of that same port now means yet another general anaesthetic at yet another London hospital for a child without the luxury of time on his side.

Everything about that last hospital trip is wrong. We are directed to the wrong ward, Silas is put in the wrong bed and initially he's taken to the wrong operating theatre. The only spark of brightness is the late evening car journey up to London with Silas by my side. Houses are festooned with Christmas lights, winking in the darkness. Silas is excited about Christmas. I promise him a tray of Ferrero Rocher all to himself. We talk and we chat and we laugh. Silas tells me all about his plans for the next year.

'I'm really looking forward to school next year, Mummy.'

'Why's that?'

'Because I'll be in the top year.'

'Yes, you will.'

His eyes spark under the street lights. 'Also, I'll get a chance to go out with the girl I like.'

'How's that?' I ask.

'Because the boy she is going out with at the moment will have left. Leaving the coast clear for me!'

Irrefutable logic from a boy whose brain struggles to know even what day of the week it is.

Silas has had a crush on this girl for a while. A few weeks earlier we made a starburst loom bracelet for him to give her. He went into school a few times, the bracelet burning a hole in his pocket, but he had failed to pluck up the courage to give it to the girl.

'She's always surrounded by her friends,' was his stock excuse. 'I'll be embarrassed. They'll laugh at me.'

Finally, when he was at school one day, Ben found him in the dining room at break time surrounded by a gaggle of girls. Ben dived straight in, seizing the opportunity.

'Silas, haven't you got something to give Minty?'

Silas paled and all the girls stopped talking, waiting expectantly.

'Go on,' said Ben. 'She'll love it.'

Silas looked at his father, drew a deep breath and dug in his pocket and pulled out the colourful, intricate bracelet. He handed it to the girl.

She slipped it on her wrist and tossed her golden hair. 'I love it, Silas,' she said, admiring the band. She gave him a hug. 'I'll always wear it.' The other girls crowded round to have a look.

Silas beamed, his chest puffed out. His father gave him a conspiratorial wink and left the room.

Back in the car, that dark night on the way to the hospital, I let my son talk about his future. I know that he'll never get to kiss the girl in question or make her happy. More than anything else this fact tears a gaping hole in my heart. Silas's needs are simple. He just wants to love and be loved in return. The only silver lining is that at least he's never going to get his heart broken and his emotions trampled on by an undeserving girl. At least I know that no girl is ever going to get the chance to usurp me in his heart or in his affections. He'll never have the chance to love any woman more than he loves me, but this knowledge offers little comfort.

~

The boys break up for the Christmas holidays. Silas throws his arms round each of them, delighted that he's no longer the only one at home.

His downhill slide accelerates. He stops initiating conversations. He still answers questions but no longer asks them. We go to buy the Christmas tree but by the next morning he has forgotten and is confused when we talk about decorating it. Later, Rufus gives him a ball that he finds in his room.

'Wow, thanks,' Silas says and throws the ball up in the air.

After a minute, he turns to Rufus and says, 'Whose ball is this?'

'Yours,' says Rufus, frowning. 'I just gave it to you.'

'Oh, great, thanks.'

A few bounces later. 'Rufus.'

'Yup.'

'Is this your ball?'

'Nope, it's yours.'

'Is it?'

'Yes, I gave it to you, remember?'

'Did you?'

'Yes.'

'Thanks.' He throws his arms around Rufus. 'You're a nice brother.'

'I know,' says Rufus, peeling himself out of the embrace, his face flushing.

Silas no longer walks. He lurches, bouncing off the walls, bumping into doorways, tripping over his own feet. His head tilts far over to the left. He wanders around from room to room, restless, reluctant to stay in one place for any length of time. I find him standing in the downstairs loo, swaying gently from side to side, a look of confusion on his face.

'What is it, darling?' I ask.

He wrinkles his brow. 'I . . . I can't remember what I was doing?'

'Do you need the loo?'

He rolls the thought around his brain trying to catch it, trying to process it, as though it's a slippery eel. His eyes drift in tune with the thought in his head, circling in his sockets. His head droops. 'Yes, maybe that was it.'

A few days into the holidays, we put the Christmas tree up and start to decorate it. Silas sits on the sofa. He doesn't engage. He keeps looking towards the door of the room as though he can hear some distant noise that we cannot, a wavelength that only he can access, as though there's an exclusive party happening elsewhere that he's keen to join.

Standing on the top of a ladder putting the star on the tree, it hits me in the solar plexus. I double over in agony as the realisation explodes inside me. He's leaving us. That's exactly what is happening. His journey somewhere else has begun. My heart pounds. I'm not ready. I'm not ready. Not yet. Please not yet. How can I ever be ready for this?

My eyes find Ben. He reads my agony. We slip into the next room.

'I don't think we have long,' I whisper.

'What do you mean?' he asks.

'I think we've got it all wrong,' I sob. 'I think it's all going to happen much quicker than we realise.'

Ben shakes his head. 'What makes you think that?'

'I just feel it,' I say. 'I feel him going.'

'You're wrong.' Ben paces across the room.

I put my hand on his arm. Tears streak my cheeks. 'I'm not. It's going to happen soon.'

He brushes me off, anger giving him strength; his eyes well up.

'We need to stop the chemo,' I say. 'We can't fight anymore.'

'We have to keep fighting. We can't stop.'

I shake my head. 'No. No more fighting; it's time to stop. Now we have to let him go. That's our job. We have to make this as easy as possible for him. If we really love him, then we have to let him go. Let's not drag this out for him.'

'How can you be so sure?' Ben asks, crumpling into a chair.

'I'm his mother. I just know.'

Christmas suddenly seems a long way off.

~

The day after we put the Christmas tree up, I ring the oncologist and say we have decided to stop the chemo. He's not surprised and agrees that it sounds like the right decision. I hang up the phone and am left wondering for how long exactly he's felt this way. Why has it been left to us, Ben and me, who have no experience of the course this disease takes, to make the call? Or do desperate parents have to come to their own realisation that they've reached the end of the road? Would we even have listened a few weeks earlier if the oncologist had put the thought in front of us? Probably not. He counts on the fact that there will come a time when we realise we're keeping our son alive for us, for our own selfish reasons. He knows there'll be a moment when we say, 'No more.'

Here we are now, stepping off that cliff into the abyss. We are freefalling.

Later that same day, Silas wets himself for the first time. The nursing team warned us that incontinence is likely. We have the pads and absorbent pants in the house already, but it's still a shock.

The strangest thing isn't that it has happened but that Silas is unperturbed by this turn of events. He sits on the sofa, an absorbent pad beneath him, and he doesn't question what has happened. He just seems to accept it. Has he forgotten that it has happened as soon as it occurred, or can he no longer make the connection between the event and what that might mean for himself? I want to understand what he's thinking but there's no way to get inside his head.

The following day, his brothers and Freddie all bundle on top of each other and Silas joins in. His right leg drags on the ground, unwieldy and heavy. His legs and arms don't work quite as he wants and we hover around him as if he's a newly walking toddler, but he doesn't complain. He smiles and he laughs and he giggles with glee. Momentarily, we can see the boy trapped in the husk of his brain. He's still there, it's just becoming harder and harder to find him.

We brave a trip to the cinema to see the latest instalment of *The Hobbit*. The other boys pester us and we give in. We borrow a wheelchair for Silas. Again he accepts this turn of events without question. The film drags on and on. Silas mutters to himself and I can see the storyline is way beyond him. We take him to the disabled loo but find it occupied. We wait and wait. Silas grows restless. He has absorbent pants on just in case, but I don't want to make him sit in his pee. He's 11 years old and this, at least, is something I can try and control for him.

Eventually, a perfectly able woman exits the toilet. She hardly glances at the wheelchair and expresses no remorse. I open my mouth. I want to let rip and yell at this woman for making my dying son suffer. Ben touches my shoulder and shakes his head. He's right. I grit my teeth. How many times in the past have I too snuck into a disabled loo for one reason or another? I'm as guilty as the next person. What right have I to pass judgement? The film finishes and we wait for everyone to leave. Silas holds tightly to my hand. Ben catches my eye and I read in his tortured expression the same thought that runs through my head. This'll be the last time we leave the house with Silas. The realisation floors us.

Other old friends and family come to visit over the next few days and there are touching moments: Silas's cousin, Selena, born only a few short weeks after him, sitting next to him on the sofa, helping him to hold the controls to play Mario Kart against his brothers; my god-daughter, Thoma, holding his cards and helping him play a big group game of Uno. Silas just accepts their help, never questioning why he needs it.

His meek acceptance of his situation worries me enormously. I can't get inside his head, this child I thought I knew so well. Does he understand what is happening to him? If so, on what level? Does he have fears? Is it simply that he doesn't want to worry me? Instead of me protecting him, is he just trying to protect me?

One evening, when it is just Silas and me, I kick the proverbial door to his future wide open.

I lie next to him on the sofa, stroking his hair. 'Silas, darling, is there anything worrying you at the moment?'

'Uh uh.' He shakes his head.

'Anything at all that you want to ask Mummy? Anything?'

'Nope.'

I kiss the top of his head. 'You know you can talk to me anytime, whenever anything bothers you, don't you? Whatever it is.'

'I know.'

'You also know how much I love you, don't you?'

He looks up at me. 'I love you the same, Mummy, so of course I know.' His attention drifts back to the TV.

'I love you more,' I mumble.

He glances at me. His eyebrows pull together. 'But just a smidgen,' he says.

I nod and squeeze him close. I steady my breathing and watch his chest rise and fall. He reminds me of a candle trapped in a bell jar, the flame sputtering and flickering as the oxygen runs out, unable to move to save himself.

Instead it is me; me who wants to rage. Rage against the dying of his light.

∼

Silas sleeps more and more and he becomes hard to wake. Not just hard, impossible, even with prodding and shouting and cajoling and shaking. One night, I carry his dead weight up the stairs. I puff up each step and fall on his bed with relief, my arms aching. I stroke his head and fight the urge to pick him up again, despite the pain, just to feel the reassuring weight of his warm body and the comforting beat of his strong, young heart.

∼

Silas talks less and less. He lies in our bed before breakfast only a few days after we stop the chemo.

'I love you, Splodge,' says Ben, kissing his cheeks.

'I really love you, Daddy,' says Silas, his eyes wandering towards the window.

'What about Mummy?' says Ben.

Silas pulls his gaze back and looks at him blankly.

'Aren't you going to tell Mummy how much you love her?' says Ben, nodding his head in my direction.

Silas's eyes focus on my face lying on the pillow next to his. 'I really, really love you, Mummy.'

'Ditto,' I say, rubbing his nose with mine. I hold my thumb and forefinger a small distance apart. 'But just a smidgen more.'

He smiles.

Those are the last words he ever speaks to us. Simple and perfect. The next day he never really wakes up.

~

In my naivety, I think things will be over quickly. Death is upon us and surely it will be swift. Silas is no longer eating or drinking. We use a syringe to put water in his cheeks. How long can this last? His mind has shut down; how long till his body does too?

'I don't think we will make Christmas,' I say to my mother. Christmas is still four days away.

The local GP tries to warn me, but my brain refuses to heed his advice. He comes to see Silas. Standing downstairs afterwards we talk in low voices.

'How long?' I ask.

'It's hard to say.'

'It's torture.'

'I know.' He puts a hand on my arm. 'This happened with my father. I've got to warn you – he lasted more than four days.'

My heart tumbles and my hand goes to my mouth. 'Four days!'

He nods. He opens his mouth and I see the hesitation in his eyes. The words tumble out. 'Silas is stronger, though. He's young and his body is full of life. It could be longer; much longer.'

My knees buckle. I put a hand out to steady myself on the wall. 'I can't do this; I can't watch him slowly starve to death.'

'I'm sorry,' the doctor says. 'It's the body's way of shutting down. It's not easy, I know.'

'Why is it I can put a dog out of its misery but not my son? What's right about that? You wouldn't be allowed to starve a dog to death in this country – you'd go to prison for that, but it's all right to do it to a child? My child. Someone I would lay my own life down for!'

The doctor nods, words meaningless. He squeezes my shoulder and leaves. At the door he looks back, his figure silhouetted in the weak winter sunshine.

'You and Ben are doing amazingly well,' he says. 'Silas is lucky to be so loved by parents like you.'

'Well, he's drawn the short straw on every other count, hasn't he.' The words tear out of me, the bitterness sharp on my tongue.

~

These days are long and hard. Silas is never alone. We read to him. Ben picks up a copy of *Peter Pan* we have tucked away on a bookshelf. The opening sentence of this book twists the knife deep in our hearts.

'All children, except one, grow up.'

Ben nearly puts the book straight down but he continues, his hand shaking. We want Silas to be able to fly away into his Neverland and dream of fairies and lost boys and adventures and boys that never grow up. That keeps us going.

We recognise much of Silas in Peter's behaviour. The forgetfulness, his need for love, the eagerness to make others happy and his love of stories.

'I'll keep the window open for you to fly back, always,' I whisper in Silas's ear. I want him to know, like Wendy knew with her mother, that I'll never give up waiting for his return.

There are times I read lines that brand my heart with the tears dropping silently from my cheeks. Never seems to be more than just an awfully long time. Never stretches into an unbearable, empty future.

Christmas Day comes and goes. We open Christmas presents lying on the bed. The boys watch *Home Alone* stretched across the covers, their roars of laughter filling the room. Silas lies still beside them. We play games of cards next to him and play all his favourite songs over and over. We sing to him and talk to him and stroke him and kiss him.

At times we're not sure if he is awake or asleep. He doesn't respond to questions with words, a moan, a nod or even a squeeze of the hand, but he will play thumb wars with his left hand clasped tightly in mine or Ben's hand. The expression on his face doesn't change until we run the head massager over his scalp and then his eyebrows draw up in response to the ticklish sensation. Never have I missed his hand curling in my hair, tugging the strands loose, but now I am bereft without it.

I lie next to him on the pillow. Noses inches apart. My eyes absorb his features, hungrily trying to sear them into my fickle memory. I kiss his cheeks constantly, reminded of the games we used to play when he was small and deeply asleep. How different these desperate kisses are now.

~

In the night, Silas startles awake and his eyes search frantically for us in the half-light. I lie next to him cocooned in our bed and whisper words of love into his ear.

We start to worry he's in pain and unable to tell us. Round and round my head circle his words from that first awful night when we discovered BOB's existence. 'I could still think, Mummy, it was just that I couldn't get the words from my brain to my mouth!' Is this where he is now, trapped inside his head, deep in a subterranean cave screaming for help with no one to hear him? I pray and I beg to whatever powers that be to take him quickly and not leave him in this gasping, twilight existence.

No one answers and the days lurch on.

The nursing team assure us we'll know if he's in pain. We've no choice but to trust their judgement. We start him on a driver with Midazolam to stop the startle seizures he's been having, and to give him his medicines as he can no longer swallow easily. We massage his legs and arms, spreading our love all over him. We turn him constantly to prevent bedsores from developing. The hospital have set up a special bed next to ours, but we don't use it. We need to keep him wrapped in our love, safe between us. We moisten his mouth with a sponge on a stick that looks like a child's lollipop, and we clean his teeth gently.

His stomach grows concave and his hip bones stand proud. All I can think of is that I should have given him the tray of his favourite Ferrero Rocher chocolates when he would still have been able to devour them. I berate myself.

People come and go. We don't want them there. We want to shut ourselves away and keep his last days to ourselves. Managing our own emotions is a constant struggle and coping with someone else's feelings of loss is beyond us both emotionally and physically. We board our feelings up behind a wall of purposefulness. We have a job to finish before the wall can crumble. We plug the gaps and shore up the structure. We hold each other up, drawing strength where there is none and persevering without hope.

The days drag on and for the second time since Silas's diagnosis I wish for it to be over. I want it done. I don't want to bear witness to this unendurable suffering of someone I love. I think about speeding the process up myself with the aid of a pillow or a hand. I talk about it with Ben. I wish I was brave enough. If Silas had been in obvious pain nothing would have stopped me. Selfishly, though, I want all the extra time: every extra minute that he draws in his breath, every extra second that he lies next to me warm and vital and still alive. I wrap my son in my arms, his heart beating wildly in his chest, fighting to survive but running on empty, and I know true, vomit-inducing terror.

~

Silas dies after a difficult night on the morning of 29 December 2013, nine long days after he stops eating or drinking. His hands are cold and clammy and his lips icy. His breathing slows and his racing heart finally admits defeat. As he takes his last few shallow breaths, lying wrapped tight in mine and Ben's arms, the sun rises and fingers of red and orange streak across the clear blue sky. The birds trill and our cockerel crows a welcome to the new day.

'It's going to be a beautiful morning,' I whisper into Silas's ear. 'You go now, my darling. Go have your adventure. I'll find you. I promise. I will find you. It's OK. You'll be OK. We'll all be OK. I love you and I know you love me.'

After

S ilas is dead.

He lies in our bed, unmoving, still. His eyes are sunken and swallowed by dark circles. I can't absorb this information. This is the moment that I've been dreading since that day we were given his diagnosis in hospital all those months ago. It's finally here and I fight it. I've known for so long but knowledge has not prepared me. How can I be prepared for this? Where has my vital bear of a boy gone? Ben and I cling to each other. We cling to our son. The tears stream down our cheeks. I hear an animal groan, guttural, a noise wrenched out of a place so deep and so dark that I can't recognise it. Is it coming from me? I feel it reverberate through my chest so it must be.

The community nurse knocks at the bedroom door. She has arrived early, summoned by our frantic early morning phone call triggered by our night of panic, by our fears that Silas was suffering in those last, long, lonely hours.

She enters the room, her face soft with compassion. She has been part of the team looking after us so well these last few weeks. She feels our loss and tiptoes round our grief. I stare at her uncomprehending. Why is she here? What is she doing in my house? Who is she? Why is she intruding at this time? Should I know her? I can't process my thoughts. They drift through my head, wispy and unformed. All I know is I want to be alone with my son. I need to be alone. I glare at her. She touches my shoulder.

'I need to confirm time of death,' she whispers. 'I'm sorry,' she adds.

I nod, shifting to let her touch my son, my boy, my baby, my love. So still, so pale, so strange, so wrong. She checks her watch. My eyes follow her, willing her to go, to leave Ben and me alone.

She moves out of the room. 'Take as much time as you need,' she says. 'There's no hurry. I'll makes some calls and if you need me I'll be down-stairs.'

I watch her leave. How many times has she had to do this before? How many children has she witnessed die? How can she bear such a burden? This one time is surely enough to rip me apart, to tear my sinews from my bones, to shred my organs and leave them in tattered, bloody heaps. I turn back to my son and fight the bitter taste of vomit as it rises in my throat. This is it! The rest of our lives to be faced without Silas by our side. Without his trademark huge hugs, his sunny morning face, his unadulterated love and his quick spark of mind. All of that is undone. I am undone. I am unravelling, strands are escaping and disap-pearing. I don't recognise this place. I don't recognise myself. I longed for his suffering to be over and only now do I understand that his release is truly the start of my own torture. There are no more lies to hide behind, no more pretences to keep up, no more putting a brave face on. Just us. Just us and the raw, bare, inescapable truth that our son is dead and our hearts are broken.

We lie next to Silas's body, unspeaking and unmoving, each lost in our own raging sea. A vast, bottomless chasm lies between us and unspeakable monsters rise from the deep. I long for them to swallow me but that would be too easy. They circle round my brain like vultures and my heart pounds in panic.

A voice breaks through my pain and claws at me, dragging me back from the abyss. I hear it. I focus on the sound. Ben's lips are moving. His voice comes from far away, muffled and strange, yet at the same time familiar and reassuring.

'We need to tell the boys,' he says.

I look at him blankly.

'We must wake the boys and tell them,' he repeats. He rests his lips on

Silas's cheek and gives him a long kiss. Finally, he pulls himself away and climbs out of bed.

I nod. I pull the lost strands of my mind back and bundle them together – haphazard but sort of intact. I have to think of the others. I can't help Silas anymore but I can try and salvage the rest of my family. I banish the monsters back to the depths of my mind and concentrate on the present. I can't begin to think about the future, that is simply beyond me, and the past is too agonising. The present is the only place I can exist, minute by minute, second by second, heartbeat by heartbeat. No forward or backward, just here and now.

The boys enter our room, one by one. Silent, struck dumb. I had four boys and now I have three. How can that be? How can the world still be turning and the clocks still ticking?

They lie on the bed with us and Silas. They say goodbye to their brother. The disbelief is etched across their features. They are lost. I see that, but I also see their grief is so very different from my own. They pay it some attention then turn away, the burden too much. They dip in, feeling the temperature with their toes, but the coldness puts them off and they pull away. It's too much for them. I look at our family and I fear for their future. Their lives are irrecoverably altered; everything in their futures will now be coloured by the death of their brother. I mourn for the end of their childhoods and I'm terrified by the potential impact of this day on the rest of their lives. Their futures have been stolen from them just as surely as Silas's, just in a different way.

We all lie on the bed, whispering and touching Silas. I cut a lock of his hair. His face and hands are so cold but his tummy and thighs are so warm. I bury my hands in his heat, the last tangible evidence of his life, before it escapes. I lay my head on his tummy, feeling his warmth spread across my cheek, my face wet with tears. I can't believe he is really gone and I cling on to the last of him.

We play his favourite songs. We kiss him, although the coldness of his cheeks terrifies me. His eyes are half-open, as they so often used to be in sleep. We try to close them but they lift again. This upsets me. My mother comes to say her goodbyes. She only lives a few minutes away. I can see she wants to stay and help, but there's no room in my broken heart and I want to be alone with all my boys. She wants to hug me but I can't let her touch me. I don't want to be touched by anyone. I think I might break or implode. I can't share this pain, this burning agony, and no one can lessen my burden. My rejection hurts her. I see that but I have no mental space to consider the feelings of others. It takes all my powers to keep breathing. In, out, in, out. I focus on each breath to keep the panic at bay. My mother lets me push her away, although I know my pain breaks her heart in turn. She leaves, crumpled and alone.

We spend some time together like this, all together, until the boys grow restless and the discolouration of Silas's skin becomes too upsetting for us. Once the heart stops pumping, the blood pools and bruises appear on the back of the neck, behind the ears, under the eyes. These are things we are not prepared for – as if we were prepared for any of it. Death is undignified and visceral and so unbefitting for a glorious, vibrant, young boy. I don't want the other boys to remember these things, so we decide it's time. Time for Silas, the shell that's left of him, to leave us. Time for him to leave the house in which he spent so many happy times, where echoes of him stampede down the corridors and his laughter reverberates off the walls.

The undertakers are called. The community nurses help to dress him, sparing me his further indignities. I choose a favourite T-shirt – a pink one that has 'Tough enough to wear pink' – scrawled across the front, a blue hoodie and trousers. I give my boy the last of my desperate kisses and hide away as his body is removed. I can't believe that I can let them take him. I toy with insisting he should stay, but I know that the other boys would freak out. I tell myself over and over that it's no longer him, that he's already past the second star on the right, but I still feel as though I am somehow letting him down, abandoning him right at the end.

I fight the urge to run out and stop the undertakers. I dig my nails into my palms and clench my jaw. I am frozen, unable to move, shivering. One of the nurses puts a hot cup of tea in my hands. An engine roars, then the silence surges over me, stifling me, suffocating me. They are gone.

Silas is gone.

~

Everything is muffled, deadened. The winter sun streams through the windows but its rays are too weak to warm me. Noises are muffled. People speak and I find myself looking at them uncomprehendingly, trying to catch the words that float aimlessly around me in fluttering ribbons of sound. I can't make sense of their meaning.

'Sorry, what did you say?' I ask.

They repeat the question. I look at them blankly, frowning as I try and decipher their words.

'I don't understand,' I say, shaking my head, trying to clear the fog. I see their mouths move but their words are disconnected, floating past me in isolated bubbles. I'm beyond the easy reach of words; language is lost to me. They see my confusion and speak slowly enunciating each word as you would to a small child. Finally, I snatch the meaning from the jumble of noise and nod in response.

Things seem to be happening in slow motion. Time has elongated, stretched. It's taut like a bowstring and could snap at any moment. For days I have wanted the clock to stop ticking and give me more time with my son, now time seems to almost be at a standstill, each tortuous second stretched to breaking point. People move around me. Wheels are in motion. No one could do anything to save my child, but now everyone is busy dealing with his death. There is plenty to do now that he is dead.

Ben walks into the kitchen and turns the photo of Silas that greets him round to face the wall. I see his agony. I can almost touch his pain; it radiates from him in jagged lines.

'You can't do that,' I say, turning the photo back. My fingers linger on the curve of Silas's jaw.

Ben looks at me in surprise. 'I can't look at him,' he states.

'If you do that and hide him away, we'll never be able to face his image,' I say. I reach for his hand. 'I know it feels too painful to look on his face now, but we have to find a way through it otherwise we'll never be able to turn the pictures back and I couldn't bear that.' Ben closes his eyes and nods, his shoulders sag. He pulls me close and tucks my head under his chin.

'I can't believe he's really gone,' he says. 'How will we do this?'

'I don't know. I really don't know.' My words are muffled in his jumper. 'I'm not sure I'm going to be strong enough.'

Did we eat that day, that long day? I don't remember. We must have because the children wouldn't have gone hungry. When did people leave us? I have no recollection. All I know is that they went in the end.

Finally alone, we take the dogs and leave the house where we've been cocooned for the last two weeks and we walk, the five of us. I roll these words round my tongue, tripping over the gaping hole where the sixth should be. Now there are five. How could that ever be the right number?

The sun filters through the woodland, dappling the undergrowth. A blackbird rustles through leaves on the ground searching for insects and the last of the fallen berries. Ben takes a picture of me and my remaining boys perched on a stile. The light is clear, the air is fresh and my son is no more. Can you read our loss in our faces? If I was to show you the picture taken that day, could you tell what calamity had befallen us? The boys are smiling. My arms are around them, a hint of a smile forced on my lips. Could you tell its false nature, the disbelief written behind my eyes, the loss imprinted on my soul? Could you see the scream clawing its way through my insides, threatening to rip me in two? Or would the picture deceive you into seeing a happy family, one not marred by tragedy? A happy family simply enjoying a walk on a sparkling winter's day. We see what we choose and we rarely delve beneath the surface, afraid of the sediment we might stir up.

We shout on the walk, all of us. Our voices lift in the light breeze.

'We love you, Silas,' we call. The boys vie to outdo each other, until they are hoarse. The birds are silenced by our outbursts. We splash in puddles that linger on the road after the spate of wet weather. Every run, jump and splash is sealed with a shout of 'Love you, Splodge!' We can no longer tell him to his face, but we toss our love into the air, hoping the ripples will reach him.

That afternoon, we update the blog. The blog has been a positive conduit for our emotions over the last 18 months for friends and family. We post a picture of Silas taken a year earlier, posing in a Usain Bolt lightning stance. The light catches his features, his strong jaw and knowing eyes. A pork pie hat sits askew on his head covering his hair loss. The picture is timeless. It speaks of strength and invincibility. It speaks of potential and possibility. We title the blog 'An awfully big adventure'. The words are simple.

Our gorgeous, funny, bright, beautiful boy lost his brawl with BOB as the sun rose this morning.

Under the picture we type: *Silas – Forever 11.*

The comments come thick and fast as friends digest the news. One, written by Silas's great-uncle, touches a chord in all of us.

There was an extra star in last night's sky, brighter than the rest. It heralded the passing of a truly remarkable boy, whose packed, eleven-year life was enhanced to the last by the devotion of two of the most wonderful parents on this earth. For a true definition of love, look no further.

If only love could conquer all!

~

When I first had all the boys, I often wished I had been blessed with a daughter. What happened to my dreams of sugar and spice, dolls' houses and glitter, hair plaiting, ballet shoes and shopping?

To live in a houseful of boys is akin to hanging out in the sweaty changing room after a violent game of rugby played during a tropical downpour. Clothes and mess litter every surface, you need urinals instead of toilets – although even that doesn't guarantee a splash-free zone. The dirt and wet permeates every piece of soft furnishing, body odours are alarming and the more attention drawn to each whiff, the more sniggering and back-slapping. A single burp triggers a cacophony of competition. Fungal infections are rife and everyone just talks over each other under the illusion that the loudest is the one most likely to be heard.

I learnt early on that I had two choices. The first was to construct myself a perfect boudoir of feminine fantasy and to retire there to gently glow whenever the ribaldry and bawdiness became overpowering. The second was to join the horde at their own game and get stuck in. Like most mothers of boys, I chose the latter, so as not to find myself lost on the periphery of the family.

I started educating myself on the male psyche. At breakfast I can often be found with the sporting pages of the newspaper spread out before me. I have learnt about googlies and square legs, offside rules and Pele kicks, a Jimmy Owen and crash balls. I can name half the players in the Premier League. I know what clubs they play for and what position they play, their transfer fees and what they get paid. I've now been to the Emirates Stadium, to Wembley, to Lords and to Twickenham. I've stood on the sidelines of numerous rugby matches bundled up and shivering from the cold; I've spent Sundays hours from home cheering on a football-mad child; I've bitten my tongue at a poor line call during County tennis matches; I've sat sweating in the sauna-defying heat of rival swim meets.

The list is endless but at least I can take part in the conversations round the dinner table. I'm not the butt of family jokes for my lack of knowledge. I join in with the family sweepstakes and have even been known, on a rare occasion or two, to shout at the referee on the television. But there are some lines that I refuse to cross – I have held off from joining the much-talked-about family Fantasy Football League because a woman has got to have some self-respect.

I used to bemoan my lack of female companionship. This was generally lost on the boys, but Silas once asked me why it mattered so much.

'My mum is like my best friend,' I explained.

'So?' He shrugged his shoulders.

'So, we have a really good relationship and I'm really lucky. I speak to her on the telephone most days. I tell her all my problems. She's always there to listen. I wanted to have that same sort of relationship one day with a daughter of my own. Now I won't.'

'I'll still talk to you when I'm older,' said Silas, putting his arm around me.

'You're sweet, my darling, but it's not the same. Sons tend to drift away from their mothers.'

'I won't, I promise,' he said. 'I'll make sure I call you every day after I'm married.'

'Your wife might not like that.'

'If she doesn't then I won't marry her!' He folded his arms across his chest. 'She'll have no choice in the matter. Not if she wants to be with me.'

'I love it that you care,' I said. 'And I won't hold you to your promise. Just don't forget about your poor mama when she's old and lonely.'

'Never,' he vowed. He gave me a big kiss and ran out of the room. 'You see,' he called back over his shoulder. 'You don't need a girl after all!'

~

That first night without Silas, Ben and I both take sleeping pills and sink into oblivion. We don't want to think anymore. Thinking is exhausting; grief is exhausting. I want to curl up and press the off button. I want to escape from my new reality. I don't dream. My body shuts down – its only defence against the constant assault on my emotions.

I wake in the early hours, my legs pulled up to my chest. I lie in the dark, disorientated, untethered and then it hits me and the pain takes my breath away. I can't cry because then the pain will devour me and there'll be no coming back. I lie motionless, afraid to move. Perhaps in the dark I can hide from the pain that is searching for me, snaking tendrils over my body. I register the comforting weight of a sleeping cat on the bedcovers, its heavy body curled up in the crook of my knees. I focus on the weight and try to hold the waves of pain at bay, but they are relentless, rolling over me, sucking at me, pulling at my insides.

I hear my heart beat, the pulse thudding in my ear resting on the pillow. The steady rhythm doesn't comfort me, it catapults me back to the last few days and the relentless, accelerated pounding of Silas's dying heart. I replay the last few moments of his existence on a repeat loop through my brain. I can't shake the image of his dying body. I know I needed to be there at his death, just as I was at his birth, and to have been absent at that moment would have been unbearable, but I now have memories that I'll never be able to erase. Memories I don't want. Memories that drown out all else. I have lost his smiling, happy face. Tears soak my pillow. I search for my Silas. I rummage through the drawers of my mind trying to find a glimpse of him, one I can hold on to, but they all flit away out of reach, taunting me with their elusiveness. The tears roll silently down my cheeks. How could all that he was be no more? The waste astounds me and leaves me gasping for air.

~

Those first few days after Silas dies, we function at a basic level. We are cut off, adrift in an ocean of sympathy. The phone barely rings, people leave us, give us time and space. Space is the last thing we need. We don't want time to think. Thinking is our enemy. Thinking rips us apart.

I am cold, so cold. We leave the heating on all day but it doesn't warm me. I want to burrow under my bedcovers and stay there, stay there in the room where he took his last breath. Although I had fought to keep him at home, I had still been worried about him dying in the house and how that would make us all feel, but now I draw comfort from his closeness. I'm glad we kept him here. It feels right.

We fill our time with practicalities. It's easier to focus on the funeral and the service of celebration than to examine our emotions. I look at photos of Silas, trying to pick out ones for the service sheet. I am cold, precise and practical. It's an exercise, pure and simple. Videos are harder to watch but we sift through hundreds trying to find clips that sum up his character, his zest for life, his madness, his enormous heart. He feels close; watching the footage keeps him close, keeps him alive somehow. The more we watch, the more surreal his death becomes. We keep our distance from our feelings.

Letters and cards start to arrive. We pounce on them greedily, desperate for snippets of information that are unknown to us or long forgotten, anecdotes about Silas that give us new images of our son. New images are what our brains crave and we find some small solace in borrowing other people's memories.

The best letters take us back to happier times: lazy summer days playing cricket; parties smashing piñatas; holidays hurtling down ski slopes or eating ice creams in Italy. Silas's godfather nails his godson's character when he recalls a conversation he had with Silas about the 'strawberryness of strawberries'.

Some letters bring vivid, forgotten images to life. A friend of ours, James, writes about how he once had to dress up as Father Christmas and dispense presents to eager children. An eight-year-old Silas waited in line. He wasn't fooled by the cheap Woolworth's white beard and dodgy outfit. When his turn came, he sat on James's knee and looked him squarely in the eye. 'I know you're not Father Christmas!' he stated. James raised an eyebrow. Silas then pulled on the beard until the elastic holding it in place stretched taut. 'See,' Silas said. 'Not real.' He turned to his younger brother. 'Told you,' he said and let go of the beard. The elastic pinged back with a satisfying snap. James let out a squeal and Silas and his brothers rolled around on the floor incapacitated by laughter, all thoughts of presents forgotten.

One note, from a family with a son in Silas's class, mentions how a letter from Silas two years earlier was the clincher in deciding where to send their boys to school. They had been so impressed with his open manner and easy conversation on a drama workshop day they had organised, and even more gobsmacked by his eloquent thank-you letter penned on behalf of the whole class, that they decided their sons should go to the same school. We knew none of this, and how wonderful it is to find out something new about our son; our son who was never going to do anything new ever again. Even better, it turns out they had kept his letter and they are quick to send it to us. We treasure it. Something so small and simple – a piece of previously unseen writing, a slice of his lost life – is invaluable to us.

Photos are wonderful. Some friends take the time to print out pictures of Silas and include them with their letters. Often these are pictures we have never seen, and we feast our eyes on his image. We steal these memories and they provide some brief solace from the other too recent images that lurk around the perimeters of my brain, snarling and snapping for attention.

For all those who get it right, there are many that pitch it wrong. It's ungenerous of me, I know, when these people have hovered their pens over paper struggling to find words, but in our despair we are unable to find generosity and understanding. We judge phrases unfairly and cannot help but note those who should but do not write.

'We are sorry for your loss.' Sorry. How does sorry begin to convey the enormity of our situation? Also, I didn't lose my son; how careless would that be? If only I had just lost him! Lost, he might still have a future. I wish I had lost him. He died. He died an undignified, awful death and left an achingly raw, unfillable chasm inside me. Words like those cannot begin to offer comfort.

The ones that drive Ben mad start with, 'There is nothing I can say.'

There is nothing I can say and I can't imagine what you are going through.

He tosses these cards aside and by the twitch of his jaw I know immediately what's written inside them. These friends or acquaintances have chickened out of addressing the situation. We both know they can imagine it but that they dare not: the horror of our situation terrifies them. They can't find the words because they don't have the courage to look for them, and we find this hard to forgive.

'I might as well go off and hang myself then,' says Ben, after yet another such letter. If only the writers of these letters knew that instead of offering a modicum of support, they chip away at our fragile hold on the situation.

I find most unbearable all the letters that are addressed to Ben, Sarah, Oscar, Rufus and Inigo. Where is Silas? Silas has been wiped out of existence. People have made a conscious decision to remove him from our lives and I can't forgive them for doing it so easily. I know many will have agonised over how to start these letters and cards, but they have failed at the first hurdle. The cards that sing to me the most are those that include Silas, those that end 'with love to you all but most especially to Silas'. There are a few special letters that get it right, perfectly right, some from people I least expect and hardly know and these start, 'Dear Gorgeous Silas'.

My mother accuses us of being too sensitive and she's right. We teeter on the edge of our self-control. We're merciless and judgemental. Words and expressions are examined through the lens of a grief-clouded magnifying glass and take on a whole new meaning.

Some good friends are brave enough to call. It's instinctive when someone answers a phone to say, 'Hi, how are you?' It trips off the tongue without thought. It's a courtesy, a habit, nothing more. Now, though, we greet such calls with silence, even when we can hear the caller desperately try and claw the words back. How can we answer such a question? Do they want to hear the truth? How my heart aches and I can barely string my thoughts together. How I have to fight against the urge to keep my foot down hard on the accelerator in the car as I round a sharp bend in the road. Do I just say, 'Fine,' and leave a meaningless word hanging in the air, just to lessen their discomfort?

Ben and I have long, strange, circular discussions on what to say when people call and utter those three dreaded words. 'How are you?' He eventually settles on, 'I'm getting by, thanks.' I just say, 'Surviving,' but I don't mean that. Survival takes effort, a desire to live, a hunger for the future, choices to be made. What I mean is existing. I exist. I am. My body functions, just. I eat when I have to, I sleep with assistance, I follow my bodily urges. I exist in a sort of half-light, crepuscular way, but that's all, and even this takes enormous effort.

Some close friends pick up on this new language of ours and instead of ringing up to ask how we are they try hard to learn new words.

'Hi, darling, just checking in with both of you,' says Rufus's god-mother, Bella, when she calls. She calls often. She senses when I find it hard to talk and doesn't force a conversation, but she keeps calling, letting me know she is there.

Others send simple kisses at bedtime. The text message pings through on my phone. I know they are thinking of us. Their efforts are touching and we really appreciate their perseverance and their willingness to cock up and try again. So many other friends disappear – too frightened to ring, too scared to stumble – and we're left confused by their absence and let down by their inadequacies.

One friend is unnerved by the lengthy silence down the phone as I digest her poor choice of words.

'I'm sorry,' she mumbles. 'I can't seem to say the right thing.'

'It's OK,' I reassure her, burying the part that wants to scream at her for her insensitivity. 'I'd much rather you'd keep trying and mess it up than not try at all!'

'Really?'

'So many don't even try, so we really appreciate it.' And it's the truth. We see how hard it is for people to step into our lives, and how unpredictable our sensitivities are. I would run a mile from me given half the chance, so can I really blame others? We are demented with grief and it would be impossible for people to get it right all the time.

Yet still we judge.

~

The boys seem to be taking it all in their stride. I think for them there is some relief that it's all over; that things can move on again. I feel a strange relief too, which induces feelings of guilt. I'm glad it's over so that I no longer have to watch Silas suffer, but I don't want life to move on. To move on would be to accept his death and I am far from there. I'm glad that the tornado has finally hit. I can deal with the practicalities of the immediate aftermath much better than the waiting and constant uncertainties of the preceding weeks, but this is all.

We talk about Silas all of the time, all of us. We make a conscious decision to include him. It's agonising and painful but feels right. These are the first few days of how we live now, and both Ben and I feel that it's important to let instincts lead us. We bring him up in all conversations, round the dinner table, watching TV, on walks.

'What would Silas make of this film?'

'Would Silas like this meal? What would he eat first?'

'I bet Silas would have eaten five fajitas!'

'Silas would find that joke really funny.'

We need to keep him alive in our memories. I'm terrified that if we stop talking about him because it is too painful, we'll be unable to hold on to him; that his essence will slip through our fingers like sand.

I see visitors blanch when we mention his name. They don't know how to respond and tiptoe round his existence clumsily. They fail to realise that all we want to do is talk about him. Talking about him keeps him with us in some small, intangible way.

~

I wander round the house that first week, confused, searching for Silas. I want to find evidence of his existence, proof of his part in my life.

I long for a room that was his that I can just hide away in, surrounding myself with his belongings, but I don't even have that comfort.

For many years the boys had gravitated together at bedtimes. They all shared a room together at the top of the house. It was a room full of noise and laughter; a room full of elaborate camps made from duvets and blankets and old boxes; a room full of whispered secrets and brotherly battles. About a year before Silas became ill, the boys had separated into their own spaces. Silas stayed in the room at the top of the house, but he was never happy there and more often than not slept with one of his brothers. After the arrival of BOB, we moved Silas downstairs next to us and he shared a small room with his youngest brother. Space was tight and conflicts increasingly common, so a few months before he died, we juggled things around and Silas went into the next-door room with Rufus. We redecorated another room and a few weeks later Rufus had a new space. Silas, at last, had his own room again but, as it turned out, it was only his for a few short weeks. Too short a time for him to make a stamp on it.

I walk around his room trying to feel his presence but he's not there. I open drawers and cupboards but I find nothing of him. He was never a hoarder like some children and possessions were not so important to him. Relationships were where he thrived and these can't be boxed neatly away. I search for his smell in his clothes, in his teddy bears, even his slippers, but it has vanished. There's so little of him in this room that I cannot find him, even the sheets are clean and unused. I panic. I find myself lying on his bed searching for bits of wallpaper that he might have worried as he drifted off to sleep. I rummage through his desk looking for snippets of writing, anything, but there is so little. I finger his watch and sniff it, looking for remnants of scent, his sweat, but it is long gone. He is gone and the remaining threads of his life are gossamer thin.

I go round the house collecting evidence. Birthday cards, Mother's Day cards, his baby teeth, the shirt he was wearing the morning he died, the lock of his hair, little love notes to me, a bracelet he bought me – anything that has come from him. I am desperate, maddened and bereft. I hoard my paltry collection in the cupboard beside my bed. My treasure trove of a love lost. It's all I have left and provides little comfort.

~

In our downstairs loo, we have a large window. The window looks straight out onto the busiest part of the garden. We didn't want to put net curtains on the window and sandblasted glass was expensive, but we had to give the occupants some privacy. We toyed with various ideas and eventually we settled on some film we could stick over the glass. We found a company that would etch what we liked into the film. There were four panes of glass so we turned each boy's name, first and surname, into an anagram that we felt reflected something of their character.

Oscar's was Nuclear Slop. Being the eldest, the mood that Oscar woke up in in the morning would often dictate the day for the rest of the house. He could be delightful but also poisonous.

Rufus's was Fuller Sunup. Rufus was a happy little boy, always smiling, until a toy was snatched by one of his brothers. He lived life in bubble of contentment.

Inigo's was Lupine Lingo. Inigo was still very young at the time but already talking. His language skills were much more advanced than the other three at the same age. Walking was hazardous with three bigger brothers so he traded movement for words.

Silas's read Pulls Aliens. His mind worked in such a different, madcap way to the others that we used to tease him that he had been delivered to the house in an alien spacecraft and we had agreed to bring him up as our own. He went along with this for a few years until his brothers started to tease him.

'You're an alien, you're an alien,' they chanted when he annoyed them.

One day, as he sobbed in my arms over some fight or other, he said, 'I'm not really an alien, am I, Mummy?'

'Of course you're not,' I said, angry for opening him up to such teasing. 'You came out of my tummy. Look, you've even got my ears.' I pointed to my non-existent earlobes.

He sniffled. 'Good. I'd be so sad if you weren't my mummy because you're the best mummy in the world.'

~

Ben and I sit in the bath. I feel close to Silas in my bathroom. Some of our best conversations took place in this room and some of our worst.

We discuss the funeral, the hymns we want, the hymns Silas would want, the readings. We want the funeral to be tiny, just immediate family, his godparents, some close friends and the families of Silas's two best friends, in whose houses he spent so many happy hours. We don't want many children there. We don't want them to have those images and memories. Not if we can help it.

'Shall we cremate him or bury him?' Ben asks.

I'm quick. 'Cremate him.'

'How can you be so sure?'

The corner of my lip lifts and I let my mind drift back to the day a few months earlier that Silas and I had this same conversation in this very bathroom. It had been a generic sort of discussion with him and Inigo about the pros and cons of burial versus cremation, and I had used the opportunity to steer the talk and garner answers.

'He told me.'

'When . . . ? How?'

'We had a conversation once. Here.'

Ben looks at me in surprise.

I continue. 'I guess that's the one advantage of knowing your child is going to die. You can winkle such pieces of information from them.'

'Are you sure?'

I nodded. 'I told him I would want to be cremated so my ashes could be scattered somewhere I loved and he said, "Same."'

I left out the bit about how he couldn't bear the thought of worms eating him and how he and Inigo then graphically discussed which soft body parts would be consumed first in a gruesome boy's own sort of way.

We talk about a bigger memorial service down the line and mull over ideas as to how we can make the service child-friendly. We settle on the idea of a wristband in his favourite colours, pink and blue, with his name spelt out using adjectives that describe him.

We throw words at each other. Sunny, silly, smiley, idiotic, imaginative, inventive, loving, lazy, laughing, loyal, amusing, adoring, active, ardent, sparkling, sporty, soft, spirited. It is nice losing ourselves in words that describe our missing boy. It draws us close again and the distance between our individual journeys of grief narrows. We find ourselves on common ground. For a brief moment, I think we can do this: together we can find a way to live without the sun. Somehow.

We delve deep into Silas's character and we finally settle on a selection of verbs that we feel best sum him up.

Smile . . . Imagine . . . Love . . . Achieve . . . Sing

⁓

In Year 4, Silas was given the task of producing an acrostic poem in class. Acrostic poems are poems with a simple structure so they are easy for children to write. The first letters of each line spell out a word. They do not need to rhyme and there is no set rhythm, but the whole poem should reflect the original emotion or idea.

Silas's teacher called me into the classroom the next morning.

'Mrs Pullen, I need to show you this.'

She slid Silas's English book in front of me. Silas disappeared to play, a big smile on his face, singing the words to a song we had been listening to in the car on the way to school.

I glanced down. She tapped her finger on a page. 'This is amazing, really, for a child his age. Not only the subject matter but the way he has really portrayed the emotion of the situation.'

I read the poem. The work was messy, there were crossings out and illegible scribbles. Neatness was never a strong point for Silas.

> Blood was pouring,
> Longer and quicker.
>
> Entertaining it was not.
> Aching inside,
> Kicking at his stomach
>
> Nothing would stop it.
> Eventually we will know.
> Soon he will be in heaven.

Stamp and he goes off.
Self-confident, he will live.

I traced down the word BLEAKNESS with my finger. 'Did he really write this?' I asked.

'Yes. Without any help!'

'Wow!'

'That's what I thought. What an imagination and he has an amazing ability with words. I told him that when he is older and he has his first book published he will have to dedicate it to me.'

'And what did he say?' I asked.

'He said, "OK, but it can't be my first one as that has to be for my mummy, because I love her best of all!"'

~

New Year falls immediately after Silas dies. The boys want to celebrate somehow. They've been stuck at home with our misery all holiday and I can see the isolation is stifling them, but I can barely put one foot in front of the other so how can we have guests or even begin to think of going out? More importantly, how can I move into a different year without Silas? I need to stay close, but a new year will rip us further apart.

Our neighbours step into the breach, as they have constantly throughout the last months. Kate drops by.

'How about coming to us for supper tomorrow night?' she says, going straight for the jugular.

I stare at her. Is she really talking to me? Does she have any idea? She smiles. I blink. Of course she does. It's Kate. Their family has been deeply affected by Silas too. His death is another country, and she may not speak the language, but at least she is standing on the same shore.

'Come on. How about it? The boys would like it. I know it'll be hard. We could have the Sherwins too?' She refers to the family of one of Silas's best friends, Harry. Last New Year's Eve we were all together. A vision of us adults dancing round the kitchen Gangnam Style, much to the embarrassment of all the children, springs unbidden into my mind. I remember cutting a chocolate log whilst dancing and singing with Silas. He wore a checked shirt belonging to his oldest brother. It was too big, the sleeves flapped round his arms as he danced. His head was bare, half bald from the radiation, but he was unselfconscious and at home with both families. In my memory, he grins at me. I close my eyes and try to hold on to the image.

These are two families who have shared the journey with us from the beginning. There are only a few others who understand our pain as well as them.

'OK,' I say finally. 'I'll talk with Ben, but I'm not sure we'll be much company.'

'I know,' says Kate. 'We're not expecting anything. You don't have to pretend with us, you know that.'

The next night we go. The kids have fun. They let their hair down with old friends. It's hard to hear their laughter but we know how important it is. Harry is lost without Silas, and that's painful to witness, but we are surrounded by people who are not afraid to remember and who talk boldly of our missing son. They are patient with us. The evening is agony. I don't know why we agreed to go. What were we thinking? I can't celebrate a New Year; it catapults me away from Silas. He was alive in 2013 but not in 2014. How can that be? I need to go home. I don't want to be here. It was a mistake to come. I catch Ben's eye. I see the same confusion mirrored on his face.

Our friends surround us with love and, somehow, we make it to midnight. We stumble home.

Another first out of the way.

~

On New Year's Day, three days after Silas dies, one of our cats disappears. It takes us a couple of days to realise the cat has gone, so wrapped up in our grief are we. The weather is abysmal; it has rained heavily for the last few days. It's still raining and I know there's little hope of finding the cat, but this cat is special and I can't bear the thought of leaving him lying injured in a ditch.

We set out to search. We call repeatedly. The cat is an oriental breed and more like a dog; coming when he's called. I check along the busy main road but see no sign of a body. The children are upset and beg me to go and ask the neighbours if they have seen him.

I can barely talk to my own mother at this stage. Finding words to share with others is beyond me. I've built a wall around my emotions. I can almost pretend that Silas is just staying with friends; it's easier than facing the truth. It's the only way I can function at the moment. This wall of self-preservation is fragile and crumbling and stray words act like pickaxes. It will only take one misplaced strike to bring the whole lot tumbling down and then there'll be nothing left to hide behind. My 11-year-old son lies alone in a funeral home and the thought of speaking to neighbours I hardly know fills me with dread, but there's no one else to do it.

I start nearest to the main road. I knock on the first door. There's no answer and I turn to go. The rain has plastered my hair to my head and droplets of water drip down the back of my neck. I hear a muffled shuffling and the door opens. A fug of warm air flows out. An old lady pulls her dressing gown tighter around her and eyes me with suspicion.

'I'm looking for my cat,' I start. 'He's disappeared. He's been gone a couple of days.'

'It's probably been run over,' she states.

'I know. But if you see anything . . .'

'Where do you live?'

'At the Rectory.'

'Oh,' her eyes focus sharply. 'It was your son . . .'

I nod, not trusting myself to speak. I can see the village grapevine has been hard at work.

She puts her hand on my arm. 'I'm sorry.' She pauses. 'I'll let you know if I see the cat.'

I move to the next bungalow. I feel the lump lodged in my throat. I can't do this, I think. I can't expose myself to strangers' pity in this way. I think of the cat. I think what Silas would want me to do. I take a deep breath and ring the doorbell. Another lady answers, she recognises me immediately and her features soften.

'You're the lady whose son . . . You lost your son, didn't you?'

The tears spring into my eyes, my throat aches as I battle the lump. I find it hard to swallow. I want to scream, 'I didn't lose him.'

'I'm so sorry, it's so dreadful,' she says. 'What are you doing out here?'

'I . . . I'm looking for our cat. It's disappeared.' I stumble over the words.

'You should be at home with your family,' she says. 'It's only a cat.'

I square my shoulders. I feel a muscle tick somewhere near my eye. A tear winds its way slowly down my cheek, mingling with the raindrops. 'I think my children have suffered enough this week and I promised them I would ask. I couldn't save my son, but just maybe I can save the cat.'

She's startled by my outburst. She stares at me and nods. 'I will keep a lookout.' She touches my cheek with her finger. 'You're a brave lady. God bless your family and your little boy.'

I stumble away, the tears coursing down my face. I've lost the cat just like everyone keeps telling me I've lost Silas. I don't seem to be able to keep hold of anything I love. All I can do is hope they have found each other.

~

Ben goes to register Silas's death. He returns home, visibly shaken, with a death certificate.

'It was so strange,' he says. 'I had to wait in a room with newly married couples and newborn babies. They were all there to register a happy event in their lives. I wanted to shout at them to make the most of it. That I was there to register the death of my 11-year-old son.'

I pull the certificate out of the anonymous brown envelope the registrar has placed it in. It's typed on grey-green watermarked paper. It's factual and impersonal. Cause of death is written as a malignant glioblastoma. Where does it say he was only 11 years old? Where is the box that says this should never have happened? My hand shakes. Is this all that is left of my vivacious, 11-year-old son – a scrap of paper? Is he just another statistic now? Isn't a certificate awarded for achieving something good? What has Silas's death achieved?

~

Silas got various school awards but the two I remember most clearly were under very different circumstances.

His first speech day at Wellesley, aged eight, he was bubbling with excitement and buzzed around us unable to stay still. When we took our seats, we realised he'd gone. As the hall filled up, we stood and scoured the surrounding seats but there was no sign of him. Pupils generally sit with their parents but we couldn't spot him anywhere.

'He's probably sculling around with his mates somewhere,' said Ben.

'Do any of you know where your brother is?' I asked the other boys.

They shook their heads.

'He isn't getting a prize or anything?' I queried.

'Don't think so. He would have told us,' mumbled Oscar.

I nodded. Silas had only been at the school for a couple of terms, so it was unlikely he'd even be in the running.

The headmaster came in and the hall quietened down. I took a last look round to see if I could spot him but there was no sign. I shrugged my shoulders and sank into my seat.

The speeches came and went and then the prizes started. There was still no sign of Silas.

The headmaster continued. 'And the Academic Prize for Class JB goes to Silas Pullen.'

Ben and I gasped. Silas popped up from one of the front rows and strode to the platform to receive his prize. He glanced our way and a big grin broke across his face. We clapped with pride.

'Why didn't you tell us?' I asked Silas afterwards.

'I wanted it to be a surprise,' he said, hopping from foot to foot with excitement.

'Well, it certainly was,' said Ben. 'Well done, you.'

'We looked for you,' I said. 'Where were you hiding?'

'I crouched on the floor in front of my seat until the headmaster came in, then I kept my head down. I knew you were looking but you didn't see me, did you?'

We shook our heads. Silas tucked himself under my arm. 'Are you proud of me?' he asked.

'Always,' I replied.

The next time he got up on that stage to receive an award the roles were reversed. It was two years later. He was in the middle of a chemo cycle and he had no idea that he was going to get anything. We knew otherwise.

Silas sat next to us towards the back of the hall, his tie was crooked and his hair was cropped close to his head. The radiotherapy had bleached out some of the colour and the hair on one half of his head was lighter when it regrew.

He fiddled with his cuffs as the prizes for his form were announced and applauded the winners.

The headmaster's voice boomed across the hall. ' . . . And secondly a special prize for a pupil who knows nothing about this. This has been awarded for courage and cheerfulness in the face of adversity and goes to Silas Pullen.'

Silas turned to us, mouth open in amazement. He raised his eyebrows and a smile flitted across his face. He stood and walked up to the stage, back straight and head held high. A huge cheer erupted from the hall.

He returned to his seat clasping his prize. I wiped my eyes, unable to stop the tears falling.

Silas turned to me. 'Did you know?' he accused. He hesitated when he saw my tears and uncertainty clouded his features. 'Are you crying, Mummy?' he said.

He put his hand on my knee and peered into my face. 'Why are you crying?'

I smiled at him and lied. 'I'm crying because I'm happy for you.' He frowned at me.

I put my arm round him. 'I'm crying because you make me so proud. You deserve that award so much.' I smiled through my tears.

He shook his head and gave me a hug. I held him close. Inside I was torn apart. I wanted to wail for everything that he had lost, everything that he had suffered and the horror that he was going to suffer. I wanted to rip my hair out for the future that was no longer his, but instead I stifled my sobs and fixed that smile on my face. This was his moment and I would not ruin it for him.

~

I find myself in the hairdresser's. Kate comes with me. There's something I need to do. The lights in the salon are too bright. The music on the radio is too loud, too cheerful. I don't want to be here. Kate knows and she squeezes my shoulder.

I sit in front of the mirror. Who is this person I see reflected back at me? Do I know her? Her skin is pale and she has dark circles under her eyes. Her eyes are haunted, fathomless. She's a stranger. I raise my hand to my face to check the reflection is mine. It moves in synchrony.

I have no make-up on. My son has been dead five days. I search my face, trying to see if I can see the loss etched on my skin. Where is the evidence of my broken heart?

The stylist pulls a chair over.

'What do you want done today?' she asks, running her fingers through my long hair. I have to stop myself from pulling away. There's only one person I want to feel wrapping my hair round their fingers. I feel the tears rise. I keep my eyes wide open, if I don't blink then they won't fall. The stylist doesn't notice. She chats away, her voice bright and breezy. Her happiness offends me.

I look at Kate. She gives a nod of encouragement and squeezes my shoulder.

'Cut it all off!' I say. Then louder. 'Cut it off.'

~

Ben and I go a couple of times to the funeral parlour. We discuss arrangements for the service. We can be clinical and detached. We agree to see the body. I can't bear to think of Silas lying here all alone, but my imagination must be worse than the reality. I'm not sure, though. How can I be sure? I've never done this before. Ben told me that after his father died, more than a decade earlier, he wished he'd never gone to see the body. He could never shake those images and it had always disturbed him.

This is different, though. We have already seen Silas dead. Those images are already burned on my mind; indelible, forever. Now I need to reassure myself that he is OK, that they are looking after him here. It's as though I need to check that this really has happened to me, that I really am immersed deep in this nightmare. A bit like pinching yourself to make sure you're awake. Will seeing him again do this, or will it fling me back to those dreadful first hours?

We are led down a softly lit corridor. The walls are hung with pictures of bucolic landscapes and welcoming sunsets. Side tables are adorned with vases of flowers and their sweet scent sickens me. The pile on the carpet is deep and soft underfoot. We stop outside an innocuous door and are left alone to enter.

'Are you sure you want to do this?' asks Ben, his face pale and strained.

'I think so,' I reply.

He nods. 'OK.' We both take a deep breath and step into the room. The cold air hits us and finds its way through the gaps in my clothing. I shiver.

Silas lies on a raised table against the far wall. It's probably some sort of gurney or trolley but it's covered by a long cloth and the details escape me. I have eyes only for my son.

He's so still, so pale, so removed from anything he had been while alive. He is so dead. It takes me a while before I can step closer to him. A blanket is pulled up to his waist and his arms are folded unnaturally across his chest. Who is this person? Do I know him? I see Silas in the face but I don't recognise him. Then I realise what's so strange. He's not smiling. His lips are pressed together in an awkward fashion. He looks so serious, so . . . so un-Silas.

'They managed to close his eyes!' whispers Ben with relief.

I nod. I bend over and kiss his head. His hair looks darker and it has lost its vibrancy. It feels coarser. Ben can't bring himself to touch his son without covering his hand with a handkerchief. I understand this. Silas's flesh looks so alien, but I need to feel the change, to know that this shell is no longer him. I stroke his cheek. It is icy and slightly waxy. I pull my hand away and curl my fingers into my palm. I lay my forehead against his and let my breath warm his skin. Where is my boy? He's not here, of that I am sure. I lean down and kiss his lips. They are bloodless and tinged with grey, not pink as they should be. They are soft still, but they don't give in the same way. Not in the way they should.

'I love you, Splodge,' I whisper. 'Always a smidgen!' I pause. 'I don't know how we'll manage without you.'

Ben's shoulders shake. He leans over Silas. 'I love you, Splodge. All the way to the stars and back and down to your tickly toes and up to your sweet buttony nose.' He brushes his finger against the side of Silas's nose.

We stand with our boy for a few minutes more, the air is thick with our pain. We can take no more. We leave.

We return to the funeral parlour the day before the funeral. I steel myself once again. This time, Silas is lying inside the wicker basket we have chosen instead of a coffin. The pale silk lining gleams and a small pillow is tucked under his head. I am glad of this small comfort. We place a selection of things in the basket with him. Sealed letters from each of us, photos of us all together in happier times, a mini rugby ball, a mini cricket bat – the one he hit so many balls with in different hospital rooms – his two favourite teddies – a polar bear and zebra – a tin of jelly beans, an Arsenal badge, a conker from the garden. We scatter some dried rose petals and rosemary over him. These had been gathered by my mother from the floor of the church at our wedding and kept ever since, a symbol of our love for one another. We stuff his pockets full of sunflower seeds, his favourite snack.

Finally, I wrap his stiff fingers around my ponytail of hair, collected at the hairdresser's. I can give him this at least. My hair is now short and boyish and cropped close to my head. In death I give him the one part of me he loved the most. My hair. It's his to keep forever. It's all I have left to give him, this beautiful, still boy of mine.

~

We wake the morning of the funeral and the rain runs in rivulets down the windows. I'm glad it is raining. There should be nothing cheerful about this day. I want the day to be dank and depressing, grey and foreboding. I want the world to weep. I want everyone to know that the laughter is gone from my life.

We all wear blue. Blue is a flexible colour. There are many shades and hues. Blue is the colour of the sky and the sea, it's the colour of forget-me-nots and Silas's favourite Smarties. It is also the colour of sadness and tears. In some countries it is used for mourning and has been embraced as the colour of heaven. For us it's simple, Silas is dressed in blue in his wicker basket and so are we.

We reach the tiny medieval church. This is a church where two of our children were christened. It's plain and simple and unadorned, with beautiful, high, boxed pews. It's a place we often walk to and it's where I had gone that day of the scan results. Ben turns the engine off. The wipers stop and the rain cascades down the windscreen. The drops drum on the roof of the car but can't drown out the noise inside my head. The children remain silent in the back. The hearse is parked nearby. We know Silas is already in the church. My breaths are rapid and

I feel the panic build in my chest. I don't have the strength. Ben squeezes my hand. I'm unable to look at him but I return the squeeze, grateful.

We run to the church, heads bowed against the driving rain. The heavy oak doors are open and there in front of the altar stands the wicker basket.

I stop.

This is the last time we will all be together as a family of six.

Forever.

The knowledge rips away the flimsy wall I have built and I am lost. I can't stop the tears and I no longer try. I steel my shoulders and follow my remaining sons into the church.

The service is short. My eyes never leave the wicker basket. The thought of Silas alone in there tears me apart. I dig my nails into the palms of my hand. I want to wake up. I want to be dreaming this nightmare. How can this be real? Silas never wanted to be alone. Silas was always happiest in a crowd. Loyal and always in search of companionship, he loved to make people happy.

The church fills with voices but I have lost mine. One of the hymns is 'When a Knight Won his Spurs', and the adjectives gentle, brave, gallant and bold must have been written for Silas. The enormity of our loss overwhelms me.

Silas's cousin, also 11, reads a small poem. Her voice rings out, clear and true. Oscar, only 14, stands in front of the small congregation and reads a passage from *Jonathan Livingston Seagull*. He reads beautifully. His younger brother lies in a coffin a few feet behind him and yet he does not falter.

At the end of the service, my boys, all four of them, leave the church together. There will be no more together again, there will only ever be an absence – a hole that can never be filled. Three of them carry the fourth, with the help of their father and one of their uncles. Inigo struggles to bear the weight of his older brother, his best friend, and he stumbles. His uncle steadies him and it is over.

I follow them, my face wet with tears. People want to touch me, to comfort me. I pull away. I don't want their touch – I can't be comforted, even by those who love me. I need to feel this pain and bear it on my own. It's all I have left of my 11-year-old son – this unendurable agony.

In the car, on the way to the crematorium, Rufus is quiet and hunched in on himself.

'Are you OK?' I ask him.

He avoids my eye. I put my hand on his knee. 'It's OK. You can talk to me,' I say.

'I couldn't cry,' he blurts out. 'Is there something wrong with me?'

'Oh, darling. There's nothing wrong with you. No one says you have to cry. Sometimes it's too painful to cry and it's easier not to. Grief is different for everyone. There's no right or wrong way to grieve. You do what feels right at any one moment and don't worry about anyone else.'

His shoulders relax and I see the burden lift slightly.

The crematorium passes in a blur. It's impersonal and I'm outside myself looking in. I'm a witness to these events, nothing more. My heart is in tatters and I step away from the pain. I touch the basket with my son in one last time.

I whisper, 'I love you, my darling. Always.'

I will myself not to be there and to close down the shutters. I see Rufus, his tears finally set free. Queen's 'Don't Stop Me Now' plays loudly over the sound system. I close my eyes and take myself to the car in my mind. I sit there with Silas beside me. We sing the words at the top of our voices as we have done so many times in the past. He grins at me, mischievous, his brown eyes sparkling. He tucks his warm hand into mine. I feel his touch.

I hear him loud and clear as he roars beside me.

~

We manage to get through the rest of that long day. The sky lightens after the funeral and the sun drives the rainclouds away. It's a beautiful sunset. We, all five of us, are exhausted. Early in the evening we all get into our bed and watch a film. This is the room where I feel closest to

Silas and that feels important. His last moments were spent here, his last breaths hang in the air, somewhere.

The next day dawns. The first day of the rest of our lives. I'm in the kitchen. Ben goes to fetch something from his study. He comes back to the kitchen, his face animated.

'Darling, come quickly,' he says, beckoning me. 'Something amazing!'

My heart skips a beat. It has been a mistake. It has all been some sort of dreadful mistake and Silas is back. I close my mind to the impossible logic. My head says no but my heart, my heart doesn't listen. If only . . . Could it be possible? A miracle?

I run and follow Ben. There in his study, curled up in the used paper basket next to the radiator, is our missing cat.

I close my eyes for a moment as disappointment floods over me. What was I thinking, hoping for a miracle?

'It's a miracle!' says Ben.

I pause. He's right. The cat has been gone six days in miserable weather. The study door has been shut all night, so he must have made his way home sometime on the evening of Silas's funeral before Ben closed up for the night. The poor creature is barely clinging on to life. He is bedraggled and his fur is matted. He's covered in ticks and he's thin, so thin, I realise as I pick him up. He can hardly walk and his back legs collapse under him. How he got home, I'll never know. Somehow he had climbed in the cat flap and dragged his mangled body to the warmest room. He must have heard our voices upstairs but he could go no further. It is a miracle all right, not the one I crave, but a small miracle all the same.

I give him a bit of water and a little food and rush him to the vet. His pelvis is fractured in several places and shunted up his spine. He has obviously been hit by a car and is dehydrated and starving, but somehow he got home in the end.

I head back home, leaving the cat at the vet's to recover.

'It's extraordinary,' says Ben.

I nod. We had both written off the cat but now he is back. Somehow.

'How strange that he should come back yesterday, of all days,' says Ben.

'I know,' I say. We are both thinking the same thing.

'Is it possible?' asks Ben.

I shrug my shoulders. 'I have to believe that Silas had a hand in his return. It's too much of a coincidence.' A thought strikes me.

'Do you remember the day Silas was christened?' I ask Ben.

He nods. 'Of course.'

'Remember my mum went back home after the christening and found her cat dead outside her front door.' This was strange enough, but the weirdest thing of all was the cat had also been called Silas. I'd always loved the name and had named the cat whilst still a teenager, never dreaming that one day I would choose the name for one of my own children.

I shake my head with disbelief. 'So a cat, his namesake, dies on the day Silas was christened and then, on the day of his funeral, another cat comes back to life.'

'It would be nice to think he had a hand in it somewhere,' says Ben. I nod and we're lost in our own thoughts, both of us fully aware that we would trade any number of cats for just one more day with our son.

~

Several good friends ask me how I am sleeping. I tell them sleeping isn't the problem and it is true. I long for my bed every night. I long for the brief period of respite sleep brings. It doesn't bring me rest; I feel permanently exhausted. Keeping feelings at bay is hard work, strenuous and bone-shatteringly tiring. Sleep is not the problem. Awake is the difficulty. If I wake in the early hours, even for a moment, then sleep has gone, chased away by thoughts that cannot be contained. I dread being awake. I fight to stay asleep. I fight to avoid the truth. When I surface, I have a millisecond before the torture begins all over again. I feel like Prometheus, waking every morning whole again, liver intact, only to open my eyes and see the unblinking eye of Zeus's eagle staring at me, daring me to move. Its talons grip the bedcovers, sharp and merciless. Its cry rips though the air. I cower and hold my breath. Perhaps if I pretend I am not here the eagle will go and find a new victim. But it always hovers over me and without warning strikes. I gasp as the pain hits me afresh.

It goes on for the rest of the day.

Relentless, unstoppable, excruciating.

~

Mess followed Silas. The whole family joked that after a meal we always knew which chair was Silas's. There would be crumbs on the floor, smears and stains on the table and splashes of spilt water. He was an unbelievably messy eater.

We have a family tradition that catches out those who put too much food in their mouth. When one of the boys loads his fork too full, or just crams a big bit of cake into his mouth, a chorus of 'Postlethwaite' starts up round the table, and there's no let up until the greedy person says 'Postlethwaite' with their mouth full of food. As a child, I thought every family did this. It wasn't until Ben looked at me in utter confusion the first time I said 'Postlethwaite' to him that I realised it was unique to my family.

Why Postlethwaite? Many years ago, my mother and her five sisters were sitting with my grandparents round the dining-room table, tucking into a succulent Sunday roast. Granny was recalling a conversation with someone that she had met that week but she had trouble remembering the person's name.

'Oh, I don't know,' she eventually gave up. 'It was something like Frobisher or Postlethwaite.' Her tongue got caught around the syllables and she lisped the last name.

There was a moment of silence. Then all six girls started laughing and mercilessly mimicking her. 'Postlethwaite, Postlethwaite,' they sang.

One of my mother's sisters had a mouthful of food and it came shooting out across the table as she joined in. Six girls rolled around the floor in stitches. My grandfather gave up trying to keep order and 'Postlethwaite' forever became synonymous with a mouthful of food.

Try it sometime. It is simply impossible to say 'Postlethwaite' with a mouth jammed full of food without half of said food spraying across the table.

Silas often crammed too much food into his mouth and was constantly caught out with chants of 'Postlethwaite, Postlethwaite' from the rest of the family.

'Pofulway . . .' he spluttered, a few stray crumbs spraying from the corners of his mouth.

'Pofallwait . . .' he tried again. Sauce dribbled down his chin. By now the rest of the table was in hysterics. Silas, goaded on by his brothers, threw caution to the wind and tried a final time. He took a deep breath through his nose and cried, 'Pofulthway.' Food flew across the table in all directions, hitting his laughing brothers in the face and scatter-bombing the table. Silas creased up with giggles and had trouble swallowing the remaining food left in his mouth. He never minded playing the clown and always had the last laugh.

~

'Do you dream of Silas?' I ask Ben, not long after Silas dies.

He nods. 'Occasionally. Not often, but I have done.'

I stare at him, jealous, unsated.

'You don't?'

I shake my head. 'I want to dream about him. I want to dream about him so badly but I never do.' *Why you and not me?* I think. *Why do you get to dream about our boy?* I need those dreams too. I need to find him in my sleep and, just for a few precious minutes, hear his voice or touch him. Just for a few minutes I could have him back, couldn't I? Or am I to be denied this too?

Eventually I dream about Silas. I wake in a cold sweat. This isn't the dream I have been longing for. In my dream, Silas dies a violent death. He falls down the stairs, and although I see him, he's dead before I get to him. Yet again I can do nothing to save him. I relive his death, his face contorted in agony as he lands at the bottom of the stairs. I am haunted by the glimpse of him.

I bury my face in my pillow. It's a new form of torture – so near yet so far.

These dreams continue. They are rare but they hit me hard. Silas is always dying, and usually violently, when I find him. In one dream he has been stabbed repeatedly, I kneel in a pool of his blood as his life ebbs away again. In another he's mangled in the wreckage of a car, his breath gurgling in his chest. In others he lies in a hospital bed once again dying of terminal brain cancer. I never have time with him. I feel the pain in my sleep and am wrenched awake, gasping, my face wet with tears. How many times am I going to be forced to watch my son die?

I long for a simple dream. I am hungry for a smile or a touch or even a word, but my mind denies me.

~

Those first weeks, we devour books on grief.

Shortly after Silas dies, my brother-in-law, William, turns up with a bag full of books. I empty them out, surprised by his thoughtfulness but at the same time shocked by his presumptuousness. Why does he think other people's words might comfort us? What does he know that we don't?

I finger through the first book, *Hannah's Gift* by Maria Housden. It is a book written by a mother whose four-year-old daughter died. I start reading, hoping to make some sense of my raw feelings. The prose is gentle and the focus is on the life of the child instead of her death. The little girl knows she is going to die and accepts it with the unquestioning ability of a small child. I rail against this. It brings to the fore all the guilt I feel about not telling Silas about his imminent death. Did I do something wrong? The book leaves me unfulfilled and questioning my judgement.

Once I start reading, I finish the other books in quick succession. It's not so much comfort that they offer but a distraction. It's as though the glimpses into other people's tragedies offers a brief escape from our own. Some write in beautiful, intense prose like Joan Didion in *The Year of Magical Thinking* and C. S. Lewis in *A Grief Observed*, and I relate to these more. Although neither is about the death of a child, they touch upon elements of grief that I recognise.

C. S. Lewis captures the proximity of grief and fear, which resonates loudly with me. At times my grief overpowers me and these moments are always accompanied by a deep, dark, terrifying fear. It rises from my stomach and clogs my throat. I find it hard to breathe. I struggle not to vomit. My heart starts racing and my legs weaken. I sink to the floor, terrified that I won't be able to withstand the onslaught. I fear that each breaking wave of grief is dragging me further and further from my son, muddying the waters of my memories. The distance between us grows cavernous and dark. It is unbridgeable, and that truly frightens me. The panic bubbles in my chest, no matter how hard I try to fight it. Where is he? Why can't I hold on to him? How can I let him go? I know he would never want to let me go, so how can I just accept this increasing distance, this impossible yawning gap?

Inevitably, by living, we have no choice but to leave the dead behind and this is the most overwhelming thing of all. I would never have abandoned Silas in life, so how can I now abandon him in death? Every living breath drags me kicking and screaming into a future without him, and that frightens me. I don't want to be alive without him. Living with his absence terrifies me. I'm not suicidal, but we have never been apart and I rage that my child has to make this journey, this last journey into the unknown, without me.

Ben reads books too, which is quite a departure for a man who is happiest reading the newspaper or *Decanter* magazine. I think both of us find some reassurance in the knowledge that we are not alone on our journey, that many others have trodden this well-worn path before us and many more will continue to do so. In a strange way, it's this that offers me the most comfort rather than the individual stories of loss. If others can get through it, then so can I.

I am not alone.

Some books I simply stop reading only a few pages in, unable to relate to their premise that the death of Silas is something I will get over and recover from, that I will be able to put behind me in years to come, that my grief will adhere to a strict pattern.

When my father died suddenly more than a decade ago, aged only 58, I was floored. Initially, his death left a gaping hole, but I had small children to deal with and a life to live. Gradually that hole filled in and became noticeably smaller and smaller until now it's merely a puddle. Things did get better. His death became easier to live with. Silas feels very different.

In my trawls of bereavement charities on the Internet, I come across a description that seems to fit how I feel and I use it to illustrate my grief to close friends who want to understand.

'Think of the loss of someone you love as a total eclipse of the sun,' I say.

I scrawl a circle on a piece of paper with a pencil and fill it in. The circle stands out on the white paper, dark and foreboding. 'This is me, this is my life right now. All the light gone. It is all encompassing.' They nod, trying to understand.

I continue. 'This was the same immediately after my dad died but over time the blackness grew smaller and you could see more sun again.' I draw another circle the same size and draw a smaller one inside it. I only shade in the smaller circle, it is surrounded by a wide ring of white.

'I get it,' they say, relief evident in their eyes.

I hold up my hands to stop them. 'With Silas it's different.' I draw another circle, again the same size. I fill it all in black again so that it looks identical to the first one. 'The blackness does not get any smaller over time. It stays the same.' They stare at me.

I draw a very slightly bigger circle outside the one I have just coloured. There is just a thin ring of white paper visible between the edges of the two circles. 'The blackness stays the same. The loss will never go away or get easier, but hopefully over time the light will find a way to grow outside of it. It will always be there, the same size, a Silas-shaped void, but if we're lucky our lives will expand around it.'

They nod in understanding and several of my friends, especially those who have yet to lose anyone close to them, have said it allowed them to picture the devastating impact of our loss, and that they in turn have used the image to help others understand.

Many months later, I ask William what made him bring all those books.

'I am not sure,' he replies. 'I just started buying them some time before Silas died. They were either ones I'd been told about or I'd read about. I did some research.'

'How did you know we would need them?'

'I didn't, but I had spoken to a few people.'

William practices as a psychotherapist, so he understands the power of words. I am touched by his thoughtfulness. I know how close he was to Silas. They spent much time together walking and talking those last few months. The loss is written deep on his face too. 'There was so little I could do to help you both and this was just one small thing I could offer.'

I thank him and I know once again that we aren't the only people to be changed forever by Silas's death.

∼

Sometimes, in the weeks after Silas's death, I find myself stranded in a public place. Not literally but figuratively. I'm surrounded by a sea of people in the supermarket, on the street or once even at Olympia Exhibition Centre in London. People brush past me going about their everyday business, wrapped up in their own lives. I stand rooted, unable to move. Why am I here? I have no place here. My son is dead. Can they not see? Why can people not see my grief? To me it is so tangible, so real

193

and raw and all-encompassing that it's incomprehensible to me that others cannot feel it, see it, taste it, hear it. Why do they not recognise it?

'Here I am,' I want to shout. 'Look at me if you dare. My son is dead. Stop what you're doing. Can you not see? Stop chatting on the phone and laughing with your friends. Feel my pain. Share it with me.' I want to hold a placard above my head saying 'Grieving Mother' so I am no longer invisible in this hectic world.

I say nothing. A few people give me odd looks and a slightly wider berth.

I get it. I suddenly understand why Queen Victoria wore black for decades after Prince Albert died. Part of me wants everyone to know the suffering I'm going through. I want them to know without me having to tell them. I want them to understand. I feel so alone and anonymous. I realise that some of the old mourning traditions and rituals make sense – wearing mourning clothes for a year and wearing jewellery containing locks of hair.

In this modern day we have lost touch with the grieving process. We have the luxury of living in a First World country where the death of a child is tragic and rare, and where life is not an everyday battle for survival. People aren't exposed to death as they were only a century or so ago. They don't want to see the bereaved and be reminded of the hurt that might one day be theirs.

It hasn't always been like this. There's a tombstone in our local church, where Silas was christened and where we held his funeral, which chronicles the death over a decade in the mid-19th century of 12 children in a single family – the Walker family. Eleanor, George, Ezekiel, Amos, Jesse and Emmer all died in infancy, but James died at seven, Ellen at nine, Sarah at 10, Thomas at 11, John at 12 and Mary at 13. Five of the older children died in the space of just two weeks in 1847, most likely of a smallpox or scarlet fever outbreak. The two parents, Ann and John, have the next door gravestone. They died a year apart in 1874. How did they live with their grief for nearly 30 years? How did it not tear them apart limb from limb? Perhaps they had other family members and friends that held them together. I sense they never came to terms with their staggering loss, as on their tombstone are the words 'Thy will be done'.

Was it any easier to bear the death of a child in those days? Were parents better then than we are now at keeping their offspring at arm's length? I don't think it can have been easier emotionally for the parents, but it was commonplace and expected for people to lose a child so the community did not shy away from death.

Victorian women were expected to wear mourning clothes for a year following the death of their child but for two years following the death of their husband. This seems the wrong way round, but it indicates the high rate of child mortality in those days. For Ben and me the eventual death of each other will be far easier to bear than the death of Silas. For my mother, so close to my boys, Silas's death has been worse, much worse, than the death of my father a decade ago.

Death has always been part of life, but in our search for immortality and longevity, and in this age of medical miracles, we have forgotten how to approach death and how to help those in the jaws of grief. Death is not an option – it is not a box you can choose not to tick. We are all going to die and yet, and yet . . . grief is an embarrassment, just as C. S. Lewis pointed out in *A Grief Observed*. Grief is raw and primal and, for those that have not been there, often easier to ignore than to confront. Brush it under the carpet; turn your back; lock it behind closed doors and keep a stiff upper lip. However, those of us deep in its throes would much rather wail and gnash our teeth or tear our hair out and have friends and neighbours do the same.

Grief is unpredictable. I see that now. I remember when I was in labour with my first son. The labour was long and drawn out   Oscar was not in the right position. During one contraction, Ben rubbed my back in a circular motion. The movement felt good and helped me relax. The following contraction, Ben, thinking he was onto a good thing, did the same. This time, though, I couldn't bear him to touch me there. It was as though he was sticking hot pins into my kidneys.

'Get off me,' I screamed at him.

He stepped back, hands raised in submission. 'I thought you liked it. You said it felt good,' he blustered.

'I did like it,' I hissed through gritted teeth, the waves of the contraction rolling over me. 'But I don't anymore!'

Grief is similar: it follows no predictable pattern. One day, a comment is OK or you can talk about how you are feeling, and the next everyone appears to say the wrong thing. What chance have friends got of getting it right all the time? None. None at all. But the most important thing is that they keep trying.

Ben and I feel most let down by those close friends who have left us alone: no phone calls, no e-mails, no contact. We know it's not easy and that the longer they say nothing the harder it becomes, but we find it difficult to make allowances. Luckily, we have many friends who call like clockwork, send bedtime texts, write long e-mails, arrange dog walks or drop by unannounced. They don't always get it right either, but they never stop trying and their love and support buoys us up.

~

One moment of excruciating pain stands out above all others. Not much more than a week or so after the funeral, Rufus tells me that he has made it through to the final of his school's annual poetry competition. I'm surprised; I've no recollection of Rufus even learning a poem.

'That's great. Well done, you,' I say.

'Will you come and watch me?' he asks.

My heart sinks. To watch him means placing myself in a hall full of people, parents and teachers. Most of whom I've not seen or spoken to since Silas died. I don't want to see anyone.

'Please . . .' he begs.

I know how important this is to him. Rufus isn't a natural public speaker. He's not one to thrust himself into the limelight. He lacks confidence. It will cost him to get up on that stage and recite his poem and I can't let him face this challenge on his own, especially as he's now at that school alone. He has never been alone at any school. Sandwiched between two brothers, 18 months younger than one and 17 months older than the next, they have always been by his side. Oscar, though, is now at a different school and Inigo is still at his primary school. With Silas gone, Rufus is suddenly alone for the first time in his life.

He needs me as much as I need Silas, and I can't let him down.

'OK,' I say with a heavy heart. 'I'll come.'

The night in question draws closer. 'You don't have to go,' says Ben, recognising my reluctance. 'Rufus will understand.'

'I know he will but that's exactly why I have to go. I have to show him that he matters just as much.'

Ben nods. He knows it's true.

I arrive at the school. It's dark. I linger in the shadows, steeling myself. I time my arrival late so that I don't have to sit around too long before the recitals start. I stand for a moment outside the double doors to the hall. I can hear the gentle murmur of voices. I take a deep breath and walk through the opening.

Small groups of people turn to look at me. They fall silent as I pass – teachers and parents alike. They part like the Red Sea to let me through. I lift my jaw and square my shoulders. I picture Silas walking beside me, exuberantly telling me about his day, and draw strength from the image. My eyes scan the room. Is there someone here who can rescue me? As I catch people's eyes they look away, dropping their gaze.

I am alone.

I blink, fighting the sudden desire to turn around and run. I think I might burst into tears. What will they all do then? My heart is thumping in my chest. The panic rises in my throat. I have to get out of here. I spot Rufus sitting with his friends. Seeing him gives me strength. I can do this for Rufus, I repeat in my head. I can do this for him. He needs me.

I see an empty seat near the back and move to sit down. I slide into the row. All around me are parents and grandparents who have come to see their offspring perform. I see parents with children in Silas's class. They glance at me and I see the pity in their eyes, but all I can think of is why haven't they written to us. All the parents were told about Silas's death. A couple of weeks was surely enough time to pen a few words for a small boy who spent happy times with their child. Was it that hard for them to put pen to paper or was his death that insignificant in their lives? These thoughts whirr around my head. I know my thoughts are irrational and unfair, but I have no control over them. My stomach churns. I want to leave but the hall is filling up. A hand touches me on my shoulder. Behind me sits a friend, someone who understands better than others. She has stopped regularly at our house for coffee over the last few months and has brought gifts of stews and casseroles. She even turned up on the last day Silas was up and about. She squeezes my shoulder and gives me a hug and I smile at her, grateful for her support.

The rest of the school file into the hall, the children are boisterous and laughing. They sit in the rows in front of me. They nudge one another and turn and look at me. They look quickly away and whisper to each other. I'm in a fishbowl. I have no escape.

The poetry competition begins. There is an external adjudicator who rings a bell before each performer.

Ting.

The noise echoes inside my head. The contestants drone on. I can barely watch the children from Silas's year. Silas made it through to the finals every year; once he had even won with the marvellous 'Pedro the Brave'. He should be up on the stage right now. The pain swallows me. My breathing is ragged. I start to recite his winning poem inside my head. I can still remember it now and the concentrated effort it requires to recall the words calms me.

Finally, Rufus climbs onto the stage. Nervousness emanates from his every pore. He shifts his weight from foot to foot. I feel for him but I also know that in a few weeks he'll need to do this again, a different poem in front of a much bigger audience at the memorial service we are arranging for Silas. He needs to show me he has the strength.

'"The Charge of the Light Brigade" by Alfred Lord Tennyson,' he says.

The words slip over my head. I watch my son. He finds his rhythm and I see him relax. He talks of death and glory, and I know that he has seen death. He is one of the few people in this room that knows there's nothing glorious about a life ending. Can I read a shadow of this in his face? Will others see it?

He finishes. I clap, proud of my son, but glad that the evening is nearly over.

The adjudicator sums up and then, much to my surprise, announces Rufus as the overall winner. There is applause. I groan inwardly. I won't be able to slip away now. Chairs scrape and voices rise. I stand up, uncertain how to proceed.

A member of staff comes up to me.

'Well done, Rufus,' he says. 'You must be very proud of him.'

I stare at the man. These are the first words he has spoken to me since my 11-year-old son died. He's one of Silas's teachers. Where are his words of condolence?

'He's a clever boy,' he continues.

I nod, unable to speak, afraid of what I might say.

He makes his excuses and moves on. I hold the back of the chair for support. Others start to come up to me – teachers and parents alike. All these people had nothing to say to me when I arrived, but now their faces are split by grins. I can almost touch their relief. It is palpable.

'Rufus did well, didn't he?'

'Well done, Rufus.'

'He deserved it; he read really well.'

'Good choice of poem.'

'You must be so proud of him!'

I struggle to breathe. My hands are cold and icy. I keep my eyes wide and try not to blink, afraid the tears will fall.

I murmur words of thanks and they leave, patting themselves on the back for being brave enough to speak with me. I spend some time with Rufus, who is staying the night at school. I hug him for a long time.

I get back in the car. I start the engine and sit cocooned in the dark. The tears fall from my eyes. I scream. I don't care who might hear. Then do the only thing I can. I call Ben.

He picks up immediately. 'How was it?'

I choke. I am wracked by sobs. I struggle to speak. 'It's . . . it's . . . it's as though he never existed,' I say.

'How do you mean?'

'No one said anything about Silas. No one. Not one person in that room mentioned our son.'

'It's hard for them,' says Ben.

'I know, but what do they think it is for me? I haven't seen any of them since he died!' I am distraught. My nose is running. 'He's only been dead a couple of weeks and all of them just negated his entire existence.'

'People don't know what to say . . .'

'I know but they could just say, "I'm really sorry about Silas but you must feel very proud of Rufus." Anything. Anything would be better than nothing.' I sniff and wipe the tears from my cheek.

'They don't want to upset you.'

'Look at me now,' I shout. 'The worst thing of all is to pretend nothing has happened. That life is carrying on as normal.'

'Everyone in that room was thinking about Silas,' says Ben, his voice quiet. 'In fact, he was probably the only thing they were thinking about!'

'I'm sorry if my grief is an inconvenience, if it makes them feel uncomfortable, but the least they could do is acknowledge Silas's existence. Don't make it harder for me than it already is.'

'I know,' says Ben. 'They are wrong and they would all be devastated to hear how much they have upset you.'

My tears turn to anger. 'It's just like that time I took Silas to watch Rufus play football after his second brain surgery. It was as though he was invisible. The two teachers at the match were incapable of talking to him. All they had to say was, "Hey, good to see you, Silas, sorry you haven't been well. We look forward to seeing you back at school!" But instead they ignored him and studiously avoided looking at him. He asked me what was wrong with them and wasn't it weird that they almost pretended he didn't exist.'

I think back to that day, 16 months earlier, and how Silas had turned it into a game. He had tried to force the two teachers into noticing him and talking to him. He kept putting himself in their line of sight or sidling next to them, but neither of them acknowledged him because they didn't know what to say. They chose to say nothing and my 10-year-old son realised that his illness made adults uncomfortable.

'Come home,' Ben says. 'Don't pass judgement. I know it's hard but we can't let other people's behaviour upset us. They don't mean to hurt us.'

'But they do upset me,' I whisper. 'They do!'

'I know.'

'I just don't want to pretend that he never existed just to make it easier for everyone else! I owe him more than that. We owe him.'

Ben sighs. 'I know we do. Just please come home and drive safely.'

I leave the school and drive. My eyes blur with tears and the head-lights of other cars bleed across my vision. I turn the radio on to distract me. The song 'Happy' by Pharrell Williams comes on. Silas liked the song, but it fills me with despair because I'm not 'so happy' and I'm not sure if I will ever be again. I can't bear to listen to it and I switch the radio off. I bang my closed fist on the steering wheel and try to focus on the road.

~

Ben and I throw ourselves into organising the memorial service. We want it to be special, more a celebration for a boy who loved life and held nothing back than a maudlin service of remembrance.

It's on a par with organising our wedding or a big 40th birthday bash, except without any of the joy. We know there are many children and families and friends who'll want to come, and we don't want to exclude anyone. But how are we to cater for the huge numbers we expect? It's rare our disparate collection of friends assembles in one place these days. I can't help feeling that for many it will be a chance to catch up with old friends and part of me resents this. I know they will be sad and wish they hadn't had to meet like this, but they'll still have a good old get-together and knock back the drinks. I wish that I could be the one standing on the outside looking in. I try and squash these feelings inside me, trample them underfoot, but I don't have the energy and they weigh heavy on my shoulders.

Our friends are generous: they give us help with the venue and the service design, they volunteer to make the floral decorations or sing. One good friend, Stevie, can't fly over from LA but calls in favours and begs time off a recording studio and records his own version of Charlie Chaplin's 'Smile' to be played at the beginning of the service. Others, including several parents of children at Silas's school, agree to play a set of Silas's favourite songs at the party afterwards. We are touched by their support and we start to feel less alone.

The themes of the service follow the words we chose to describe Silas on the wristbands.

Smile . . . Imagine . . . Love . . . Achieve . . . Sing

It gives us a structure to work around and helps us to build his essence into the day.

Ben decides that he will do the eulogy. I know that this is a tough decision but he feels that no one else will do justice to Silas. He writes his speech over several days.

No father should ever have to sum up the life of their 11-year-old. A life barely begun. I can see the strain it puts him under in the sag of his shoulders and the bags under his eyes.

He reads it to me. We are sitting outside in the damp January air. We both have tears streaming down our faces. It's an honest, heartbreaking tribute to his son and it is so filled with love. Love cascades from his words. I'm drowning in a sea of love. The speech is not maudlin or sentimental or self-pitying. It's a glorious tribute to our boy – rich in the nuances of his character and tales of his madness. I know without doubt that everyone who enters the church that day will leave knowing Silas as intimately as his closest friends. Ben has done the impossible. He has shared Silas, heart and soul, in 10 short minutes.

I know that Ben will struggle to retain his composure on the day and we put an emergency plan into action if he can't finish the words. He visits the doctor who prescribes him some beta blockers. Ben has spent a lifetime speaking in front of audiences and playing a part, but we both know that this'll be the hardest part he ever has to play. I make him a promise. I won't cry during the service until after his eulogy. I'll keep my agony at bay so that he will be able to draw from my strength as I draw from his.

∼

Ben was a hands-on parent from the start. He never shied away from nappy-changing duties and would roar with laughter as yet another one of his sons peed all over him on the changing mat.

He was an actor when we met and his work came in dribs and drabs. We courted in the wilds of Wales on the set of a film called *Prince Valiant*. Idyllic memories ensconced in soft, warm hotel robes in places with strange-sounding names that rolled musically off the tongue.

After Oscar was born, we rented out our flat in London and took off to New Zealand for a couple of years so that he could film a TV series there. Long tramps with a baby in a backpack cemented our love for the outdoors. We debated about staying but family eventually lured us back to the UK.

Acting gave Ben freedom to spend days lazing in the sun with his growing boys, rousting on the grass and playing endless games of tickle monster. He was the father every small boy dreams of having.

He played loud games of football or cricket in the garden. He invented new games like 'Rugball', a mix between football and rugby, which involved two opposing sides kicking rugby balls into football goals. Points were scored from balls that were caught or found the back of the net, but points could also be given to the opposing team by dropped catches. I was inevitably roped in to make up the numbers and calculate the scores.

Ben built treehouses that defied all rules of gravity. He took the boys for white-knuckle rides in a trailer behind the tractor mower. He would throw them onto sofas, beds, anything with a modicum of cushioning. They screamed in excitement and he just had fun.

In truth, I didn't have four small boys. I had five – albeit one a little bigger than the rest.

Ben had no respect for health and safety and I was forever the small voice of reason. One holiday, we were staying in a cabin in the Blue Ridge Mountains in North Carolina, USA. We had been swimming in the New River daily, a short walk through the woods. We spent a whole wonderful day kayaking a 20km stretch, just the six of us. I remember as a child having to coax and cajole my father into anything wet, even a swimming pool. Ben was the exact opposite – always the first in, throwing himself under the water, no matter how cold. The next two days of our holiday, the heavens opened and rain pattered onto the roof of the cabin. We snuggled up watching videos and playing games, but as soon as the sun found a break in the clouds Ben suggested a swim. The four boys leapt up and raced to put their trunks on. We heard the river as soon as we left the cabin. It roared through the woods, its waters swelled by the rains. It was in spate and the water level had risen over five feet in two days.

'You can't swim in that,' I said aghast, watching branches roll through the muddy water. 'The boys will get swept away.'

Ben thought for a moment.

'I've got an idea,' he said. He disappeared back in the direction of the cabin.

'Aw c'mon, Mummy,' said Silas. 'You always ruin the fun.'

'There is no way any of you are swimming in that,' I said.

Ben reappeared with a thick coil of rope in his arms. He set about tying one end to a tree.

'What are you doing?' I asked.

'We'll tie the rope around them and haul them back in,' he said. 'That way no one will get swept away.'

'You're crazy.'

'I'll test it out first.'

'You are not tying my kids to the end of some moth-eaten rope and letting them swim in a flooded river. No way!' I crossed my arms over my chest and squared my shoulders. I was ready for battle.

He looped the rope around his chest, tying a knot. 'It'll be all right, you'll see.' He waded out into the river. The current sucked at his legs. He leant into it and slowly made ground. When he got deep enough, he let the river take him. Within seconds, he was swept out of view. The rope went taut. I grabbed it and started hauling it in.

When he reached the bank and climbed back out, his grin split his face in two. 'That was great,' he whooped.

'Can we do it? Can we do it?' the boys all chorused, their eyes alight with excitement.

I shook my head.

'It's fine,' Ben said. 'You worry too much. The boys will be fine. Watch.' He beckoned Oscar over and started tying the rope around his chest.

I stepped forward. 'No!'

'Please, Mum. Please, Mum.' Oscar's green eyes beseeched me.

I tutted and blew my cheeks out, my resolve weakening, and that was all they needed.

The next half hour was one of the hardest in my life but Ben was right. The boys were fine and they loved every minute of it. They jumped in the water and the current ripped them away. Then they were hauled back in and did it again and again. My heart stayed in my throat and I know that we were lucky – the knot on the rope could have slipped undone; they could have become tangled in underwater debris – any one of a number of tragedies could have occurred, but it didn't and they still talk about that afternoon with wonder and excitement.

That is Ben; fun, inventive and exciting, as all fathers should be. I'm often a foil to his exuberance, a brake on his excess. His lack of a desk job and a daily commute meant he spent more time with his boys than most fathers do in a lifetime.

Eventually, he stopped acting and set up a production company of his own, but he still works from home most of the time and is just as good at soothing fevered dreams and cobbling together a meal as me.

~

A few days before the memorial service, the phone rings. It's a local reporter.

'I've read your blog,' she starts.

'What?'

'The blog. It's great!'

'But it's private. How did you get hold of the web address?'

'Oh, let's not worry about that. I want to write about Silas for the *Faversham Times*. Can I ask you some questions?'

I don't know how to respond.

We need time to think. I don't want the blog laid bare for all and sundry. I don't want people to ogle over our tragedy with their morning cup of coffee or read about it on Twitter. I know tragedies sell newspapers, but not mine!

'Can you give us some time?' I ask. 'Can we just get the memorial service out of the way?'

'Er, sure. I'll call you in a week.'

I'm upset. The blog address cannot be searched for via any search engine. The privacy settings are high. The only way the reporter could have got hold of it is via a friend, someone who we had given the address to ourselves. I feel betrayed. My father spent a lot of time in the public eye. I know not only how persistent reporters can be, but also how they can twist your words and tread roughshod over people's feelings.

'How could someone do that to us?' I ask Ben.

~

The day of the service arrives. It's Ben's birthday. This isn't an oversight on our part: none of us feel like celebrating birthdays anymore. Family and friends descend on the house. It's full of noise. Everyone is dressed in blue and pink in honour of Silas.

The church fills up. It's not our small village church. It's a big church in our local town. Two years ago I sat here for the funeral of a young man I played tennis with. He was 23 and his death was tragic. Now I'm here for a service for my 11-year-old son. I pinch my thigh to make sure it is real. I feel the sharp pain. There's seating for 500 but we still end up with people standing. Our boys and their cousins act as ushers. They relish the involvement and I know how much Silas would like to be standing with them. They give everyone a Ferrero Rocher to be eaten during the service. The church bells ring out as we take our seats. I close my eyes and I see Silas hanging on the bell rope in our little church near the house, ringing the single bell, his face split by an enormous grin and I cannot help myself, I smile.

The piano crackles over the speakers and Stevie's voice echoes through the church, singing 'Smile', his voice rich and moving.

Ben sits next to me in the pew. The boys are on the far side of him. We have positioned ourselves so that a pillar is between us and most of Silas's school friends. I have some privacy if I need it, but I stiffen myself; I've made Ben a promise.

Our three boys rise and walk to the centre of the church. They are joined by one of their male cousins. Four boys stand still, a hole is momentarily filled and my heart skips a beat. There will never be four again. They read a poem, written by a friend, entitled 'Imagine'. It's full of magic and eagles and pixies and toadstools oozing with snails. It's right up Silas's street, crammed with wonder and limitless possibility. Their voices ring clear and true, and even Inigo, only nine, doesn't falter.

I shiver. The church is cold, so cold. I pull my coat around me but the icy air slithers under my clothes. I clench my jaw to stop my teeth from chattering.

Silas's friend Harry reads a passage about love. His voice wavers and I know that Silas is the only person he would do this for. His courage is immense. A friend's two sons sing Bob Dylan's 'Forever Young'. The younger boy is a chorister in Canterbury Cathedral and his voice is pure and powerful. The congregation is stunned into silence. I focus on the stained glass window in front of me. I will not break my promise to Ben.

Freddie, a loyal and true friend to Silas, says a few words that he has written, a taste of their friendship and their shared laughter. Both him and Harry have lost their best friend and I know they will carry him in their hearts forever. This thought reassures me that Silas will live on in others.

Ben says his words.

'What can I tell you about Silas that you don't already know . . .' he starts. 'Some people have a secret side to themselves that many don't glimpse and some folk shelter the softer sides of themselves out of harm's way – but not Silas.' His voice cracks and he takes a deep breath. 'What you see is what you get with Silas. He faced outwards towards life, wore his heart on his sleeve and looked at all life threw at him and he threw at life, square in the eye. Seemingly unstoppable . . .'

I know that he has a picture of Silas next to him on the stand. Hidden from view, Silas gives him strength. I see him look at it and touch it when his resolve wobbles. People laugh and cry during his speech. He has judged its content with perfection. I will him through it, sending him waves of strength. He catches my eye. I smile. Inigo sneaks his hand into mine. I squeeze it tight.

Then it's over. Ben is back beside me and the school choir gets up and files to the front. I see Silas's favourite girls, all of them are there, wearing pink headbands and scarves. My resolve falters. Ben is done. I kept my promise to him. The tears start down my cheeks. Their voices ring out across the church and the words to 'Sing' by Gary Barlow fill the nave. Silas loved this song. It was yet another he would sing loudly and always just slightly out of tune. The girls do him proud.

I have no real recollection of the party after the service. There are too many faces, blurring in and out of focus. I greet and I talk but I remember nothing of to whom or what about. All I want to do is stand

and look at the video montage Ben has put together of Silas. It's projected onto the back wall of the venue and he is so real, his broad smile and his hazel eyes. I feel him all around me. There are children milling everywhere. I have a moment when I catch a glimpse of the back of a familiar head. I draw in a sharp breath, I swear that it's Silas and I push through the crowd. My heart pounds. I know it's madness but my heart refuses to listen to my brain. I have to know for certain. Someone puts a hand on my arm, they want to offer their condolences. I brush them off. I scan the mob of people. I spot him. The child turns and I see it is a friend of Rufus.

Silas isn't here. Of course he's not here!

The music starts. James, the son of a friend, has written a song for Silas. He's autistic and he did this off his own bat, without prompting. His mother is amazed as he does not deal in feelings and yet the song is full of emotion. He sings it in front of everyone.

> *Everyone look at the sky.*
> *Right above us in the sky.*
> *Do you see the star?*
> *It wasn't there before.*
> *Can you see the star?*
> *It wasn't there before.*
>
> *As it shines above us,*
> *I can't express the sadness,*
> *For the loss of you.*
>
> *I saw the seasons change.*
> *I saw you slip away.*
> *Do you see the star?*
> *It wasn't there before.*
> *Can you see the star?*
> *It wasn't there before.*

As it shines above us,
I can't express the sadness,
For the loss of you.

As I look up in the sky.
I see your star shining so bright.
I miss you.
Everybody sends their love.
We all miss you.
Everybody sends their love.

It is poignant and packed with loss and love. I look around and see faces wet with tears. I am detached. The band starts. Everyone is having a good time. Children are dancing. It's surreal – all these people having fun in front of me. I know this is what we want. This is how we want Silas's friends to remember this day. Will I ever be able to remember how to have fun? I think about how much Silas loved having fun. He would never pass up such an opportunity. The band play 'Little Lion Man' and I shout the chorus out for Silas, swear words and all. It is what he would be doing, and in his absence I feel an overwhelming need to do it for him, to draw him close. The room pulsates with energy; all around me kids are yelling, their faces bright and their eyes sparkling under the flashing lights.

The band close with '500 miles'. Ben and I stand close. I slip my hand into his. The crowd is jumping. Arms ringed with blue SILAS bands are raised in the air. They will remember this night.

In the car later, on the way home, Inigo is buzzing.

'That was one of the best nights of my life!' he says. He realises what he has said and is quiet for a moment. 'Obviously, I wish Silas was there . . .' he starts.

'It's OK,' I say. 'I'm glad you had fun. We wanted everyone to have fun. That's the best way to remember Silas. You don't have to feel bad about it.'

I gaze out of the window. It is a clear night and the stars are bright. The moon casts a glow across the fields. 'Today was for you, Splodge,' I whisper. 'I hope you had fun too.'

~

Silas didn't only love to sing. He loved to dance. He wanted to learn how to waltz, how to do the foxtrot, how to jive. The Dashing White Sergeant could have been written for him. What could be better than stomping feet, twirling girls around and generally making a fool of yourself? Burns Night at school was a highlight for Silas and he was the first to volunteer to learn the next dance.

I have video footage of Silas dancing robot style round the kitchen. His movements are jerky and automated. His expression blank. He folds in half and hangs suspended at the waist as though his batteries have run low. Then he twists upright. His eyes wide and staring. His arms bend and then straighten and only then do I realise his hands and lower part of his arms are encased in blue rubber. He looks like a surgeon on the cusp of an operation, hands slipped into surgical gloves. It's unnerving until I realise he's wearing an old pair of blue washing up gloves. I laugh and shake my head at his strangeness.

Silas used to do a weird chicken dance sometimes just before bedtime. He'd stick his neck backward and forward, lift his feet up high, picking his way carefully over the carpet. His arms were bent and held in close to his chest, his hands near his chin, more T. rex than chicken. He would strut across the room to an invisible tune in his head. His lips would turn up at the corners as he struggled to keep a straight face. Then, just as suddenly as he began, his arms would drop, he'd relax and hop under the covers in one swift movement. He'd catch my gaze and see my smile. His eyes would twinkle and his mouth twitch.

'What you lookin' at me for?' he'd say, and a grin would stretch across his face.

~

The day after the service, we all troop out into the garden. Ben carries a large axe over his shoulder. The blade is sharpened and glistens in the weak winter sun. We gather in front of a large horse chestnut tree. The light streams through the bare branches and dapples the fallen leaves on the ground. An earthy, damp smell seeps upward. This tree is our guardian of the dead. Under its spreading limbs we have buried many of our pets: cats, guinea pigs and even a fish or two. Ben has fashioned headstones and plaques from tiles and wood and even bits of concrete. I can read the names: Quncy, Cato, Bella, Finn, Alfie and Jonesy. Each name triggers a flash of memory of soft fur or a snuffling nose.

We stand in a small group in front of the tree – Ben, me and the boys. With us are Ben's brother, William, and his sister, Sam, as well as her husband and their two children. Rooks caw above our heads, warning us that we are in their territory. They will soon start their annual nest-building on the tall sycamore tree behind us.

'Each of us is going to make a cut in this tree,' says Ben.

Ben hands the axe to Oscar. Oscar spreads his feet and balances his weight and then swings the axe. The blade thuds into the trunk of the tree, leaving a narrow cut in the thick bark. The other children follow suit trying to hit the same spot. Inigo and his cousin Gus have difficulty hefting the heavy axe but they leave their mark. We each have a turn and the cut gradually widens until a section of dark bark peels away. I run my fingers over the wound. The tree weeps, my fingers are moist with sap. Its pain mirrors my own.

Ben lays his hand on the rough trunk. He turns and faces us and the children watch him expectantly. 'The wound on this tree symbolises the pain that we are all feeling without Silas. I read somewhere that it was a custom of the Cree Indians in North America to select a tree to help them mourn. They stripped away the bark and would return to the tree over time to see the wound heal. As the wound in the tree healed slowly so the wound in their heart would eventually heal. It gave them a visual representation of their grief.'

212

There is silence as we stare at the weeping gash, each lost in our own thoughts.

'Can we go now?' says Inigo, breaking the moment, drawn away by the lure of playing with his cousin and unwilling to waste any more time staring at a tree trunk.

He disappears and their laughter echoes across the garden. Ben puts his arm round me and smiles ruefully.

'I like it,' I say. 'It's a nice idea.'

He squeezes my shoulder and we turn and head back indoors.

~

Everyone leaves and we are on our own. The days after the service are long and difficult for Ben and me. Our focus is gone. Planning the service gave us purpose and kept us anchored. Now the rest of our lives stretch endlessly in front of us. We are adrift without a compass in the sea of eternity. Other people have closure and now they can move on, but it's not so easy for us. Somehow we have to pick ourselves up and find a new way to live.

I start by clearing out Silas's room. There's not much of him here but there are bits and pieces: some loom bands, some dog-eared Match Attax cards, a couple of notebooks with a few scribbles in. I turn every page looking for a snippet of writing that I can be certain is his. So little. I pick up the last book in *The Hunger Games* trilogy. We never finished it, he and I, and now I know I never will. I sniff the pages, breathing in deep, hoping to find a trace of him but I find just the crisp, memory-evoking smell of paper and ink.

I start to empty his drawers. I sit on the floor, his clothes spread around me. Each item transports me to a different location, a different time, a different memory. The striped blue, grey and brown T-shirt takes me straight to a pebble-strewn beach in Wales. Silas turns to me, his mouth smeared with chocolate ice cream. He purses his lips and blows me a kiss. The Union Jack T-shirt he wore when we went up to Wembley to watch the Olympic football, our last outing together before BOB arrived. The reindeer slipper socks that kept his feet warm and that nurses always commented on.

I take my time, savouring the memories until the pain is too much and I bundle the clothes into piles. A pile of those that hold too many memories I throw out. I don't recycle them to a charity shop. I couldn't bear it if I was to see a stranger wearing his clothes. They go in the bin. A pile that I put aside for Inigo – one day he might find it comforting to wear his brother's clothes. A few find their way into Rufus's cupboard as Silas and he are of a similar size. I hold up the teddy bear onesie that Silas made me buy only a few short months ago. I can see him so clearly messing around with Inigo in the kitchen, both in their onsesies, both soft and cuddly. I bury my face in my hands. I can't believe that he's not here. Sometimes it hits me so hard. I curl the onesie up into a ball and cling to it. I lie there on the carpet and give in. The tears are unstoppable. It's as though a dam has burst. I draw my knees up to my chest. I howl but I am soundless. The sound is trapped somewhere deep inside me, clawing its way to the surface. The pain is physical: so intense, so real, I think I might be dying. I cannot survive this agony. I'm being ripped in half. Is this what death felt like to Silas? No one can survive this. It is animal. I want to disappear into myself, keep folding in and in until there is nothing left, until I am no more. I stop fighting the pain and give in to it. I cry until I am empty.

'I'm sorry,' I say, over and over. 'I'm sorry that I couldn't save you. I'm sorry that I didn't tell you.'

I beg forgiveness from my dead son and the tears flow all around me. I am misery. I never knew it was possible to be this consumed with pain. I'm drained, exhausted and depleted. I can cry no more. Strangely, this is a release. My sobs recede and I find I can pick myself up and carry on. The outburst gives me new strength, strength to pack away my emotions again and carry on until the next time.

~

Four days after we say our public goodbye to our son, a friend of mine from university commits suicide. He hangs himself. Friends knew he was depressed and struggling, but nobody saw this coming. Do they ever?

I haven't seen him much over the last few years, and wasn't close to him, but his death still leaves me reeling.

I can't believe that anyone could willingly put their family through the pain that we're navigating. I'm angry at my mate. Here he was, healthy and alive. He chose to take his life, throwing it away for nothing when I had been fighting tooth and nail for every extra day for my son. My anger is irrational, but I'm furious at the sheer wanton waste. Didn't he know how precious life is? I can't reconcile myself to the situation.

I know that he must have had his reasons. I also know that depression is a horrible illness. I know all this but I find it hard to forgive him.

I spend the next two weeks agonising over whether to go to his funeral or not. Ben is reluctant to let me go. The truth is, I'm in no fit state to attend. I'll be exposing myself in public at my most raw. I'll be facing people I haven't seen for years – some who will know about Silas's death and some who won't. I don't want to see all these people that'll remind me of the happy life I once had. I remember the poetry competition. It'll be worse. I don't want to catch up with old friends and see the pity in their eyes. It's a recipe for disaster.

In the end I go. The night before the service, I dream about my friend. I wake up knowing that I have to go to his funeral. I'll never understand why he has done what he has but I need to forgive him and I need to say goodbye.

I time the event with military precision. I arrive late and the London church is already full. I slide into a pew. The smell of incense is strong. People turn and look at me. I recognise many faces from the past and there are whispers and nudges. I see Bumble, Silas's godmother. She gives me a smile. She knows how hard this is for me. In fact, all my children have at least one godparent in the congregation. I'm amongst many friends, but as I look round the church I see faces of people who didn't make Silas's service for one reason or another and yet here they all are. A sharp stab of resentment flicks through me. They've dropped everything to make this funeral. I take a deep breath; I know I'm being unfair but still the knowledge sits heavy inside me.

The congregation stands and the coffin is carried into the church. My legs buckle at the sight of it and I'm thrown right back into a small countryside church. It was a mistake to come. Ben was right. It's too soon. I try to take slow, deep breaths. My heart is pounding. I look down and focus on the hassock by my feet. I follow the stiches with my eyes, picking out the individual colours: red, blue, yellow. I try and empty my head. I banish thoughts of Silas.

Somehow I get through the service, but the words are a blur. I say goodbye to my friend, and I feel the weight of his death lift. 'Please look after Silas,' I whisper.

As soon as it's over, I tuck my head down and make a break for the exit. I push past people, girlfriends, old boyfriends. I don't want to stop and talk. I don't want to wonder why that person hasn't bothered to write to us. I worry that the floodgates will open and that's not fair to his grieving family. Today is for him, it isn't about me. I have done what I needed to. I head home.

~

The local newspaper prints a double page spread about Silas, but the reporter is sensitive to our wishes and she agrees not to publish the link to the blog. The strapline is not about his death but about his life.

Our beautiful son Silas touched so many lives.

We are grateful.

Shortly afterwards, a friend turns up for coffee and confesses to leaking the information about the blog. It was an accident, clearly a mistake, and she has been beating herself up about it. I hug her, pleased no one let us down deliberately.

~

When Ben rings my mobile, the ring tone is Silas's voice. He just says, 'Daddy, Daddy, Daddy, Daddy.' It gives me a shock the first few times after Silas dies. It doesn't really sound like Silas, but I know it's him. It upsets me but I can't bring myself to change it. Silas recorded it for me months ago and to remove it somehow feels like a betrayal of him. So I leave it and, strangely, over time I come to savour it.

Silas messed about with my phone often. Somewhere in my settings he has referred to me as beautiful Mummy and just occasionally this pops up in headings. It catches me by surprise, always. It's like a kiss from him floating past me in the air.

One day, a few weeks after he dies, I'm in the car and I use the voice memo app to record a message. When I play the message back later, I see there are several others already recorded and stored in the phone. The dates indicate they were recorded 10 months earlier. I frown. I have no recollection of these.

I press play on the first one. It's Silas singing 'How Much is that Doggy in the Window'. I catch my breath. How good it is to hear his voice. In that instant, I can picture him clearly, wandering around the kitchen singing into my phone.

I play the next one. Silas sings a made up song. The words tear a huge gash down my already shredded heart.

'I can't even begin to tell you how much I love you. Oh, you're the best mummy. How, I can't say, how much I love you.'

These are the first new words I've heard from my son in weeks. He's standing right next to me at that moment, tall and solid. He might as well be singing in my ear. It is a gift. It's an unexpected gift from him, pure and simple, and it takes my breath away.

There's one more recording. I take a deep breath and touch the play arrow.

'I can't begin to say how much I love you, Mummy,' he sings. 'Oh, I love you, yes I do. Oh, I love you, yes I do. You are the best mummy in the world.' His voice cracks on the high end-note. I sit, silent, the tears flowing. How had I not found these months before? I smile through my tears. I know how much Silas would love for me to have been caught out like this. It's painful but the best present he could ever have given me.

~

What am I now? Am I still a mother of four? What do I tell people who ask those innocent questions: 'Do you have children? How many do you have?'

Do I say four and hope they leave it at that? What if they ask how old they are or why I only have three with me? How do I answer strangers' questions? Do I jump straight in and say, 'I had four but one died'? Not exactly a conversation starter. I don't want to open myself up to their scrutiny and pity. They don't know me and they hardly deserve to be thrown into my tragedy, off-guard and unprepared. And yet . . . I can't deny Silas's existence. This would be a betrayal of him and everything he was. I'm unable to do this.

Where does this leave me? It's a dilemma we encounter often.

The mother of a friend of Oscar's writes us a letter two months after Silas dies. She nails it. She has four sons too: older than mine. Her youngest and my oldest are the same age. She has always given me delicious insights into living in a house full of boys. She was the one who told me to feed them a loaf of bread and a hunk of cheese before taking them out to a restaurant to save on the bill. She tells me that these days, when she takes her family out, she feels like a VIP film star with an entourage of strapping, handsome bodyguards. So she feels my loss. She knows that each son is as precious as the next. She has spent many years living in Africa where her husband works in the oil industry.

She writes: 'In Africa, I have noticed that a mother always introduces herself as a mother of eight or a mother of 10, even if some of her children have died. This way, no child is ever forgotten. Ever. Sarah, you are a mother of four boys forever.' Her words give me some small comfort and the strength to always include Silas in our family unit and weather the awkward pauses.

A stranger turns up at the house some months after Silas dies. She is the mother of a friend of my brother-in-law's. She is dropping him off after a meal. We invite her in politely. We stand chatting. Two of my sons walk past and I introduce them.

'You have three sons, don't you?' she says, with conviction.

It's a punch in the solar plexus. I reel back and put my hand on the wall to steady myself. I don't know what to say. How do I respond to such a question? Thoughts swirl around my head. She must know I had four in order to say with such certainty that I have three. So what's she trying to do? Is she trying to force me to tell her about Silas or is she just interested to see if I will deny his existence? Either way it is unforgivable. I want her out of the house in that instant, this woman I don't know, this woman who is happy to tread roughshod over my emotions.

'Get her out,' I hiss to Ben in the kitchen a few moments later. 'Get her out or I'll say something I will regret.'

A few moments later, she is gone.

The boys face their own moments in the months after Silas dies. Inigo is at school in an English lesson. His teacher wishes to illustrate a point.

'So, for example, let's take someone like . . . someone like . . . Inigo.' The class turn to look at Inigo, sniggering in expectation as small children do. 'We could ask him something like, I don't know, how many brothers and sisters he has?' The teacher looks at Inigo enquiringly, waiting for a response.

'Er, three brothers, sir,' says Inigo.

Another boy pipes up. 'He's only got two brothers, sir.'

Inigo is confused as to how to respond. 'Two, no three . . . Yes, three.'

An awkward silence descends on the class.

The teacher in question will have been squirming in his seat, wishing he had asked anyone else, but he didn't and Inigo found himself in the unenviable position of either denying his brother's existence or being called a liar. It bothers him enough to want to talk it over that night.

'You just have to do what feels right at the time,' I say. 'The truth is you do have three brothers, just one of them is elsewhere. You should never be ashamed of that. There might be times you don't want to explain this to people and that's OK too, but nothing will ever change the fact that you are the youngest of four boys.'

~

At times, I get the sense that people think we could afford to spare Silas. We had four boys. That's plenty and the loss of one is careless but not insurmountable. Instead of an heir and a spare, we had three spares.

'You'll be all right; you've got the others,' a really close friend says one evening.

'What do you mean?' I hiss.

He blunders on, oblivious to my distress. 'Well, at least you've got the other boys.'

I see Ben clench his fist beside me, a muscle twitches in his jaw. 'They are not a substitute for Silas!' he growls.

I know this isn't what the friend means but he has phrased it badly. He blusters, uncertain where he went wrong. 'I only mean that at least you have got other children.'

'That makes it better, does it?' I say. 'You think it would be harder to be without him if Silas had been our only child.'

'I suppose so,' he says.

'You don't know what you are saying,' says Ben. He stalks off in disgust. Our friend is bewildered.

'I didn't mean to upset you both,' he says.

'I know but you can't tell us his death would be worse if we didn't have the others. They are not him and will never take his place. Silas was a person and all that he was is gone forever. This is the same no matter how many sons we have. Yes, in some ways the other children help me get out of bed in the morning, but they don't make not having Silas any easier. They don't fill in that hole. The hole would be the same no matter how many children we had.'

'I didn't think . . .'

He is sheepish and contrite but he's not the only good friend to make this suggestion to us. Each time it cuts deep.

The other children do give us purpose at times, it's true. They are hard to ignore and are hungry to live. Sometimes, though, I think it would be easier if Silas had been an only child, then I could give in to the madness of my grief and not force my other children to make this journey beside me.

'When will you and Daddy be happy again?' asks Inigo.

I shake my head. It's a question I don't know how to answer.

~

Friends say, 'Silas wouldn't want you to be sad.'

My mother says, 'Silas wouldn't want you to be sad.'

They are right. I know this to be true. He would hate it if I was sad. However, I also know deep in my heart that Silas couldn't bear it if I was happy without him. So where does that leave me? How can I explain this to them? Can the two emotions coexist? Can I not be sad but at the same time not be happy? Living in a sort of emotional vacuum. Is this even possible?

My son talked about not being able to live without me. Yet here I am without him trying to find a way to live with his absence. Is this yet another betrayal? My head whirls trying to make sense of my feelings.

~

We collect Silas's ashes. I have a thought that we will put some of them in the graveyard with a little plaque, so people can visit. We'll scatter the rest either in places he was happy or under a tree in the garden.

When I hold him in my arms again, though, I find that I can't part with him. It feels good to have him home in this small way, although the strange weight of the ashes in the box unnerves me. I had envisaged the ashes as soft, like flour, but I can hear them grate as the particles rub over each other, reminiscent of a wave tugging on a sandy beach. It's hard to imagine that this is all that's left of my smiling, joking son. Ben and I both feel that we need to keep him with us for now and we put off making a decision about what to do with the ashes. We both know that there's only one place Silas would want to be and that's here with us.

Maybe there will come a time when we can part from him again but it's not now, not yet. Maybe never.

~

We have conducted lots of life-saving operations on our kitchen table. These are tortuous affairs involving lots of screaming and wriggling.

It starts with a child. Any child. Perhaps one who has been a little naughty or disrespectful or simply been in the wrong place at the wrong time.

'I think an operation is in order,' Ben will say.

'Hmm, agreed,' I nod.

We will then grab the screaming child and haul them onto the table. Ben will hold the arms and I'll hold the feet. Then with a spare hand each, we set about the procedure. This will usually involve liberal use of imaginary scalpels and retractors. Organs will need to be removed and stitches sewn.

One hot summer afternoon, we had Silas on the operating table.

'Stop,' he squirmed.

'No, we've only just begun,' said Ben. 'Anaesthetist,' he called, turning to me.

'Here I am,' I confirmed. 'Just going to give the patient an injection.'

I pinched the inside of Silas's leg lightly. 'Right, the patient is ready.'

'Nooooo' screamed Silas. His scream shattered into laughter as Ben lifted up his T-shirt and scrabbled about with his fingers on Silas's bare stomach.

Ben drew his finger in a line from Silas's sternum down to below his navel. Silas giggled and writhed.

'Right, nurse, we just need to remove the stomach,' said Ben. His fingers deftly tickled Silas's stomach, working their way into all the most sensitive parts of his anatomy.

'No,' laughed Silas. 'I can't take it.'

'Now we're moving on to the kidneys,' said Ben. More tickling. Silas bucked on the table, his shrieks cutting through the air.

'I beg for mercy,' he gasped between snorts of giggles. 'I beg for mercy.'

'All right, nurse, I think the patient has had enough for now. Stitch him up,' said Ben.

I thread an imaginary needle and get to work nipping the flesh together. There is more writhing and giggling.

'Good job, nurse. I don't think the patient will require staples.'

Silas rolled off the table panting with relief, a broad grin on his face.

'My turn next,' said Rufus, clenching and unclenching his hands in anticipation.

~

A letter arrives in the post. I open it. It contains a single sheet of paper. At the top are two words – 'For Silas'. Underneath is a poem.

> *I am the light that soared.*
> *Bursting from nothing into brilliant being!*
> *When the dark sky wraps a thousand dreams*
> *In a blanket of winking stars . . .*
> *There I am.*
>
> *I am the brightness in heavenly streams*
> *Of consciousness.*
> *I am in each particle that floats*
> *And spins on moonbeams.*
> *I am the almost imperceptible warmth*
> *That melts frost-spiked leaves.*
>
> *The normality of variety.*
> *Life in all its random games.*
> *The breadth and depth of thought.*

The expectation of experience.
The journey ahead, around, above and beyond
Each path you tread.

I sing exuberantly
In a voice that clears the shadows!
Poised, watching, sure.
I am the answer to silence.
I am the love that will endure.

I am ready, steady, go!
The ebb and the flow
Of hope, potential.
I was and always will be
Playful, sparkling
Possibility

It's beautiful. It makes me cry. It's for Silas. It's a gift from our friend
Gabby, an author and wordsmith. We are touched by her thoughtfulness.

~

The winter jasmine unfurls its profusion of yellow flowers and the cro-
cuses break through the ground by the front gate. The days grow
warmer. Spring is coming.

I don't want the arrival of spring. Spring suggests growth and life and
the future. I want to push it back under the ground. I planted the cro-
cuses by the front gate a decade ago. The splash of colour that greets me
when all else has yet to surface from the winter gloom always lifted my
heart. Now it reminds me of the passing of time. I want to stamp on the
flowers and I feel a strange sense of delight when the first few buds are
nibbled off by rabbits. Let me stay forever in the bleakness of winter. It
matches the ice that resides in my heart. I cannot thaw. I don't want the
constant reminders that life carries on without Silas. The stasis of winter

suited me fine. The newborn lambs leaping in the fields give me no plea-sure. I took Silas to feed the lambs at our neighbour's house last spring. He laughed as they tugged hard at the teat of the bottle he held and giggled as they butted his leg, impatient for more.

I feel as though I am being pushed forward on the relentless conveyor belt of time. I search for the rewind button but it doesn't exist. I scrabble at the walls until my fingers are raw but there is no way off. Each second takes me further from Silas and there's no way back. I rail against this increasing distance from my son but to no avail. It's inevitable and it fills me with fear. I'm afraid that I'll forget the way he ran, the way he stuck his tongue out when he was concentrating, how he threw his head back and laughed with total abandon. I'm afraid of the fickle nature of my memories. How will I hold on to him as time passes?

～

Car journeys are my nemesis. Sitting alone in the car, driving on auto-pilot, gives me too much time to think. I take myself back to those last few days. I torture myself by replaying Silas's last few breaths. I can't rid myself of the images. Is this post-traumatic stress disorder? Can I get such a thing from watching my son die?

I know I should try and bury these thoughts, but they have the lure of a newly frozen pond, glistening and beckoning me to test the ice. I try to stay away, but I'm always drawn back and the fragile ice never holds my weight.

I hound myself with questions. Did we do everything right? Was he in pain? How much did he know? What was he thinking? These are questions that I'll never find the answers to, but I find it impossible to stop asking. The one that sits in my heart the heaviest is whether we should have tried harder to keep feeding him. This might have dragged out the mechanical process of his dying, but I can't bear that essentially we starved him to death. Knowing now how long Silas lived without food or water, I would have tried so much harder to get sustenance into his body, using feeding tubes or other methods, but at the time I thought he only had a day or two. What did I know? We weren't prepared for his body to fight so long and hard. No one warned us, not really. What if he lay there all those days unable to communicate but aware of ravenous hunger? Did he wonder why we weren't feeding him, this boy of mine who took such pleasure in eating? He had to go cold turkey. One day he ate a good breakfast, lunch and supper and the next he had next to nothing.

I try and chase these thoughts away; I focus on the tail lights of the car in front but my mind returns on an endless loop of recrimination and despair. I turn the radio on desperate for distraction but it is 'Let Her Go', a song Silas loved. I can't escape and I cannot let him go.

Straight after he dies, I'm unable to listen to any music. Music reminds me of happier times – of dancing round the kitchen and singing in the car – but it also reminds me of those last few days. The days I lay in bed with him with my head next to his on the pillow. Our breath mingled and I breathed him in as I played song after song that he loved. Every song I hear now reminds me of Silas. In time, I'm able to listen to them again. There's something comforting about music I know he too has heard. It connects us even though he is no longer here to listen with me. New songs become the enemy, songs that his ears have never heard. They're untethered to our life together. They make new memories in which he plays no part and I can't bear it. I switch them off in disgust even though he would have liked them. New ground is harder than old.

This is the same with places. To begin with, Ben and I are filled with trepidation when we return to places we have been with Silas, but we soon learn that old places are easier than new. We prefer to be able to picture him with us, to know that his eyes have gazed out across the same view rather than generate memories in which he has no part. We need to be able to put him in the landscape with us. New places are an act of betrayal. They are a sign that our life is carrying on without him, that we're forging on ahead. We avoid them as best we can, reluctant to leave him behind.

Others don't understand. They think we don't want to be reminded of Silas all the time. They think new experiences will be good and are scared to dredge up too many old memories. They are wrong. We want to keep Silas alive in our minds. Old memories offer a way of holding on to him. We want to talk about him constantly, but hardly anyone else dares. They talk about everything but Silas. I find myself compensating for this by dropping him into the conversation more. Those close to us stop shying away from him. They learn to include him with natural ease and we are grateful. I've lost him in the flesh but I don't want to lose him from our lives. However hard this may be.

~

Mother's Day arrives. The boys leap on my bed and the springs groan in protest. They have all made me cards. They are too old to be forced, so I'm touched. They know how hard this day will be.

Rufus surprises me the most. He has put a lot of thought into his card. He has drawn it in blue and pink and on the front he has written 'Smile Imagine Love Achieve Sing – Always'. Rufus is the least demonstrative of all my boys. Communication has never been his strong point. He talked late, finds spelling hard, more often than not prefers his own company. He's like a cat in his affection, only giving love on his terms.

Ben and I would often tease him about this and we'd throw ourselves on his bed, hemming him under the covers. He'd struggle, but we would rain kisses on him. 'Get off me,' he'd yell, shaking his head from side to side, trying to avoid our questing lips. 'We will,' we'd say, 'but only if you give us both a hug and a kiss.' He'd sigh and roll his eyes, extract an arm and give us both a perfunctory kiss and a momentary half-hearted hug. Then he'd push us away.

Since Silas has died, he has tried hard to make up for the love Silas showered me with. He senses that I need it, and he forces himself to fill the hole. I know how much this costs him and I love him all the more for it. Over the months, I sense that this is getting easier: his arm round my shoulders feels more natural; his kisses more relaxed. Perhaps this

227

will be Silas's legacy to him. Inside his card, with the startling clarity of a child, he states.

'I love you even though I rarely say it.'

This simple sentence blows me away.

When the boys have chased each other downstairs and I am on my own, I pull out the last Mother's Day card Silas ever gave me from the cupboard beside my bed.

It reads. 'Dear My Mummy. You are the most wonderful, most beautiful, most lovely and the prettiest mother in the world. I can't explain how much I love you. No one has a better Mum than us because we have you. Love from Silas your son.'

I have another Mother's Day card from him when he was younger, that reads simply, 'I love you because I can curl your hair.'

I sit for a few moments absorbing his words of love. They sing to me. I close my eyes and imagine his warm body next to mine on the bed, his hand curling in my hair. For a brief second I can hold him there, then he's gone. I am bereft.

I open a little Mother's Day present that I bought for myself. It's a necklace. It has several little silver hearts, one has Silas's fingerprint on and his writing engraved on the back. Ben took the imprint on Christmas Day as Silas lay in our bed. I had phoned the company up after speaking with a mother whose daughter had died. She said she wore a necklace with her daughter's fingerprint. I wasn't sure at the time. It seemed a little tacky, but I know Silas would have loved tacky so, after he died, I chose the necklace with as many hearts as possible. It's not the one I would have chosen, but I know that it's the one he would have chosen for me.

~

Like all small boys, Silas was a thrill-seeker. He loved that bottom-falling-out-of-your-stomach feeling. He squealed with delight on fairground rides. He'd beg to be swung round and round by the arms until he was so dizzy that he could no longer stand. He'd stumble to the floor, doubled up with laughter, breathlessly shouting, 'More, more, more!'

When the boys were small my mother still lived in my childhood home. It was a wonderful, old, beamed Kentish hall house, bordered by a hop farm on one side and a small river on the other.

To get to my mother's from our house you had to snake through a myriad of tiny lanes. The highlight of the journey for my boys was a small humpback bridge.

The bridge was sited on a narrow lane, there was only room for one car to pass at a time. Going one way you had to be careful as you couldn't see what was coming, but going the other way, if you were lucky, you had a clear view up the hill the other side. If the coast was clear you could floor the accelerator and take the bridge at some speed.

The excitement would build in the car as we neared the bridge. The boys were all strapped into their car seats, their heads craned forward. As soon as they saw nothing was coming, they would chant, 'Faster, Mummy, faster!'

I'd increase the pressure on the accelerator. We'd crest the bridge and the car would feel as though it lifted free of the road for a brief moment and then we would come down hard on the far side. The boys would all squeal in delight at the strange feelings in the pit of their stomachs and their faces would flush as the endorphins rushed through their little bodies.

'Fast enough?' I'd query.

'Nope,' hollered Silas. 'Next time go faster still!'

No matter how fast I dared to go, it was never fast enough for him.

~

The boys seem to be doing well and we are relieved, but we know it's early days and events like this have a habit of coming back to bite you years later, so we organise a counsellor to meet with them. I might not want to talk to anyone myself, but I want them to know that it's OK if they wish to talk with someone outside of the family.

The counsellor is bearded and approachable. Inigo thinks he looks a little like Father Christmas. He's most practiced at dealing with the traumatic, sudden deaths of children – car crashes and murders – but he has worked at hospices too, and although Ben and I started our grieving process many months before, the boys had only a little time to know Silas was dying. His death was traumatic for all of us, and it happened too quickly – far too quickly, even if it wasn't sudden.

The counsellor gives us worksheets to wade through with Inigo. He talks to the boys. They are articulate and open. In just one session we realise that he isn't what they need. Not for now at least. It's a door we will keep ajar for the future, but so far they seem to be dealing well with Silas's death, as far as children can.

Sometimes I resent the fact that the boys all seem to have absorbed Silas's death so easily into their day-to-day existence. They dip in and out of their grief. They are able to pack it away in a manner impossible for me. I'm jealous of the ease with which they do this. I don't want them to be sadder or paralysed with mourning, but I envy the way their waking day is largely free of the burden that weighs me down.

I know that it's not that they miss him any less than I do, they are just better at not thinking about it. The immediacy of childhood gives them some protection. And yet, his death has derailed them. Oscar comes to me with every headache, worried that he must have a brain tumour. Inigo hates to be alone – in his bedroom or even going to the loo – and jumps at every shadow or creak of a floorboard.

Those normal securities that children take for granted no longer exist for them. Their parents can't keep them safe. Sometimes we can't stop bad things from happening. They know this now. All children work this out eventually, ours have just got there a little earlier, when they don't yet have all the necessary tools to face this truth.

Inigo lies in bed at night, fearful of intruders.

'No one can get in and hurt you,' I say, kneeling next to him, stroking his forehead.

'How can you be sure?'

'Daddy and I wouldn't let them.'

He thinks about this for a moment. 'But what if they killed you and Daddy?'

I change tack. 'Has anyone ever broken into this house before?' I say.

'No, but . . .'

'Well, then, nothing bad is going to happen to you.'

'How do you know? You can't see into the future.'

'You're right, I can't, but has anything bad ever happened to you in this house?'

He shakes his head, his eyes large in the dim light.

'You see,' I say.

He hesitates. 'But it did to Silas.'

How do I respond? His 11-year-old brother died in this house and I was unable to prevent his death, despite all my efforts. In his eyes, what power do I have to keep him safe?

None. None at all.

I come at it from a different angle. 'What's the worst thing that will happen to you if someone breaks in?' I ask.

'They'll kill me!' he states.

'OK. So the worst thing is you would die?'

He nods.

'If you die, who'll be waiting for you?'

He shrugs.

'Silas!' I say. 'Silas will be there, so maybe dying won't be so bad after all. You'd get to see Silas.'

He looks at me as though I am mad and I realise it's only me who finds this a comforting thought. I'm no longer afraid of dying if there's just the smallest chance that I'll get to be with Silas again.

'I don't want to die,' Inigo whispers.

The tears spring into my eyes. 'I know,' I say, pulling him into my arms. The thought 'neither did Silas' floats around the air between us, but we leave it hanging there, unsaid.

~

231

I start writing again.

I wrote my first book before Silas got ill. I had always wanted to write and Ben encouraged me.

'If you don't do it now, you'll never do it.'

He was right. I didn't want to be yet another one of those people who felt they had a book in them but never did anything about it. So I did and I'd loved doing it. I had finished the first draft of my book just before BOB entered our lives.

As soon as the battle with BOB began, I shelved the book and spent hours reading research papers instead.

My book was written for my boys. I read the first draft to Silas in the first months after his diagnosis. I knew it needed work, but he loved it and every night he would say, 'Just one more chapter, Mummy. One more chapter, please.' He would make his eyes big and tilt his head to the side and beg for more. 'Pleeeaase, Mummy.' More often than not, I'd give in to his pleas.

After his death, I wonder whether I'll be able to write. Will I be able to shut myself away in a room, alone in my head? I know I won't be able to go back to that first book, not yet anyway. So I decide to try starting a new one.

I had discussed the storyline of this second book with Silas in the months before he died. He'd given me some suggestions to flesh out the characters and the plot. So starting it brings him close. It also turns out that writing is a release, as when I'm lost in the story I can't be thinking of Silas. I escape for a few hours each day, and yet I still hold him close as I'm writing for him, for all my boys. It's easier than I think and the words flow.

Before the final paragraph is typed on the page, I know what I must do next. It's six months since Silas died and I feel further from him than ever. I know that I need to bring him back close and to do this I need to write our story – his story. I have no idea whether I'll be able to do this, whether it'll be too painful or whether it'll end up being cathartic, all I know is that I owe it to him.

I start, and once I start, I can't stop. The words come out fast and furious and *A Mighty Boy* is born. Ben says I vomit the words out and in a way he's right, they come from a place deep inside me. I write with the tears streaming down my cheeks and a picture of Silas smiling in front of me.

~

I see blue SILAS bands everywhere – on adults and children alike. Everyone keeps wearing them in the months after the service, even Silas's headmaster. Ben and I marvel: we know people must be reminded of Silas every day and this gives us comfort. The worst thing would be for people to forget him.

I get a text from a friend in Lincolnshire. 'I saw a picture of someone in this weekend's newspaper wearing a SILAS band. It's amazing. Who was that?'

As it turned out, it was my younger brother. What was truly amazing is that someone many counties away recognised the band and knew that it was for Silas.

Several months later, I bump into an old friend I have not seen since the memorial. He's still wearing his band. This meeting is unexpected so he hasn't put it on specially. The writing has rubbed off, but I know what it is and I am touched to see it still on his wrist.

'You're still wearing your band?' I say.

'Yes, I haven't taken it off.' He touches the band. 'I had a job interview this week and you would've laughed if you'd seen me trying to hide it up my shirtsleeve. I was worried it would slip down during the interview and I would look unprofessional.'

An image springs into my mind of him wriggling on his chair trying to hide the band. He could have so easily taken it off but he chose to leave it on and my heart leaps.

In his address at the end of the summer term, Silas's headmaster, Simon O'Malley, cleverly weaves the themes of the SILAS band through-out his 30-minute speech. He mentions Silas at the beginning and, although it's not obvious to the unaware, his entire speech revolves around Silas. It's little things like this – little gestures of support and understanding – that help us continue to get out of bed in the morning.

~

One afternoon in the summer, I go out to check the horse chestnut tree. The wound we made in its trunk is still weeping, still raw. Sticky trails of sap darken the trunk. It shows no sign of healing. I worry that we've done some permanent damage to the tree. What will it mean if the tree never recovers? What if the tree dies from some terrible canker that we've allowed to gain entry? Will that mean my grief will never heal? Or is it simply too soon and the whole process will take much longer? Part of me is glad. I don't feel healed in any way. If anything, I miss Silas more. The days are harder now than they were at the beginning. Is this normal? Or is it just that there is no normal, not anymore?

People ask if it is getting easier.

I shake my head. It doesn't get easier. The load doesn't lighten. I can't imagine that it ever will, but maybe there is a slight difference. The burden feels the same, but the muscles I use to carry it perhaps feel a little stronger. Imagine soldiers traipsing across the moors with back-packs stuffed with rocks. Every step is agony, but over time their muscles strengthen and after weeks of training they grow accustomed to the weight.

Perhaps this is like that.

Can I really grow accustomed to carrying this burden?

~

Silas played games. Not mind games, but real games. He liked nothing more than sitting round a table amongst a raucous group of children and adults, a board spread out before him and the dice gripped in his hand. He loved to pit his wits against everyone. He liked all the usual games – Monopoly, chess, Trivial Pursuit and Scrabble – and was keen on card games.

His favourite game of all was The Game of Life. We spent hours bent over a board, spinning the wheel, collecting money and mansions, paying fines and stealing salaries. We'd count up all our shekels at the end and the winner would be announced with a great fanfare.

Why did The Game of Life strike such a chord with Silas? On some level, did he perceive that this was as close as he was going to get to building a future, falling in love and having children? Sometimes he would be an actor and sometimes a lawyer. Home was a static caravan, a chalet in the hills or a mansion in the home counties. He would break the bank or he would be broke. He chose to be gay or he chose to be straight and sometimes he even chose to be a woman. He wanted to experience life any which way he could. He lived a hundred lifetimes through this game and, although his future was stolen from him by BOB, he had already played it out many times in his head.

~

The world is full of firsts. First Mother's Day, first holiday, first time we have chicken fajitas, first birthday, first father-son cricket match, first week, first month, first six months, and first year looming. The list is endless.

'You're both coping so well,' say our friends. 'You're amazing.'

We nod and keep the smiles pasted on our faces. Ben knows how much effort this takes out of me; this pretence at a normal life. He knows that after a weekend with people in the house, or a family gathering, or an event to raise money in Silas's name, there's always payback for me. The harder I try and quash my feelings and emotions, the more they bubble and boil to the surface until they finally erupt, long after everyone has gone or we are back home.

Usually it happens late at night when my defences are down and my resolve weakens. Sometimes I can stave it off with a whispered, 'Not tonight, Silas. I can't let you in tonight; I'm too tired.' Other times, it only takes a tiny trigger, like a glimpse of Silas's photo out of the corner of my eye, and I feel the tears slide silently down my cheeks. The urge to let it out overwhelms me. I can no more stop it than I could a charging, mad-dened bull.

I creep out of bed, trying not to wake Ben, although I hear him stir. He knows to leave me alone. I head downstairs, my vision blurred. I shut myself in the kitchen and I double over, wracked with soundless, heaving sobs. I retch and white hot agony explodes inside me. I shut myself in with my pain and misery and let it stomp all over my soul. I cry for the love I have lost and the future my son no longer has. I cry for the stupid waste of it all. I cry for the wreckage my family has become. I cry for all those mothers who can no longer clasp their children tight. I cry until the snot streams out of my nose and mingles with the tears on my chin. I cry until I am spent and then I blow my nose and lean back against the warmth of the Aga. I hug my knees to my chest and rock myself back and forth, lost in thoughts of my son.

The screech of our resident owl rents the night air, dragging me back to the present. I haul myself to my feet and rest my head for a moment against the nearest photo of Silas. I tiptoe back upstairs and climb into bed. Ben rolls over and his hand finds mine under the covers. I cling to him and fall into a dreamless, exhausted sleep.

Over time, these episodes reduce in frequency. I read somewhere that they have a name. They are known as 'grief spasms'. They still catch me unawares, but I think I must be making progress. Then I have a week, six months or so after Silas dies, when I find myself crying on and off during the day, every day. Ben is away and I panic. Maybe I need help. I think about ringing the doctor and asking for some antidepressants. I've never taken pills like this in my life, but perhaps this is what I need now. My hand hovers over the phone, but I don't call.

Instead, once again, I turn to books.

A book called *Kadian Journal* by Thomas Harding arrives in the post. I ordered it after reading a newspaper article the previous weekend. The author's son, Kadian, died in a tragic bicycle accident, and he'd written about his journey with grief. I bought it because of a single line in the article. It mentioned that he wore his son's name on a plastic band on his wrist, just like I do, and I feel connected to him in this small way.

The book is an honest, unembellished journey through grief and the loss of a child, and it resonates with me on many levels. It's full of love and I read it straight through. The most beautiful thing of all is that I put it down feeling I have a real sense of his son.

Importantly, the book enables me to see that grief doesn't follow a prescriptive pattern; that in grief, anything goes. There will be weeks that are worse than others and weeks that feel easier. I know that I am not alone. That others have tramped this path before me, and others will follow behind me. I find fresh strength to carry my burden and accept that this is just a bad week. I mustn't expect things to progress in a linear fashion, if at all. Bad weeks will keep happening and that is OK. I just have to recognise that's all they are. It's normal, so far as any of our lives are normal anymore.

I feel liberated.

I understand that I've been stifled by other people's expectations. I've been sensing that people expect us to be moving on. I sense it in stray comments. The way people casually talk to me about their child's cold or sore knee. Why are they telling me this? Can't they see that I am only feigning sympathy. My son is dead. Why would I care about their coughs and sniffles? Or they confide in me how much they are going to miss their daughter when she goes away on a geography field trip for a week. 'I don't know what I'll do. She's never been away from home for so long. It'll be really strange without her.'

They tell me how lucky I am that my older boys only weekly board as their teenager heads off to full boarding. Can't they see I don't want to hear these things? I want to scream at them. I'll never see one of my children again. He will never run through the front door and throw his arms around me ever again. These friends care, I know they miss Silas and feel his absence, but their lives are accelerating away and they expect ours to follow. Our loss is merely a ripple in the ocean of their life.

Even my mum somehow makes me feel that we should be moving on. Every year the boys play in a tennis tournament in Rye. Last year, Silas played with his friend Ed, although his tennis had crumbled when he lost the feeling in his right hand. They played and laughed and the score didn't matter. Oscar wants to play this year. I agree, but get someone else to take him as I don't want to go and see all the same kids running round having fun without Silas. My mum is planning on going with some friends to watch Oscar and she asks me why my other two boys are not playing.

'I don't want to go,' I say. 'I just can't face it.'

'Well, it's not really fair on them. When will you be able to go? Do you think you'll be able to face it next year?'

I snap. 'I don't know, Mum. Maybe I won't.'

'There's no need to get cross, but you can't put their lives on hold.'

'My son has only been dead six months and you want me just to carry on business as usual.' I am being unfair but I lash out all the same.

Reading books like *Kadian Journal* helps me to see that I don't have to work to anyone's timetable. I call my mum and we have a long chat. I explain that she sometimes makes me feel I should be getting over Silas by now. She's upset. She's devastated by Silas's death too. I know this, but I want her to understand my sensitivities. She says that she doesn't know what to say to me anymore as I always seem to take her comments the wrong way. I know she speaks the truth. I'm in fight or flight mode still, and there's no in-between. I don't have the energy to try and work out what people mean when they say something. My judgement is clouded and my brain is working in bottom gear. I know she just hates to see me so unhappy and it feels good to clear the air.

People need to understand that they can't cure us or make us better. There is no better. No magical pill or carefully selected comment that will take our pain away. This is it. People need to accept our pain. This is who we are now. I think that in a world full of solutions, death is the one thing that we cannot solve and as a species we are not good at being helpless. People can't make it better, but they can choose to hold our hand and walk beside us.

A strange coincidence happens only a week later. I find myself in conversation at a cricket match with the cousin of the author of *Kadian Journal* – they are less like cousins and more like brothers. I impress upon him how the book made me feel less alone and ask him to let his cousin know.

'Tell him thank you for sharing his story and for letting me get to know his son,' I say. The desire for people to know my son burns strongly in me too. I don't want people to forget him.

~

The actor Gregory Peck's son committed suicide. Many years later during an interview he was asked if he still thought about his son every day.

'I don't think of my son every day,' he replied. 'I think of him every hour of every day.'

Ben's head and mine are full of Silas. He's the last thing we think of when we go to bed and the first thing we think of when we wake up. He fills our waking hours.

This is exhausting but we can no more stop it than the beating of our hearts. The moments we are free of him are brief and unexpected. After he has finished work for the day, Ben takes refuge toiling in the garden. I hear the roar of the chainsaw or the dull thud of an axe splitting wood. He keeps busy.

'Sometimes I look at my watch and I realise that I have spent half an hour without Silas,' he says, surprised.

For me, hitting tennis balls helps. I can't fill my brain with Silas whilst focusing on attacking a second serve or sprinting to pick up a drop shot. I sometimes get pulled up momentarily by a stray thought, 'What am I doing here? Is this really my life? My son's dead; this can't be real.' But then the next ball comes whizzing at me and I'm forced to respond.

These brief respites feel like a small act of betrayal, but they are necessary to keep us breathing.

I start running. I hate running but I've agreed to a charity run to raise money in Silas's name. I'm surprised. Not by the running – I still hate it and Silas jumps around my head while my feet pound the road – but I am surprised by how good I feel afterwards. The endorphins released by my brain during the run make me feel energised and remind me that I'm alive and vital.

Here I am, my body shouts. Hear me roar.

~

Silas hated us to argue. I remember a Saturday afternoon, the leaves were turning on the trees and the temperature was beginning to drop. Silas was eight. Ben and I drove to pick up the older boys from school after their rugby matches. The traffic was heavy and Ben impatient. He weaved from the fast lane into the slow lane to undertake a Volvo that should have pulled into the empty lane. The Volvo suddenly swung into the slow lane blocking Ben so he swerved back out without indicating, furious with the driver. I gripped the handle, my knuckles white.

'Don't drive like that with the children in the car,' I said, my teeth clenched.

We launched into a row. I accused Ben of poor driving and teaching his children bad habits; he told me to hush and not question his driving ability. Silas and Inigo sat in the back, their faces pale.

Ben and I rarely argued, but this time I wouldn't let it go and the more vociferous I was the more irate he became.

'Please don't argue,' said Silas.

We ignored him and continued, our voices raised.

'Stay out of this, Silas. We're not arguing. Your mother is just being silly,' said Ben.

'That's great,' I snapped. 'You're the one driving badly and putting our lives at risk. I think that's pretty silly.'

The argument quickly escalated into a slanging match.

'I don't want you to argue,' shouted Silas. 'Why won't you listen to me?'

We ignored him and continued to snarl at each other.

He burst into tears, huge guttural sobs that choked him.

'Hey,' I said, turning round to look at him. 'It's OK.'

'No,' he sobbed. 'No, it's not. You'll get divorced. I don't want you to get divorced. Please stop arguing. I want you to stop!'

'We won't get divorced, darling. We still love each other.'

'Exactly,' sniffed Silas. 'You love each other so you don't need to be mean to each other.'

Ben and I looked at each other. He was right. Ben pulled into the school and parked.

'OK, no more arguing,' Ben agreed.

I nodded my head.

'Now you have to kiss and make up,' said Silas.

I leant over and pecked Ben on the cheek.

Silas scooted forward in his seat. 'A proper kiss, like you mean it.'

I rolled my eyes and this time we kissed on the lips.

Silas smiled and wiped a sleeve over his tear-stained cheeks. 'That's better,' he said.

Silas liked to be surrounded by love. Most boys will turn away in disgust when their parents become too lovey-dovey.

'Eww, go somewhere else,' they will say.

Not Silas. He would chant, 'Give her a kiss, give her a kiss,' when Ben gave me a cuddle. He loved to see us show affection towards each other. It made him happy to see how much we love each other. More often than not, he would squeeze under our encircled arms until he was squashed in the hug between us. Then he would turn his face up and kiss each of us in turn. For several minutes we would be raining kisses on each other.

'Just a Silas sandwich,' Ben would say. 'A delicious, squishy Silas sandwich.'

~

Ben and I are on different paths. They run parallel to each other but they are separate, distinct. He can't cross over to mine nor I to his. Sometimes they are close enough that we can touch hands; other times an unbridgeable gulf yawns between us. On rare occasions, our paths cross. They intersect for a brief moment. I'm reminded of a Scalextric track, each car on its own track, the two converging as the lanes cross over. What happens if we arrive at this intersection at the same time? Will it end in a collision and knock us off our respective tracks?

Ben is a father and I'm a mother. These are two different things. They are not interchangeable. We can't journey down the other's path. We are together but on our own. This simultaneous grief has ripped us apart. My loss is not greater than his, and his is not greater than mine, but they are not the same. We recognise this, and I hope that this recognition will enable us to continue to support each other from afar. We talk and understand each other's need to grieve differently.

I sometimes wonder how our marriage can survive this destruction and yet I know that I wouldn't be able to make this journey without Ben by my side. People have mentioned to us the high rate of divorce in bereaved parents. Supposedly over 70 per cent of marriages end in divorce after the death of a child. Why would they tell us this? What are they trying to suggest? Can this be true?

I do some research. It turns out there is no empirical evidence for this spurious statistic, although it's often bandied around as a fact, and I'm relieved. Some parents do divorce, the stress of grief too much on an already strained relationship, but it's not an inevitable outcome. I breathe more easily. There is one less monster hiding in the cupboard of grief waiting to pounce on me.

Much more worrying are the other studies I stumble upon showing the significantly increased mortality rates among bereaved parents in the first three years after a child's death. It seems our chances of dying of a disease or an accident are much greater in the wake of Silas's death. I'm not so surprised. I know my judgement is off, my reactions are slow and I'm quick to anger. I'm an accident waiting to happen. Both Ben and I are showing physical signs of the stress we are under. We both have strange eczema-type patches on our skin and other anomalies and pains.

We need to stay well. We are aware of this and stop drinking so much. I've never been a massive drinker but I've had a glass of wine or two every night since Silas died. It takes the edge off the pain and helps me fall asleep. In the last nine months I have come to rely on it. I need to manage without. We stop drinking during the week.

~

I'm fed up with what I see as Ben's half-hearted parenting.

I always seem to be playing the bad cop. He doesn't want to discipline Inigo anymore. He lets things slide. He lets bad behaviour pass unpunished. I know why: he thinks it's less important now and wants to avoid the confrontation. I know Inigo has had a tough time, we all have, but I think he's wrong to go so easy on him.

I think Inigo needs his boundaries firmly in place. He is confused without them. He learns very quickly to play us off against each other and Ben falls for it, undermining me in front of him.

'Mummy, can I stay up to watch the football match?'

'You have school tomorrow so you can watch the first half – but that's it.'

'But it's Liverpool versus Real Madrid!'

'I don't care who it is. First half only.'

He turns to Ben. 'Daddy?' he pleads.

'I don't see why he can't stay up longer,' states Ben.

'He has school,' I protest.

'He can watch it with me. It'll be fine.'

'Yippee,' sings Inigo, giving me a little sideways glance.

This happens often. The more Ben undermines me and the easier he is on Inigo, the worse Inigo starts to behave. I'll be chiding Inigo over some misdemeanour and Ben will come in and tell me I'm being too tough and I should let Inigo off. Inigo's face will crease with delight and he'll go off with Ben, practically sticking his tongue out at me as he disappears.

I am quick to anger, I know that. I'm miserable without Silas and cannot find the patience I once had. I become a disciplinarian as I try to pick up the slack that Ben has left. The more space Ben gives Inigo and the more he gets away with, the ruder Inigo is to me and the harder I try to reinstate the missing boundaries. It's a catch-22.

Oscar comes home one weekend.

'Inigo's out of control,' he says, after Inigo gives me a torrent of verbal abuse. 'You need to do something. We would never have got away with behaving like this!'

He's right, of course.

Ben is doing the washing-up one evening. He's cross and feels that the boys are not doing enough to help clear up after supper. I'm upset after yet another disagreement with Inigo. We exchange a few heated words and it quickly escalates. All my frustrations come out.

'I'm fed up with being the bad guy round here,' I yell. 'Why am I always the one trying to keep the discipline?'

'You're always shouting these days,' counters Ben. 'You need to let some things go. Not make such a big deal out of the little things.'

'I only have to do that because you won't!'

'I think there are more important things to life than getting cross with my son.'

'Don't you see what is happening?'

'What?' he challenges. 'What is it that you think is happening?'

'Do you think it makes Inigo happy because you let him get away with murder?'

He shrugs.

'It doesn't make him happy,' I continue. 'It just confuses him. He doesn't know where any boundaries lie anymore. He knows he can twist you round his finger and get what he likes. Great. In the meantime, I have to work twice as hard and he ends up hating me.'

Ben spins round. A wet plate in his hand. 'Silas is dead and forgive me if I don't want to be in a battle with my youngest son.'

'Do you think I do?'

'Cut him some slack then!'

'Don't you get it?' I shout. 'He needs us both to be his parents. That means sharing the hard stuff and the good stuff. You need to discipline him. You're not doing him any favours. Silas will always be dead. We can't change that but we can change this.'

Ben shakes his head.

'I need you to help me. I need us to be on the same page. He needs us to be on the same page,' I say.

Ben looks at me, his eyes wild. He shakes his head. 'Don't you get it?' he yells. 'I can't.' The tears spring into his eyes. 'I can't do it.'

The boys are quiet in the other room, shocked by our outburst. I know what Silas would do if he was here. He would run into the kitchen, a look of worry on his face, and say, 'You are not going to get divorced, are you?' And then he would say, 'Now you have to kiss and make up!' He's not here, though, and that is the problem.

Later on, when we both calm down, we agree to try and meet halfway. Within a few weeks, Inigo's behaviour is better and the house is calmer.

~

I don't shy away from the boys seeing me cry.

I've spent much time teaching them about empathy over the years. I read all the usual childcare books when they were small. They were full of stark warnings about the difficulties boys have in expressing their feelings or connecting emotionally with others. So I would sit all four of them in the bath together and we would play a stupid game. I would make a variety of expressive faces and I would get them to guess what emotion I was displaying.

'Anger,' they would yell, as I drew my eyebrows down and squeezed my lips together.

'Surprise,' they chorused, as I widened my eyes and drew my head back.

I tilted my head and looked up out the corner of my eyes and lifted up one corner of my top lip. They looked at each other and shrugged. I scratched my head.

'Confused,' the oldest two finally shouted.

I hunched my shoulders and let my mouth droop. 'Sad,' said Oscar, delighted to get one over his younger brothers.

'Don't be sad, Mummy,' said a three-year-old Silas, putting a wet arm around my shoulders and planting a soggy kiss on my lips.

Over the years, I tried to get them to recognise these feelings in themselves. After a fight with a brother, I would ask, 'And how does that make you feel?' or, 'Can you tell me whether you feel angry or just misunderstood?'

So why would I hide my feelings from them now? I know this is hard for them. Inigo sees silent tears fall down my cheeks on many occasions and he's now alert to the triggers. If a sad song comes on the car radio, or a song that Silas loved, Inigo sticks out a hand and rests it on my knee or pats me on the arm. He cranes his neck to see if my cheeks are wet.

I reassure him. 'It's OK if Mummy cries sometimes,' I say. 'I'm very sad about Silas and sometimes I have to cry. Crying makes me feel a bit better for a while.'

He nods, accepting the strangeness of adults, wise beyond his years.

He has heard me sobbing in the bath and gets out of bed and comes to join me. Sometimes my tears trigger his and we cry together. He has lost his best friend and biggest fan and he needs to cry for Silas too. He needs to know that this is normal and no one will judge him or think less of him for it.

The other boys see me puffy-eyed and wet-cheeked and they give me enormous bear hugs, drawing me into the circle of their strong arms. I'm comforted by them but reminded, yet again, that I will never feel Silas draw me close this way. As they overtake me in height and rest their chins on the top of my head, I know that Silas will never reach this milestone that all sons dream of and I am further derailed.

Several months after Silas dies, Rufus asks me a totally unexpected, perceptive question. We are in the vegetable garden, kneeling on the dirt, digging out stubborn weeds. Summer is on the way and the runner beans are already coiling around their canes.

'Do you think it would have been easier for you and Daddy if Silas had been 40 when he died?' says Rufus, without lifting his head.

I'm floored by the emotional intelligence he displays. I think about my reply and take a deep breath.

'I don't think it would ever be easy to face the death of a child at any age, but in certain ways it might have been easier if Silas was older. He wouldn't have needed us so much. He would already have left home and made a life for himself. Maybe he would have children of his own so we would have had some part of him left, but at the same time it would have been harder in different ways. Hard for his children and his family.' I pause and imagine a little round-cheeked son of Silas running around. I close my eyes and the image vanishes. I turn and look at Rufus. 'He was very little and he believed and trusted in us. He never questioned our ability to make him better. He needed us and that makes it harder for me. So the answer to your question is yes.'

He nods as though he expected this response.

I continue. 'But I have a friend who texted me after Silas died. She lost two babies, one a stillbirth and the other in his first week of life. She told me that she envied every day that we had got to spend with Silas. Does it make it harder that we had Silas for 11 years and got to know him so well, but that she never had a chance to get to know her babies? I think so, but I also understand that we were lucky to have had him for the time we had.'

I know none of my boys will ever truly understand the enormity of our loss until they have families of their own, but at least they are not shying away from it.

At times like these, I think, 'Maybe we can do this. Maybe we can make this journey and pull the pieces back together. Maybe we can salvage something.'

~

I am driving to meet Katie, one of my oldest friends. I know she worries about me. She too has four children and can imagine the hole left by the loss of one. She's the one I confided in many times over the years. She knows how happy I was. She knows that I always felt blessed. Like me, she knows how lucky she is to have four healthy children. We were the same, but now we are different. Although this tragedy has not happened to her, I know she feels my pain, truly feels it, and I know she blunders around in the dark trying to help me.

We are meeting for lunch. Such lunches are exhausting for me. Most of the time it's hard to talk about how I'm feeling. To put my agony into words leaves me floored. It's like giving someone a glimpse into the stable that contains the horror, and then trying to shut the door without letting the horror loose. It takes all my strength to bolt that door again. Sometimes I don't do such a good job and the beast gets loose.

We've agreed to meet at a pub halfway between us. The route to the pub takes me within only a few miles of my childhood home, which my parents owned for 40 years.

I drive to the pub on autopilot. I know the roads well. The radio is playing and pop songs blast from the speakers. Anything to drown out the noise in my head. I don't like the music but I prefer it to my thoughts. Spending too much time in my own head gives too much space to Silas.

The car lifts as I drive over a humpback bridge. My heart catches in my throat. I can't breathe. I hear echoes of Silas all around me.

'Faster, Mummy. Drive faster.'

'This time go really fast!'

I pull into the kerb and stop the car. The tears stream down my face. I wind down the window.

'Where is my boy?' I scream at the clouds scudding across the blue sky. 'What have you done with him? How can he no longer be?'

~

I cannot help but wonder why this has happened to us. Did we deserve this pain in some way? I read Rabbi Kushner's book *Why Bad Things Happen to Good People*. He argues that bad luck is random, a simple case of being in the wrong place at the wrong time and has no reflection on how well you live your life in the eyes of God or your fellow humans. I know the statistics. I'm not the only mother grieving the loss of a child. Three hundred 10–14-year-olds die in the UK every year and more than a quarter of them from cancer. The other largest killer of this age group is accidents, and we've had many close shaves over the years. Life is a risky affair. Maybe the way to look at it is not how unfair life is and how unlucky we have been, but simply how lucky we were to get the brief time we did.

This is hard to get my head around and I look at some of my friends with intense jealousy. All I can see are people in their gilded cages living perfect lives with their perfect, talented children. Their biggest worry is where to go on holiday next. Do they even know what despair feels like? I know that my thoughts are irrational and uncharitable, but I confess to having them all the same. I don't wish our misery on them, but I am jealous. I bury these feelings deep inside me, but I find it hard to go to the school play or concert and see the parents of Silas's friends puffed up with pride over their offsprings' achievements. Then I remind myself that Silas of all people would not begrudge his friends their lives and their success. He would be the first to give them a standing ovation. That's just who he was and I am ashamed; ashamed of my envy.

Ten months after Silas died, we go for a walk. We go with two of Silas's friends and their families. I'm worried that seeing these boys and spending any length of time with them will bring all these feelings to the fore, but my fears are unfounded. It's hard to look at these boys, these sons of theirs, who spent so much time with mine. It's difficult to hear their laughter ring through the crisp autumn air. The green-eyed monster still stirs inside me, but I picture Silas running through the beech woods with them and I catch glimpses of his silliness in them. It's not so painful being in their company, after all. For the first time, I see how watching them reach the milestones that Silas can no longer reach might be all right one day. Silas will be beside them every step of the way.

~

Silas knew how to pay a compliment. In a house full of boys, my attire can slip by unnoticed and unremarked upon. It can take days before a new hairstyle is even clocked.

Silas was different. He'd notice the smallest changes, especially in my hair, which he considered more his than mine.

On evenings when Ben and I were going out, I'd come downstairs all glammed up. The boys would be watching TV, a fire burning in the grate.

'We're off now,' I'd say, stealing a kiss from each of them.

'Uhh,' they'd grunt in vague acknowledgement.

Silas would kiss me, his eyes still fixed on the film. 'You smell nice,' he'd say, sniffing the air. Then he would lean back and look me up and down.

'That's a pretty dress you are wearing, Mummy. You look beautiful. You must be the prettiest mother in the world!'

It was enough to buoy me up for the evening ahead. It's all a harassed mother needs.

Sometimes, when I wasn't sure which outfit to choose, I'd ask Silas his opinion. He'd come into my room and lie on the bed kicking his legs as I changed.

'No, I don't like that one,' he'd say. 'I think you look prettier in the red top.'

'This one,' I'd ask, holding up an embellished red shirt.

'Yes,' he'd nod. 'But I think you should wear it with your big chunky necklace.'

Once I'd dressed, he'd run over and give me a big hug and a kiss. 'Beautiful Mummy,' he'd say and skip downstairs.

~

I have a tattoo!

I look at my arm in amazement. Here I am, 43 years old, and I have just endured the sharp pain of a tattooist's needle for the first, and most likely the last, time.

Ben has been talking about a tattoo for a while. He first suggested it shortly after Silas died and has kept the topic alive. I'm reluctant. I've plenty of reasons: I'm too old for a tattoo; my mother will be horrified; my children will be embarrassed; friends will think I'm crazy. Ben persists. He would like to mark his body in some permanent way, a constant reminder of his dead son. As if we need reminding! He wants us to do it together. Grieving mothers of the Lakota tribe in North America used to cut off part of their little finger to remind them of their loss so, all things considered, a tattoo seems an easy option.

I agree, but only if the tattooist can scan Silas's handwriting and stencil this onto my skin. I half expect a negative answer, but I'm wrong. It is possible. There's no escape now.

I choose the words and decide where to put them. I could hide them away where only I can see them, but then I'll not see them much either. If I'm going to do this then I want to be able to read them every day.

We go to the tattoo parlour. The smell of ink pervades the waiting room. All the employees are tattooed head to toe. I stare at their bulging muscles, the ink rippling on their skin as they move. One even has a tattoo over his scalp and eyelid. Ben insists I go first.

'If you can't take the pain then I know I won't be able to,' he reasons.

I grin at him. 'You forget I've given birth to four of your children. Pain doesn't scare me.'

I lay my arm across the table and the tattooist, Sam, gets to work. Thirty minutes later I hold out my arm to survey his work. I catch my breath. There on the inside of my wrist in blue ink are the words:

> *I love you*
> *Silas*

It is perfect. It looks as though Silas has just walked up to me with a biro in his hand and scribbled across my wrist. I hug my arm to my chest, peeking at the words every now and again. They comfort me. They are a permanent reminder that my son was real.

Ben has more writing. He has words taken from a story Silas wrote when he was seven.

> *You will see the light. That is where I am.*
> *I will be waiting at the far shore.*
> *I love you*
> *Silas*

As I write this, I glance down at my wrist, as I will never tire of doing, and the words make me smile. How strange that such a simple thing can give me such enormous pleasure. It's a constant reminder of the love and open heart of one small boy.

~

I read books that talk about the proof of heaven. I search for meaning and comfort in these stories of near-death experiences. I'm sceptical – perhaps they're just trying to raise funds to pay expensive medical bills or convert unbelievers. I want to believe, I really do. I want to know that one day I will get to be with my son again. This is the only thought that gives me some comfort; the only thought that will help me through these next decades without him. The possibility is enough. I come to the conclusion that all religion must have been invented by those in the throes of deep grief. It's the carrot on the stick, isn't it? The afterlife. It's what keeps driving us forward and our moral compass swinging true. I'm a scientist first and foremost, but I can't just accept that I'll never clasp Silas's hand in mine and hear his booming voice ever again. That's too much to bear. So I have to leave myself with the possibility that he exists somewhere, whole and entire, just out of reach.

Instead of convincing me of the existence of heaven, the books I read give me a different peace. They suggest to me that the brain can play wonderful tricks on the body as it is starved of oxygen. The resultant flood of chemicals causes neurons to fire and induces a flood of euphoria and happiness and a sense of overwhelming love.

I cling to this. It reassures me that this is how Silas felt in those last few hours of life, surrounded and cocooned in love both physically and chemically. The terror of those hours haunts me, but the burden is easier to carry if I know he was spared all awareness.

Several books I read suggest that I will sense Silas's presence. Joan Didion felt her husband near her; Una Glennon in *Ciara's Gift* talks about seeing her murdered daughter; even Thomas Harding writes about the presence of his son at his inquest. This isn't unusual, many of the bereaved do: an astounding percentage, actually – more than half.

I understand that there's a lot we have yet to understand about the power of the brain, and even the spirit world. I look for signs that Silas is near me: in a smell, a vision, a shadow flitting from the corner of my eye. I want to find a trace of him; proof, less of the existence of heaven, but more of his earthly existence; proof that he was not a figment of my imagination. I am open to this, I truly am. The night before my father died, he telephoned me in a dream. He had been in intensive care in hospital for the last 10 days so it wasn't beyond expectation that he would die. In my dream, my father told me he loved me and that he was sorry for leaving me. He told me that he didn't want to hurt me but he had no choice. I dreamt with such clarity that night and it felt so real that I awoke in the morning and told Ben, 'Dad's going to die today!'

Ben looked at me in disbelief, rubbing his sleep-filled eyes. 'Why do you say that?' he asked.

'Because he came and said goodbye,' I replied. There was no doubt in my mind. It was as clear as the knowledge that the day was a Thursday.

Ben got on a plane later that morning to fly to New Zealand for filming and the hospital rang a few hours later to tell me that my father wouldn't last the night. Punctuality was a big thing in my father's life. He even got me to the church early on my wedding day and I had to drag him back as more guests hastily edged through the door to find their seats. His death was no different; he didn't keep us waiting.

My mother had a similar experience. We were up in the north of Scotland on holiday. I must have been about 11 years old. The day before we were due to leave, she suddenly announced that she needed to get home. She couldn't explain her reasoning, she just felt a strong need to go straight home. My father was in an indulgent mood and we made the 12-hour journey back to Kent. My parents opened the front door and a sickly stench hit our nostrils. Our elderly house-sitter lay on the sitting-room floor in a puddle of her own excrement. She had had a stroke many hours earlier and had been unable to move. My mother saved her life by getting us to leave a day early, and to this day she doesn't know what the trigger was. She just knew she had to get home.

So I search for Silas everywhere, just in case, but I am denied. Is my belief not strong enough? I feel cheated. Why should the authors of those books be sent such comfort and not me?

One afternoon, I am running. I'm on the Crab and Winkle Way, a cycle path that runs between Canterbury and Whitstable. It is high summer. The heady scent of meadowsweet is carried on the light breeze. Cyclists brush by me, their tyres kicking up small stones on the path. I pass two women walking dogs. Their laughter drifts back to me. I'm hit by the realisation that I will never laugh in that carefree way again. The tears sting my eyes. I want to go back. I want to go back to a moment two years earlier, before BOB. I want to capture the essence of happiness that I had then and bottle it. I want my life back, unencumbered by this terrible burden. My feet continue to pound the path.

'I just need a sign, Silas,' I whisper. 'I just need to know you are OK.' I know it is hopeless but I ask anyway.

'Please,' I say. 'Anything. Just let me know you're OK.' I raise my eyes to the sky and am startled by a perfect heart-shaped cloud. I stop dead in my tracks. The cloud is small and bright, its colour heightened by the blueness of the surrounding sky. It is flanked on both sides by larger, rounded cumulus nimbus but floats there on its own. I can't believe what I am seeing. I fumble with my running belt and pull out my mobile. I want to take a picture for Ben. I want to have proof that this is happening. I glance down at the phone and by the time I look back at the sky, the cloud is already dispersing, blown on the light breeze, its edges blurring. I drop my hands, the phone forgotten. I stand there and watch the cloud, trying to stretch out the moment before I have to admit that it has gone. The tears are running freely down my face. I know it's just a coincidence, but I also know that if Silas was ever going to send me a sign then that would be the one. I cling to this thought as I brush away my tears with my sleeve and continue with my run.

'I see you, Silas,' I whisper.

~

Two things have happened in the last month that show me we are moving in the right direction.

Firstly, we find ourselves dancing. I can't recall the trigger, but Ben and Inigo and I are dancing round the kitchen. It's after supper and the remnants of the meal still lie discarded on the kitchen table. Loud music is blaring from the computer and we are dancing and singing. We haven't done this for nearly a year – the last time we did was with Silas to 'Always Look on the Bright Side of Life' and '500 Miles'. Part of me wants to stop – I'm not happy so I shouldn't be dancing – but strangely it feels right to dance at this moment. All three of us are aware of the significance of this event.

'Silas would like to be dancing with us right now,' says Ben.

'He would,' I agree. 'He would be throwing his best moves.' We smile at each other: a smile full of loss and love. Something is different. It takes me a while to put my finger on it. Then I have it. Instead of being overwhelmed by sadness that Silas is not here with us, we are thinking about how much he would love to be here, how happy he would be. It is a small shift in our way of thinking but it is a shift all the same.

The second thing is I dream about Silas. I have difficulty falling asleep one night and the tears fall on my pillow. 'I just want a hug,' I think to myself. 'I just want a hug from my boy. It's not so much to ask.' I eventually fall into an exhausted sleep. I dream and Silas is with me. For the first time since he died he is whole and alive and vital. He's not dying some horrible violent death or lying paralysed by a brain tumour. He runs towards me and throws his arms around me. 'Mummy,' he calls. I feel the heat in his body and hold him tight. Part of me is aware that I'm dreaming, and I'm afraid that if I consciously acknowledge this he'll disappear in a puff of smoke. I cling to him, trying to hold on to this moment, this figment of my imagination. It feels good, so good. I don't have him for long but I have him back for a moment and it is precious, so precious. I wake and lie there in the dark. The breath catches in my throat. I swear I can still feel the weight of his arms around my neck.

~

For months I have been tortured by the question of whether we did the right thing by not telling Silas that he was dying. My doubt gnaws at me constantly. One night, when Ben is away, I find myself typing some words into the search engine of my laptop. My fingers move of their own accord. I know I am opening a door that I might not be able to close, but I can't stop myself.

'Should I tell my child he is dying?' I type. I hit return before I can talk myself out of it.

One of the first sites I click on talks about the importance of talking with the child, and says that some parents believe they can protect their child by withholding the truth, but that most children know or suspect that they are dying. It talks about the importance of honesty, so that you can help your child feel less anxious and both have closure, no matter how hard this is.

As I read these words, icy tendrils curl around my heart. Did we get it wrong? I read about looking for signals that the child is ready to talk, like the child talking about the death of someone else. I feel sick. Silas talked about death a lot in those last couple of months, not his death but mine. Was he trying to get reassurance about his own death?

When he said that he couldn't live without me, and he would have to kill himself if I died, did he want to know if I would feel the same about his death? Was he seeking reassurance that my life would be unbearable without him, or was he trying to find out if I would somehow survive? Did he want to know what would happen to me without him?

It all falls into place. Silas knew. Of course he knew. He knew he was going to die. He wasn't stupid. He noticed the changes in his body. He knew. How could we have been so stupid? We were waiting for him to ask if he was going to die, but he never asked because he thought we didn't want to talk about it. He tried to protect us, just as we tried to protect him. Instead of putting all his fears and anxieties to rest, we let him carry the burden of his death on his own.

I gag. It all seems so blindingly obvious now: Silas asking about death; his getting tearful at bedtimes; his refusal to ask why he was wetting himself. The realisation hits me like a slap in the face. I let him down when he needed me most. I thought his mind was too far gone, but I was wrong. It smacks me like a sledgehammer. I double over in agony and the sobs are wrenched from deep in my body. I howl – deep, guttural, animal howls. I cry till I am spent. I cry for my son and for my pain, but most of all for his loss of innocence and for the burden he carried on his own.

I know I can't do this to myself. These are questions that I'll never be able to answer, but in my gut I know the truth. He knew, and in our desire to protect him we were blind to his knowledge.

Through the tears, I stumble across another site that informs me that parents who tell their child they are dying never regret it, whereas parents who try and protect their child from the knowledge often struggle with regret. It's no comfort to me that others have found themselves in the same boat. Why did no one tell me that this would happen? Why was I not advised to tell him by someone? The fear that I got it wrong when he needed me most is overpowering and I sink under its weight.

When Ben returns, I talk to him about my fears through a veil of tears. He is quiet beside me. I know I'm forcing him to go somewhere he doesn't want to tread. He refuses to let himself think about whether we did the right thing or not. He knows the pain is too much to bear and that we will never find the answer. All he can say is, we did what we did out of love and the most important thing is that Silas knew how much he was loved.

He's right, I know, and I force myself to step away from these destructive thoughts. I have to hope that in our discussions about death, I gave Silas the answers he was looking for. I hope that I gave him the belief that our love would transcend all earthly restraints, that anything was possible and that death would only be a temporary separation. Would he have wanted us to confirm his imminent death? Would that information have made his journey any easier? Knowing Silas as I do, I think he would most likely prefer our bubble of pretence to the stark barrenness of his reality.

Still, the knowledge nibbles away at me.

~

As the anniversary of Silas's death draws near, the loss swallows me again. All around me there is talk of Christmas and celebrations and happiness. I dread every day. I am catapulted straight back to those last few weeks. What was happening this time last year? These were the last few days I had with my son and the memories are vivid. As hard as I try, I can't bury them. I cry constantly – in the car, in the bath, in bed, cooking supper. I cry on the shoulders of people I hardly know who are kind enough to ask me how I am coping.

What happens when I pass the year mark? What happens when I can no longer think of what I was doing with Silas this time last year? Picturing the two of us still together in the previous year has given me comfort during the long months. Suddenly the anniversary looms, dark and ominous – another unknown, another irreversible step away from him. The distance from him yawns in my mind, the gap stretching and stretching until it must reach breaking point. His friends are celebrating their 13th birthdays. Their lives are moving on; everything moves on – a slow trudge towards the future, each step pulling the past further away, out of my reach.

'Take me back,' I want to scream. 'Take me back just for a moment. Give me longer with my son. I'm not ready to leave him!'

We make the decision to go away for Christmas, far away. There will be no Christmas without him, not this year. We go, just the five of us, a shrunken unit. Our decision is tough for our families, but we know we need to rebuild on our own without the pressure of expectations and emotions. We go on an adventure and take Silas with us in our hearts.

Going away does not make our loss easier. In some ways it makes it harder. There are constant reminders of what we are missing. The gap that looms large in our lives. We can't avoid it.

Every restaurant hammers home the hole in our family. All tables are laid for four or six. The five of us constantly find ourselves sitting at tables with a spare, empty chair. It glares at us, daring us to ignore it. It shouts, 'How can you be here when I am not?'

All families of five must have to deal with this extra chair. But for us, this is new, uncharted territory and our missing boy screams from his empty seat. We all sit and stare at the empty chair until Oscar gets up and moves it, sliding it under a nearby table or backing it away against the wall. This simple action in itself feels like yet another betrayal.

It doesn't stop with a chair, though. It seeps through into other aspects of our trip. A canoe excursion means one of the boys has to team up with the guide in two-man canoes. This has never happened before. Before, we were a neatly presented self-sufficient unit – three neatly presented pairs. One of us is now always left out on a limb, having to share with strangers or sit on their own. Wherever we turn, there are constant reminders of what we were and what we no longer are. It breaks my heart every time.

And yet, and yet . . . There are good times. Times filled with fun and laughter. We let Christmas pass us by, unannounced and without celebration. We play charades on the day that should be Christmas and the air is filled with giggles as I try to mime a zebra.

It hurts but we can find fun without Silas. We have to search a little harder for it, and it's more fleeting than before, but it hasn't gone for good. I watch the boys' spirits lift as they see that all is not lost. Things have changed, but they see we are clawing our way towards a new future with Silas tight by our side.

~

Silas is still with me. He's not here in the flesh and I can't pretend that I feel his presence around me, as much as I long to, but I know he is inside me.

The memories are there, of course, but there's more than that. I still carry him inside me. I carry his very cells in my body.

During pregnancy, foetal cells cross over the placenta into the mother's blood supply and vice versa. They help to program both the mother's and the baby's immune systems to accept each other. This is called foetal microchimerism after the mythological Greek monster the chimera, which was half-lion and half-goat.

Recent research has shown that foetal microchimerism is much more prevalent than previously thought. Most women are thought to carry cells from their babies long after giving birth. In some cases, cells from the foetus can survive for decades in the organs of the mother's body, including the skin, liver, spleen, heart and brain. They integrate into the tissue and become one.

It's even thought that foetal stem cells can help heal the mother in times of sickness. Following a stroke or a heart attack, foetal cells have been shown to congregate round the damaged tissue and help to heal it. It makes sense – it's in the foetus's interest to keep its mother well and healthy for the duration of the pregnancy. Now scientists have shown that this repair activity can happen even decades after the child is born.

So, part of Silas might live on in me. Just a few cells, perhaps. This fact delights me and I hug this secret to myself. I'm sad that this miracle is only available to me and not Ben. I would share him if I could, even now.

If he lives on in me, I can't help but wonder whether maybe it will be Silas's very cells that will hold the secret to healing my broken heart. It's a far-fetched but wonderful thought.

~

A short cycle ride from our house is a pub called the Rose and Crown in the middle of a wood. Our house is 350 feet above sea level so we are nearly always heading downhill. However, both the Rose and Crown and Perry Wood are higher than us. The cycle ride is hard work but the lure of a cold drink always keeps tired legs pedalling.

There's a beautiful walk through the woods behind the pub up to the top of the hill and the Pulpit. The Pulpit is a wooden tower or viewing platform that has been built on the site of an old semaphore tower. These towers existed in networks across the country in days before electricity, and messages could be sent between them on clear days using a system of blades or shutters.

I can see for miles from the top of the tower. We have a large, distinctive turkey oak in our garden and I've even been able to pick out our tree on a haze-free day.

We've spent many wonderful summer afternoons playing hide-and-seek in the woods. Shrieks of laughter from the children; dogs sniffing and digging in the undergrowth; that evocative smell of crisp, dry bracken that takes me straight back to my own childhood making dens with fronds weaved together to make a roof. It's a magical place.

On one such walk, when Silas was about six, he bent down on the steep path up to the Pulpit and picked something up. He held it close to his eyes.

'Look, Mummy,' he said, holding the object out for me to inspect. 'It's a shell.'

He was right. In his hand he held a perfect seashell. He fell to his knees and searched the side of the path, his fingers scrabbling through the dry bracken. Little pebbles clattered away back down the hill.

'Look, there are more,' he said, his voice high with excitement. He gathered a handful of small shells.

'Why are there shells on top of the hill?'

'Because where we stand now probably used to be under the sea at one time,' I said. I now know that the hill is made of chalk topped with ancient seabed deposits from the Eocene epoch.

We climbed the last few steps to the top. I shaded my eyes from the sun and looked out towards the distant sea, miles away at Whitstable. The sun glinted off the blades of the offshore wind farm. Silas followed my gaze.

'But the sea is so far away and we are high up?'

I heard the confusion in his voice as he turned the shells over in his hand.

I bent down to his level. 'Once upon a time, a long time ago, this was all underwater. Ancient sharks swam here.' He looked at me, his eyes wide. 'Then over many years the plates of the Earth moved and all this—' I swept my hand around me '—was pushed up and out of the water. Then the trees grew.' I touch the shells in his hand. 'That's why we have trees and shells on top of this hill.'

Silas was silent for a moment, absorbing the information.

'Wow,' he said eventually. 'The earth is amazing. I'm so lucky to be alive!'

I nodded my head. He slipped his hand in mine and we traipsed after the others.

~

There is no going back, no rewind. The only replays I get now are in my head. I am journeying down an unknown road, on a path far from the one my feet were skipping along a few years ago.

My heart may be broken but I'm not afraid of this journey. I know it's a process. I can't avoid it. It's like that wonderful children's book *We're Going on a Bear Hunt* by Michael Rosen. There's a line in that book that I have read many times to my children.

'You can't go over it. You can't go under it. Oh no! You've got to go through it.'

This is what I am doing. I'm going through it. There are no short cuts. No sneaky exits. I have to learn to live without Silas. I have to confront my grief, my anger, my regrets, my despair. No one else can do it for me. And I will do it, somehow.

I find comfort with other mothers. I am introduced to a mother whose daughter, one of four vibrant girls, died from a brain tumour a decade or so earlier. She gives me hope. Hope that we can navigate our grief and somehow rebuild our lives. I see her family, years further down the line than us, the girls all grown up and flying the nest. I see their strength and unity and zest for life, and I am awed. They hold their daughter close, and clearly the hole is still there, but they fill their days with laughter and adventure and love, so much love; love for each other and love for their missing girl. They live for each precious moment, and for the first time, I see that it is up to us to find the light at the end of the tunnel. I still can't see it, not yet, but I know I have to keep searching. If we keep moving forward, we will find a way out of the darkness and find a new way to live.

Not long afterwards I meet up with a newly bereaved mother whose daughter has been killed in a tragic accident. I know her through our children's primary school; her daughter and Rufus were in a class together. I am still mired in my own tragedy and don't feel in any position to comfort or give strength to others but it feels surprisingly good to connect: to talk freely about our children; to cry; to be angry; to be brutally honest about our misery. We stay in touch and meet regularly. One day she tells me, 'Some days I can't face getting out of bed. Then I think of you still going a few steps further down the line and it gives me the strength to keep moving. I think, "If you can do it then so can I."'

Here we are, all of us, finding our own way 'through it'. In the process, we draw strength from those that have gone before and help haul up those who follow on after.

None of us are alone on this journey.

~

So we stumble on, step by agonising step. I remember how I felt when we were first given Silas's diagnosis. When we were first told that our son would die. I remember how I screamed at Ben that first night.

'I wish he had been killed in a car crash!'

'No, you don't,' he said.

'Yes, I do. I can't do this journey. I can't watch him disappear before our eyes and die an agonising, slow death. He doesn't deserve that,' I sobbed.

Here I am, just over two years later, and I have done this journey. I am doing it. Silas didn't deserve it, and I didn't choose it, but I have done it. We've done it, all of us. We are surviving. In the process of learning to cope with death hanging over us, we've had to remember how to live, how to make every day special, and how to exist in merely a moment. Despite everything the last few years have thrown at us, we have had happy moments; ecstatic moments; belly-busting, rolling on the floor moments. Silas is a part of everything we do and always will be. We will carry him forward into the future with us. It will never be enough, not really, but it is all we can do.

So, although I would always choose to spare Silas his suffering, I am grateful for every minute we got to spend together, for every extra memory we made and every moment of delight we had. Those days are irreplaceable and I would go through it all again just to have one more day with my son, no matter how much pain it caused me.

Ben was right, after all. A car crash would have been swift in comparison, but it would have stolen those precious extra memories from me. Every day, every moment we had together was priceless and I cannot trade that in. Not now, not ever.

ACKNOWLEDGMENTS

First and foremost, my thanks go to all those who subscribed to this book and helped to make its publication possible. Without you, it might still be sitting on my hard drive. Several other people were instrumental in getting this book published: Camilla Burge, who encouraged me from the beginning and pushed me in the right direction; Euan Thorneycroft at A.M.Heath, who never stopped believing; and the whole team at Unbound, especially John Mitchinson, Phil Connor and DeAndra Lupu, among others, who knocked it into shape. I'd like to thank, too, our marvellous local Community Nursing Team, the team at The Royal Marsden, Sutton, and all the doctors across the UK who did their best for Silas, in the face of insurmountable odds. The last few years have been far from easy for my family but there have been many people who have supported us and picked up the pieces; far too many to mention in one short paragraph, but they know who they are and you'll find most of their names in the back of this book. Lastly, I would like to thank all of you who showered Silas with love in his short life. It means more than you can imagine, and I would like to thank my mother, Barbara Spens, for just being there, and my husband Ben, for shoring me up and never letting go.

Those seeking further information about some of the issues raised in the book may find the following organisations useful:

The Brain Tumour Charity
www.thebraintumourcharity.org

CLIC Sargent
www.clicsargent.org.uk

Child Bereavement UK
www.childbereavementuk.org

The Compassionate Friends
www.tcf.org.uk

The author's proceeds of this book are being donated to the Silas Pullen Fund, a fund set up after Silas's death to accelerate research into paediatric brain tumours, under the umbrella of The Brain Tumour Charity. Brain tumours currently receive less than 2 per cent of all cancer funding and yet are the biggest cancer killer of children. The Silas Pullen Fund hopes to help change this.

https://www.facebook.com/SilasPullenFund

www.itisanobrainer.com

You can play 'Song for Silas' and find some of the videos mentioned in the book by searching online.

IN MEMORIAM

Joanna Butterworth 9.7.64 – 3.10.12.

Sasha Sky Crathorne, aged 8.

Matthew Denbow; my beautiful son 17.11.1990 – 29.07.2001

Louis Lawrence Dighton. (Dizzle)

Oscar Tulinius Hughes 18.02.05 – 03.05.14

For Chris Moon, dearly missed

My dad, Dr Jon Pritchard, who dedicated his life to
researching and curing childhood cancers

Rosemary Roberts
Grandmother of Camilla, Florence, Edward, Tavy,
Jasper and Oscar.

Harris Savides

SUPPORTERS

Unbound is a new kind of publishing house. Our books are funded directly by readers. This was a very popular idea during the late eighteenth and early nineteenth centuries. Now we have revived it for the internet age. It allows authors to write the books they really want to write and readers to support the books they would most like to see published.

The names listed below are of readers who have pledged their support and made this book happen. If you'd like to join them, visit www.unbound.com.

Mark Abbott
Jessica Joelle Alexander
Natalie Allen
Annie Allison
Lesley Allwright
Joanna Antoniou
Charlotte Asprey
Samantha Bain
Stephanie Banham
Frances Barker
Emma Barrett
Susie Barter
Sharon Barton
Ed Baxendale

Harriet Baxendale
Richard Beaugié
Pam and Simon Beaugié
Elisabeth Beccle
Emma Beckham
Catherine Bedford
Colin & Anne Bell
Edward Benbow
Warren Benbow
Richard Bennett
Sharon Bennett
Alex Betts
Sara-Jane Biddle
Madeleine Bioletti

Arabella Bishop

Moray Bishop

Adam Bissill

Maria Black

Keira Blackwell

David Blair

Sam Blair

Jessamy Blanford

Graham Blenkin

Anna Blunt

Anna Boggon

Karen Botha

Gail Boucher

Gary Bourne

Christian Bouvet

Helen Bowen

Sally Bowness

Rebecca Bristow

Cinders Brooks

Anne Mason Brown

Charlotte Brown

Selina Bunting

John Burdett

Camilla Burge

Emma Burnham

Hugo Burnham

Jolyon Burnham

Rufus Burnham

Rebecca Burton

Katie Bushell

Camilla Canellas

Anna Carlisle

Katie Bonham Carter

Abby Charles

George Charles

Hamish Charles

Michael Charles

Rory Charles

Sarah Charles

Clare

Lliane Clarke

Rosemary Clarke

Keith Claxton

Siobhan Clayton

Heather Clifton

Andrew Clover

Ali Cobb

Lyn Collins

Robert Cook

Anne Coombs

Tim & Bridget Corry

Samantha Corsellis

Serena Courage

Elizabeth Cox

Harriet Cox

Cally Crathorne

Annette Cremin

Tanya and John Crone

Emily Curson-Baker

Venetia Curtis

Suzie Darlington

Frankie Davies

Susie Davies

James Dawes

Valerie Dawes

Gabby Dawnay

Claire de Giles

de Moubray family

Ana De Quinto

Lana de Savary

Fernando Delgado

Sandra Denbow

Louis Lawrence Dighton. (Dizzle).

Jean Dixon

Lauren Dorman

Natasha Douglas

Lindsay Dowding

Jo Dunne

Georgia Dussaud

Justine Edelman

Anna Emery

Marie-Claire Erith

Flora Fairbairn

Francesca Fairbairn

Annabel Falcon

Mave Fellowes

Kate Fenwick

Phoebe Flood

Alex Fontanelli

Faye Fowler

Alice Fox-Pitt

Andrew Fox-Pitt

Arabella Fox-Pitt

Fenella Fox-Pitt

William Fox-Pitt

Angus and Jenny Fraser

Linda Fraser

Clare Friend

Gilli Fryzer

Alexandra Fuller

Juliette Gale

Mary Garcia

Joanne Garlinge

Fiona Gault

Nancye Gault

Phil Gibby

Gilly Gilchrist

Frances Gillies

Caroline Godfrey

Dominic Gold

Henrietta Stark Goldie

Dennis Gooch

Sophie Goodhart

Jess Grant

Annie Green

Valerie Green

Francis Grier

Sally Gross

Stella Grove

Mich Guilford

Carmen Gunther

Lucy Guthrie

Jackie Hakim

Rory Hammerson

Marion Hanbury

Jo Hancock

Miriam Handley

Lorraine Hardy

Tracy Harmsworth

Bridget Hasler

Tom Hasler

Sophie Hayes

Lucy Haywood

Emma Healy

Colin Heber-Percy

Paul Heber-Percy

James and Claire Heming

Lucy Hewett

Bindy Higgins

Paul Hillier

Ruth Anne Hinckley
Diana Hooper
Pippa Horlick
Peter Hoult
Louisa Stewart Howitt
HR Pratt Boorman Family
    Foundation
Francesca Hulme
Luna Hulme
Su Hunt
Honor James
Monique James
Antonia Jamison
Mateo Javier
Jane Jeffs
Simon Jeffs
Sarah Johnson
Fiona, Mark, John and Peter Jones
Natasha Jones
Lichen June
Maureen Kechriotis
Clare Kemp
Melanie Kent
Dan Kieran
Richard King
Gilly and Charles Kinloch
Caroline Knight
Richard Knott
George Latham
Jimmy Leach
Victoria Leake
The Leckie Family
Gemma Ledger
Philippa Lennox-Boyd
Sarah Liesching

Penelope Linell
Hazel Linforth
Kate and Adrian Linforth
Emma Loder-Symonds
Jane and James Loudon
Candida Machin
Dinah Mackay
Tali & Dickon Mager
Noa Maiman
Fleur Malik
Mark and Emma
Victoria Markou
Lucie Marsh
Archie Martine
Maria Mateo
Jamie McCallum
Sandrine McClure
Angela McHale
Kimmy McHarrie
Lucy Medhurst
Jay Milborne
John Mitchinson
Miriam Moloney
Mary Moore
Sophie Moreland
Caroline Morris
William Morrison
Heather Mott
Jonathan Mount
Lucinda Mullins
Lucy Murphy
Lexy Muscat
Omar Nash
Carlo Navato
Camilla Neame

Lucie Neame

Sarah Neaves

Piccia Neri

Angela Nichols

Stephen Nockolds

Cathy Norbury

Debbie Norrish

Camilla Norton

Emma and Richard Norwood

Simon and Katy O'Malley

Nicky O'Sullivan

Meg Officer

Ollerenshaw Family

Veronica Olszowska

Rudi Owen

Melissa Owston

Vivien Owston

Graham Page

Silvia Papana

Emma Parlons

Arabella Parr

Jane Paxton

OSCAR's PBTC

Lisa Jayne Pearson

Kirsty Peart

A Pellumbi

Fiona Dix Perkin

Vanessa Perkins

Phillips family

Jan Pilkington-Miksa

Ben Rawlingson Plant

Laura & Francis Plumptre

Juliet Pollard

Justin Pollard

Simon Preller

Nicola Price

Amy Prior

Helen Pritchard

Angela Benbow Pullen

Ben Pullen

William Pullen

David Ralli

Rachel Raymond

Francesca Reed

Clare Reeve

Sophie Rena

James Richardson

Heather Roberts

Roberts Family

George Rodd

Melanie Rollinson

Victoria Rowe

Natasha Royds

Vanessa Ross Russell

Susanna Sait

Melanie Salmon

Tom Sanderson

Rachel Saunders

Ruth Scholfield

William Scott

Maryam Seyf

Rachel Sharp

Raz Shaw

Madeleine Shepley

Elisabeth Sherwin

Patricia Sherwin

Sarah Sherwin

Ciara Shobrook

Sophie Silocchi

John and Caroline Simmonds

Rachel Sisley
Lottie Skuthe-Cook
Patricia Smallwood
Elisabeth Smiley
Barbara Spens
David Spens
Mallowry Spens
Patrick Spens
Will Spens
Miranda Stainton
Roger Stainton
Marion Stent
CJ Stephenson
George Raymond Stevenson
Belinda Stewart-Wilson & Sonny
Sebastian Stoddart
Beth Stokes
Jamie Strauss
Emma and Richard Street
Gail Sturgis
Amanda Taggart
Beverley Tarquini
India Taylor
Lucy Taylor-Smith
Sophie Taylor-Young
Ceri Barnes Thompson
Jo Thompson
Olivia Gideon Thomson
Joanna Tollemache
Jessica Tomblin

Rupert Turnbull
Andrew Turvey
Jonathan Eric Tyrrell
Sophie Van den Bogaerde
Lucy Verner
Sally Villiers
Simone & Timothy Vince
Sasha von Meister
Martin & Sue Walsh
Trina Walters
The Wanendeyas
Fiona Warner
Daryl Webster
Gavin and Anne Wetton
Giles Wheatley
Heather Wheeler
Isobel Whitehead
Philippa Wigdahl
Emma Wilcox
Rachel Wildblood
Lorraine Wilding
Liza Wilkes
Jo Williams
Zoe Wilmoth
Stephanie Wolfe
William Wollen
Fiona Wormwell
Terrie Wratten
Nona Wright
Katie Wyatt